Last of 4 volumes.

Good Reading

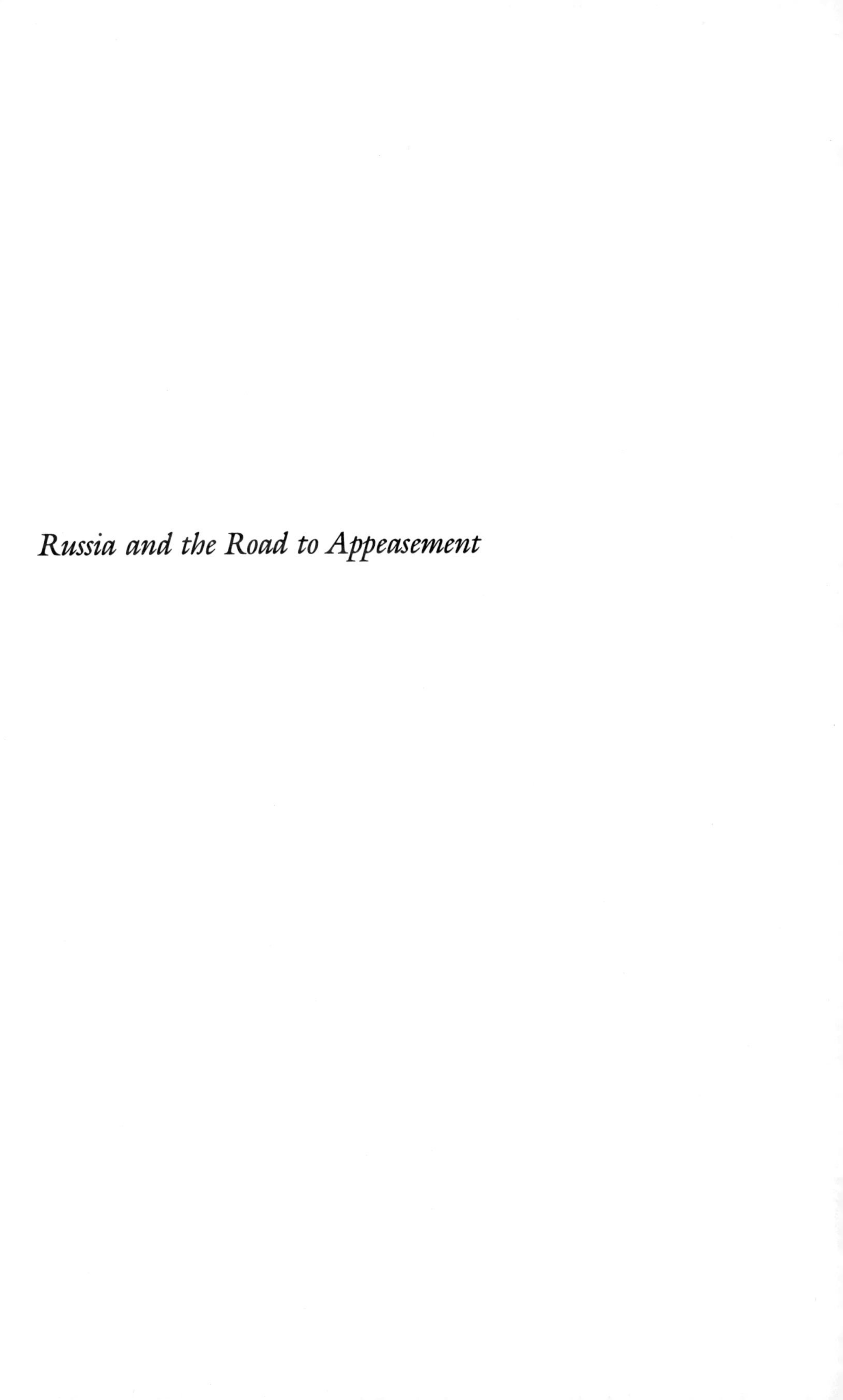

Russia and the Road to Appeasement

Other volumes on Russia and the West by the author:

QUEST FOR EQUILIBRIUM: *America and the Balance of Power on Land and Sea* (1977)

CAREER OF EMPIRE: *America and Imperial Expansion over Land and Sea* (1978)

RUSSIA AND WORLD ORDER: *Strategic Choices and the Laws of Power in History* (1980)

Russia and the Road to Appeasement

CYCLES OF EAST-WEST CONFLICT IN WAR AND PEACE • *George Liska*

THE JOHNS HOPKINS UNIVERSITY PRESS
Baltimore & London

Copyright © 1982 by The Johns Hopkins University Press
All rights reserved
Printed in the United States of America

The Johns Hopkins University Press, Baltimore, Maryland 21218
The Johns Hopkins Press Ltd., London

Library of Congress Cataloguing in Publication Data

Liska, George.
Russia and the road to appeasement.

Bibliography: p. 253
Includes index.
1. World politics—1945– 2. Soviet Union—Foreign relations—1945–
3. Soviet Union—Foreign relations—Europe. 4. Europe—Foreign relations—Soviet Union. 5. Soviet Union—Foreign relations—United States. 6. United States—Foreign relations—Soviet Union. I. Title.
D843.L54 327'.0904 81-48188
ISBN 0-8018-2763-9 AACR2

For Ian, Anne—and Suzy

CONTENTS

PREFACE

This is the final volume in a sequence of four books dealing, in historical perspective, with the rise and the present role and rivalry of the two superpowers and, thus, in their fashion, with the both classic and increasingly critical problem of the West's relations with Russia, and Russia's with the West. In the present instance, the correct order in a collective title for the quartet would be "The West and Russia," so as to indicate the gradual shift in the balance of concern and emphasis from the (Anglo-American insular) West, in *Career of Empire: America and Imperial Expansion over Land and Sea,* to the Russian (as part of the continental European) factor through, first, *Quest for Equilibrium: America and the Balance of Power on Land and Sea* (published a year before *Career,* but conceived to follow it thematically) and then *Russia and World Order: Strategic Choices and the Laws of Power in History,* to this, the comparatively most Russia-centered, volume. The so-called Third World is an important background factor and reference point throughout.

Because, with the exception of the first two companion "American volumes," no initial plan presided over the entire sequence, each of the four volumes is self-contained. However, they do share a general outlook, a basic method, and a range of analytical frameworks, hypotheses, and propositions spanning the dichotomy between empire (and preeminence) and equilibrium (and parity) as alternative great power–focused foundations of world order and, secondarily, between the conflictual state system and its putative, more benign, community-type alternative or successor.

The basic policy thesis, as it takes shape over the succession of volumes and is fully developed here in its manifold aspects, starts from the premise (established in the essential "empire" volume) that America's development as a nation is as much reducible to the common denominator of progressively expanding empires within a global balance of power system (delineated in the "equilibrium" volume) as is Russia's (sketched out, within the preestablished framework, in the present volume). Within this analytic setting, America's recent partial retreat from an imperial role is not reversed by concentrating national policies and energies on either liberal-humanitarian substitutes for military empire (the "world-order" volume) or on the strictly preventive task of impeding the expansion and inducing the erosion of the rival empire by a too mechanical, if ideologically inspired, application of elementary balance-of-power methods (by the Reagan, as distinct from the Carter, administration—the present volume). The situation requires instead the direction of strategic intelligence to the task of managing the equilibrium process in terms of a guarded progression toward complementing nuclear-strategic parity with geopolitical parity. If the purpose is to integrate Soviet Russia into the international system as an accepted role player in the maintenance of mutually acceptable world order, a means to it is to integrate, into U.S. policies toward Soviet Russia, a sophisticated concern for the policies' bearing on internal Soviet evolution in the post-Stalin (and, it is argued, properly postcontainment) phase, keeping in mind the bearing of developments in the world at large on both American and Russian national interests and foreign policies. At the end of rational policies on the part of both imperial rivals is the enlargement of the historic West by Russia's inclusion in an all-occidental concert, from which to channel the eventual assimilation of the Third World (or, the farther "East") into either a restored international system or an incipient world community.

Borrowing in one way or another from all three preceding volumes (and echoing here and there theses from my still earlier writings), but also substantially adding to them and synthetizing their main themes, this present volume is most closely related to *Russia and World Order.* In retrospect, the latter becomes an extended introduction, elucidating points and propositions about the West and the international system in general only alluded to or even but implied here—and making explicit my biases.

Personal history merges with general history only in the case of major actors on the international stage, but it can influence the interpretation and uses of general history by the mere student of international relations as well. In this book, I elaborate upon the ways I myself have been employing history as a basis for policy prescription in the overall framework of an analogico-historical approach and a conservative outlook. It must suffice at this point to say on the latter score that I stress a gradualist, or organic, unfolding of trends and am dogmatically resistant to ideology (right- and left-wing) as a policy determining factor. Although my basic philosophy is conservative, the policy I recommend is more liberal toward the Soviet Union of the future (as I see it) than is the approach of the self-consciously tough-minded liberal convert to anticommunism—or conservatism. However, I do not see the policy effectively and consistently applied by a soft-mindedly liberal policymaker aspiring to a world free of conflict and a future cleansed of past aberrations.

The case for a guardedly permissive foreign policy toward Soviet Russia implies showing sympathy for traditional Russia's case against the West. Making a fuller statement would require allowing more space to the negative aspects of both traditional and contemporary Russia, as well as placing more emphasis on constraints upon the latter in the proposed strategy. However, the task of the foreign-policy scholar is to produce internally coherent rather than balanced statements of a position or policy. His and the statesman's tasks are separate and different; the scholar is safer indulging in a *reductio ad absurdum* than offering ready-made blueprints for instant application.

I hope there is some truth, if not all of it, in what follows. If so, the effort of an expatriate from eastern Europe to recapture a gleam of insight from a troubled past may point to a more hopeful future for a West restored to its fullness than seems presently in the offing. An intuition of the conditions of private peace may dictate a workable prescription for public appeasement. Who else is to take the risk of projecting insights from an accomplished past into an uncertain future if not one who was arrested in time by the loss of place and, compelled thus to bestride two worlds in different historical time zones, lacks assured footing in one of the worlds if it remains unreformed, and in the other if it is unenlarged? The expatriate's musings can be a menace to the public good only if a one-sided doctrine conceals the origins of sentimental bias behind the reasoning (as easily happens, not only with the foreign-born commentator on Soviet matters). And their possible benefit would be lost if an overly elaborate doctrine were to hide an essential, simple point: as presently constituted, the West must begin changing its pervasive cultural bias toward the nearest East before uncorrected limitations of outlook can turn into incorrigible deformities that invite major policy disappointments. As this is written, the circumstances are not propitious for such a beginning.

It is now some years since I first analyzed the state of world politics after the American disengagement from a career of empire by analogy with the pre–World War I great-power triangle.* More recently, "rumors of war," based on analogy with events preceding either World War I or II, have made their appearance in many places including the normally nonspeculative columns of a major newspaper and popular bestsellers.† Where the analogy with pre–World War I events in the *Foreign Affairs* article is explicit and limited to the war's origins, the analogy between World Wars I and III in the fictional account is more implicit, especially as regards the course of conflict.

**Quest for Equilibrium: America and the Balance of Power on Land and Sea* (Baltimore: Johns Hopkins University Press, 1977), pp. 118 ff., and passim.

†Cf. Miles Kahler, "Rumors of War: The 1914 Analogy," *Foreign Affairs* 58, no. 2 (Winter 1979/80): 374–96, Drew Middleton, "Does It Seem Like 1914? 1939? Or Just Jittery 1980?" the *New York Times,* 6 May 1980, p. A2; Sir John Hackett et al., *The Third World War: August 1985 (New York: Macmillan, 1978).*

All the aforementioned discussions differ from mine in that they offer what might be called literal or formal analogies. Actors or events are compared or implicitly equated without first making explicit the relevant structures of power and the framework of analysis that would help in identifying what is comparable and equivalent. But, in the absence of a disciplining framework, it is impossible to segregate the essential from the accidental. Similarities and differences risk then being superficial or irrelevant as regards major as well as minor actors and both protracted processes and dramatic events. Thus, little is gained by citing Balkan antecedents to the World War I in connection with a possible World War III, by updating technologically the battle of the Marne as a way of stopping a hypothetical Soviet offensive in the west, and by positing one more outburst of end-of-war disaffection by the Asian subjects of the Russian empire as a way of finally dissolving it in the east.

My approach is to make explicit the structures of power that have implied consequences for basic attitudes or functions and thus also for what is apt to happen and when. It is possible that the drawbacks of such a schematized approach exceed its expository and didactic virtues, quite apart from its predictive potential. But the underlying issue of the use of analogy in the study of international relations is sufficiently fundamental to be of interest in itself. Contested among academics, the use of historical analogy is commonplace in the state papers written by the greatest practitioners of diplomacy. This alone suggests the reasons why scholarly doubts about the method are exaggerated if the method is properly applied, and are also somewhat beside the point.

One reason is that the circumstances in which statecraft operates are so opaque, the nature of responses to which it is exposed is so unpredictable, and information available at any time on all counts is so inadequate, that any identifiable reference point is valuable. This need imparts a highly attractive quality to already completed and known actions and reactions, and their consequences. The valuable analytical aid is, moreover, also a reassuring psychic support for what is at best a highly problematic speculation or action with portentous social implications. Because of the great potential benefit, it is possible and may be necessary to accept the risk of a wrong analogy or even of a misleading use of analogy in the wrong hands.

Closely related to the subjective reassurance analogies give to the formulator of grand strategy is another reason. The use of historical analogy can impress the audience with an authority difficult to establish by other means. Writing on grand strategy is intended not only to illuminate a problem but also to persuade, not only to devise approaches but also to encourage their adoption. It is important that such writing inspire confidence, not only by virtue of the power and plausibility of the proponent's insight but also on the strength of a quality easier to assess—his professional expertise. If the "brilliant" conception is to be taken seriously, it must be profiled against a solid background of cumulatively acquired competence.

In this respect, again, because the inherent quality and validity of strategic thought is difficult to judge and nearly impossible to be widely agreed upon in a highly competitive market of ideas, there is no surer evidence of expertise, even in our technology-conscious times, than the apparent mastery of relevant history. Indeed, its authority increases relative to all kinds of technical know-how as the issues at stake rise on the scales of "high" policy or "grand" strategy. Although the kind of preferred history will vary—thus panoramic history will attract the speculative strategy formulator and pragmatic history the active foreign-policy strategist—statecraft and history are in either case as closely linked as is social science and, say, the participant observation of small-group behavior.

Because the historical focus of this book is on the question of "Russia and 'Europe,' " the discussion inevitably spans two separate but interconnected issues that can be conveyed by two dates: 1914 and 1984. The first of these is associated with an event and the second with a thesis or theses: those of George Orwell and Andrei Amalrik, anticipating respectively the degeneration of Soviet totalitarianism and its catastrophic demise. I have been much less keenly reacting to these imaginative constructs, identified with a year that is fast approaching, than to the catastrophe associated with the year now long past. And most acute of all has been my awareness of a doctrine—that of containment—associated with the author of another, more celebrated, *Foreign Affairs* article.* It has actually become little by little a challenge to write a species of "Y" to follow upon "X" (the symbol under which the article was anonymously published). To even make the attempt meant dovetailing historico-cultural themes with a geopolitical perspective.

When fundamental issues of long-range strategy are at stake, the link between the structure of power among states and the structures of authority and control within them becomes so close as to be inescapable. Even a foreign-policy "realist" who habitually treats domestic sources of high-risk policy as subordinate to external constraints and imperatives cannot but acknowledge the link. I was led, as a result, to reecho the questions raised in the literature on totalitarianism, while at the same time discounting the more pessimistic prognoses on the strength of the unfolding evidence and my own value-based instincts. Rightly or wrongly, what started out as a narrowly policy-oriented essay—a polemical tract for the times—has turned as a result into a minor dissertation on abiding themes: war and peace, tyranny and

*See the footnote on p. 249 for closer identification of the article to which I refer. Andrei Amalrik's *Will the Soviet Union Survive Until 1984?* (New York: Harper & Row, 1970) is, in both title and content, an update of George Orwell's *Nineteen-Eighty-Four* from the viewpoint of a dissenter familiar with, and highly critical of, Soviet reality after Stalin.

liberty and necessity and choice; forms of power and spirit, justice and guilt—forces for alienation and terms in appeasement: all sources of ambiguities and dilemmas that confer tragic form on otherwise trivial functions.

The variety of subjects alone accounts in part for the book's complex structure. Another partial reason is inherent in the essential simplicity of the main thesis. Being essentially simple, the thesis is also one that cannot be conclusively proven by either demonstration from historical evidence or by means of a wide range of practical applications in policy terms. As a result, the only way to make the case I could think of was to enlarge the universe under discussion in order to generate an overall impression favorable to persuasion. The hope is that the resulting delineation of a viewpoint or mind-set will be perceived as deserving a place in the spectrum of opinion to be considered on a subject whose importance exceeds even its complexity. If a more than desirable amount of repetition attended the effort, the compensating advantage is that individual chapters or parts of the book can be read separately, depending on the reader's primary interest. They are largely self-contained even if, one hopes, also significantly interconnected in the larger scheme.

ACKNOWLEDGMENTS

There may be no better time for me to acknowledge at long last my indebtedness to Henry Tom, the Social Sciences Editor of The Johns Hopkins University Press, for his unflagging sympathy and his unvarying support of my efforts over a number of years. I could not be more grateful.

Jane Warth brought grace to the editing of the manuscript.

I also thank the Hon. Lucius D. Battle, Chairman of the Foreign Policy Institute at the School of Advanced International Studies (SAIS) of The Johns Hopkins University, for setting aside, from the institute's limited resources, a stipend for the editorial assistance of Mr. Steven Metz, a graduate student at Hopkins.

The strategic concept outlined in this book was originally presented on 8 May 1980 at the last regularly scheduled discussion meeting of the Washington Center of Foreign Policy Research at the initiative of its director, Simon Serfaty, who also took a more than casual interest in the manuscript's early version.

As the more directly policy-related complement to teaching at Hopkins' Department of Political Science and at SAIS, the Washington Center played a vital role in my professional life over two full decades, from the day in 1960 when the late Arnold Wolfers invited me to join its activities (and write what was to become *Nations in Alliance*), until 1980, when the center formally expired and its main activity was merged into the Foreign Policy Institute. For all it is worth, I wish, therefore, this book to stand alongside the other volumes in the West-and-Russia sequence as my last, fond testimonial to the disinterested public function that the center and its members, associates, and guests performed when monitoring in round-table discussions and recording in a variety of published formats the major developments and the often stirring events that took place in the "real world" during its institutional lifetime.

PROLOGUE.

The Conservative Idea and the Issue of Traditions

To consult the past without assuming that it can be reproduced in full is the first impulse of the philosophical conservative. It ought to shape the conservative idea as it struggles for expression in American foreign policy. Properly understood, the conservative idea rests on the basic belief that social change, in order to be beneficial and lasting, ought to be gradual; that each phase or stage of the change ought to grow out of an anterior one. A derangement of that rhythm will set off an upheaval tantamount to revolution. But even when there has been a sharp break in either growth or decay, it will be neither complete nor final. It will be reabsorbed in due course into the evolutionary flow as order is restored and as restoration amends some features among those that set off the upheaval and shaped its course, while it alters or aggravates other features.

If public action and affairs are to have meaning, the flow of change must be reducible to a pattern, however general. If it is to be more than an intellectual abstraction or an ordinance from above, moreover, the pattern must have a relationship to both innate drives and conscious purposes. It must have such a relationship no less than social order must match drives with duties if it is to be stable, and must fit man's duties to his station if it is to be also fundamentally equitable. Such an order is never fully realized either within or among organized societies, any more than is a clearly discernible and wholly pervasive pattern of change. But both order and pattern can be postulated as an ideal norm and act then as a constant summons to individual and collective perfomance that is more than haphazard. As part of such performance, states qua powers, too, have drives to channel, roles to play, rank to uphold and deserve, and duties to perform in both the wider system of states and the larger scheme of things if the rights and prerogatives they claim and enjoy are to be rooted in more than superior force.

Within such a view, just as perception and action must reflect a sense of history as something more than a random collection of events, so too must both perception and action be guided by a doctrine that is neither simply a statement of ethical purpose nor a mere recipe for operational success. A reading of history disciplined by attention to present trends and emerging needs will secrete a correct doctrine; the draft on history will rectify a too abstract theorizing about matters social and political without barring a speculative approach to past and present statecraft. The doctrine itself will correct for history when it is translated into a strategy that heeds the lessons from past misjudgments and derangements. If the speculative mode does not raise the sights, history is the subject of anecdote after the event, and statecraft the object of conditioned reflexes before the event.

This suggests that the American fact and the conservative idea stand to one another in a contradictory relationship suggesting incompatibility. America was conceived in the act of breaking with what her founders saw as a wrong, alien, and despotic rule; she was schooled by rejecting history for right, innate and unfettered, reason. When approaching adulthood she produced only a bastard conservatism, as the despondent musings of a few Europeanizing elitists gave way before the home-grown vitality of the provincials. This brand of conservatism matched states' rights and free enterprise at home with geopolitical isolationism and, most recently, militant—or military hardware-oriented—anti-Sovietism abroad.

Isolationism ignored future probabilities just as anti-Sovietism has since denied them. What the former lacked, the latter has stunted—the sense of history, which teaches the certainty of flux. Isolationism was from the beginning doomed to flourish only provisionally. It might have faded safely and perhaps even beneficially at a more gradual rate if, at the decisive moment of passage from the nineteenth into the twentieth century, Americans had viewed with greater detachment the evolving configuration of power abroad.

Anti-Sovietism by contrast might usefully fade faster than it has done actually. It expresses, as did isolationism, not only a fixed—and then idealized—image of self, but also a frozen image of the "other" as diabolical. It is immune to any real empathy for the (Russian) past, as that past catches up with the (Soviet) present, nor has it any real sense of what the future may call for as it drifts out of America's once-determining grasp. As only superficially its opposite, anti-Sovietism rejoins isolationism as a revolt against seemingly new complexities as they revive the intricacies of either the national or the larger past. It, too, is profoundly ahistorical. It is, furthermore, profoundly antidoctrinal, while at its most doctrinaire it serves as the warrant for a crude form of will-do policy pragmatism often verging on opportunism.

Thus doctrinaire anti-Sovietism is right-wing without being philosophically conservative. Its votaries view Soviet Russia and America outside proven sequences of events, evolving structures of power, and past strategies that either permitted or aborted organic change. They isolate the relationship of the two nations and powers from the global and intercultural settings of threats and opportunities, and supply no key to an acceptable denouement. Least of all do they suggest how evolution could resume after it was disrupted by systemic revolution, stimulated by great-power competition, or by the dissolution of a major state, without destroying in the name of modernity or humanity more of what still remains in world affairs of valid and viable tradition.

The right-wing American pseudo-conservative is suspect of lacking a concrete idea of what is to be conserved or of what is to be sought. His intellectual poverty is equaled only by the psychological obtuseness of American, or any other, liberalism. Because he sees foreign affairs through the prism of his philosophy of domestic affairs, and is anxious to be as authentically American as is the liberal with his more genuinely indigenous pedigree, the pseudo-conservative limits his vision to a certain idea of freedom and a certain form of its denial. He speaks, and on occasion acts, as if either the abstract notion or the crude denial of freedom could supply a more efficient master key to understanding and shaping the arena of world power than either did in and for the marketplace. The stark fact that the field of interstate relations is *not* the same as the marketplace never surfaces; and thus the American conservative is unequipped for "free" competition with cultures that rank different aspects of freedom differently.

Such conservatism becomes indistinguishable from liberalism when its votaries assume that the human predicament within and among nations can be expressed, and dealt with, in terms of one idea or value alone; that state power can be reduced to either brute force or subtle skill in policy without delving into the nether layers of national cultures and mentalities; that the social dimension of faith is confined to formal—or formally free—church worship; and that religiosity as a state of mind can do without the gift of wonder at the frequency with which the ways of power again and again defeat the man-chosen objectives of the will to power.

When the American would-be conservative allows himself to be repelled by the diabolical, he loses the ability to be dialectical. He cannot think of contrasts and oppositions as events that might complement one another within a grander design than his political culture teaches him to regard as expedient, and over a longer trajectory than he has become accustomed to as relevant. Cut off from doctrine, the self-styled conservative ends up being dogmatic. He exhibits self-satisfaction, whereas his liberal counterpart is tempted by self-depreciation; he insists arrogantly on inherited gains, whereas the other abjectly seeks to purge a share in inherited guilt.

But there is a better way to domesticate the conservative idea in the making of American foreign policy: to steer international relations closer to traditional modes, but also as much away from mere repetition as from the distortions wrought by two world wars and the disguises staged in two world organizations. The authentic conservative would direct the emerging world system of states toward orderly hierarchies and equilibria capable of checking the spread of anarchy; if necessary, he would not shrink from policies liable to the charge of appeasement in one—the great-power—arena and of anachronism in regard to another—the smaller-state—arena. For charting such a way it is necessary to rethink relevant history in terms of categories that are sufficiently broad to have relevance for grand strategy, with regard to events sufficiently specific to be meaningful for policy in the immediate future, as well as in a remoter one. And it is equally necessary to stop believing that, in order to uphold free choice and moral responsibility in politics, one must repudiate the very notion of historically evidenced regularities and tendencies.

Without the rudder of traditional doctrine, America's ever more direct intrusion into shifting currents of European politics before and during World War I deflected inevitable changes inside Europe into aimless drift and global dispossession. The inevitable consequence of this intrusion set in when America abruptly slipped into the leadership of the Atlantic West during and after World War II. Then, untempered in will and unapprenticed to skills, American society and its elites were equal to the new tasks only so long as issues were straightforward, and responsive to sheer material weight. The power lost its compelling force when the world began to fall back into a more complex condition, compounding apparent with real anarchy, and the charm of hegemony lost its potency when, almost simultaneously, American substance faded without bearing the late fruit of either a new sagacity or a finer sensitivity. A society no longer innocent but seemingly unfit to become imperial, neither truly religious nor authentically worldly, set about subverting the institutions of the State while the State itself failed to hold fast and steady the moorings of the Occident.

The infant heir on trial to a great epic has not ceased soon enough and for long enough to behave as the spoiled infant of world history. It is largely, if not only, of historical interest whether America rendered a service or a disservice to old Europe by intervening in her affairs at a time when Britain's preeminent power was due to pass into other hands one way or another. The present danger is that American policies might be less hypothetically damaging to the West at large. The epic of the West is in danger of ending on a note unworthy of its earlier shapers and its main thrust; its empire in danger of coming up for auction again if it is not to cease being either empire or western. When matters have reached such a pass, only new blood can invigorate even as it dilutes: only he who stood outside so far is still fired by the insiders' past greatness; only he has the will to make image reality again—and the reality, his.

It is not yet the time for the war of succession to America. But the time has come when Russia is the Occident's last and needed reserve of strength. If her bid for coregency is ignored, the threat she poses is of usurpation. Yet for the bid to rest on more than strength, and spare all the trials of usurpation, the Soviet regime will have to go on opening itself up to the humane instincts of an older and happier Russia, while keeping intact the reward for her adversities, ingrained tenacity. It must do both if sharing leadership in the enlarged West is to coincide not only with Russia restoring Europe's standing in the world, but also with Europe resuming her internal history at the point where the Latin, Anglo-Saxon, and Germanic architects had let it pause.

Russia's delayed rise to her place in the genealogy of historic Europe—and to new world power—need not reduce the "American century" to an interlude of only a few decades. Nor need it reduce American preeminence to a random sidetracking of the gravitation of power away from societies and civilizations sturdy enough to bear the ordeal of greatness along with its ornaments. If it does nonetheless, the fault will not have been with the stars, but with a Brutus-like inability to marry aspiration to aptitude. There is a better way to conciliate East and West within the total Occident than was the path chosen by and for—for and by—Germany. The unity should, but need not, be larger than Europe's only; it must run deeper than can be wrought by diplomatic strategy alone.

The omens for avoiding past errors in the interest of a less than catastrophic future have not been favorable when, in the first year of a new decade, self-styled neoconservatives took over from old-style liberals the control of American foreign policy. If anything, their ingrained tendency to view immediately unattractive change as something to be forcefully stopped, rather than to be creatively controlled and channeled, was reinforced by the condition of world politics in general—and of U.S.-Soviet relations in particular—left behind by the immediately preceding regime. The transfer of power has been meaningful for once in terms of domestic politics. But it merely highlighted the essential continuity—or continuous fluctuations—in American policies toward Russia. It is a policy that depends on chance events more than on a steadying sense of evolution, and is buttressed by the easy convergence of liberals and conservatives on the platform of a tough anti-Soviet stance. Any Soviet act or set of acts will offend that cannot be explained or justified in terms of either the "reasonable" conservative's conception of businesslike behavior or the "idealistic" liberal's view of humane conduct; responses will converge whenever the ideological conservative's anti-Sovietism is given a new lease on life for what, from his vantage point, have always been the right practical reasons, while the ideological liberal's greater willingness to take a more hopeful view of Soviet Russia is once again shown to have been always based on the conceptually wrong reasons.

The issue came to a head when, in late 1979, Soviet tanks rolled into Afghanistan. At that point, the West indulged under liberal American auspices once again in affirming an instantly cost-free principle on an eastern matter. It neither made a show of political realism nor stood back to see whether third-world adepts at *Realpolitik* could be shocked into appropriate response. Having defied Islam with palpable force, Russia was thrown down an idle challenge. Every act of official U.S. reprisal amidst crescending affirmations of a wider peril signaled submission to counsels of either instant panic or immediate expediency. It also advertised the continuing indisposition of the American people to rise to reactions that would do more than broadcast a virtual inability to act effectively. Had the evaluation of Soviet intentions been accurate, the threat would have called for actions well beyond the nation's physical ability to carry through. Instead, the threat's exaggeration disarmed the government psychologically; it could only pose as if ready to lead the world into another spell of the cold war; and it actually relied on a punitive use of bread (the grain embargo) and games (the Olympics boycott) for maiming Russian force and defending the West's supply of fuel (Middle Eastern oil).

It is a moot point whether the cold war prolonged World War II for an additional generation or replaced World War III for its duration. In either case it quieted down when spheres of superpower control or influence were at least provisionally delimited; when the right of each major power to maintain control within its sphere by all necessary means was recognized; and when a less than immediately vital sector of effectively unassigned new countries was provisionally consigned to the ambiguous status of nonalignment. Attempt at détente languished when the drift of American policy and the retreat of American power expanded the zone of countries no longer earmarked for privileged access by a major power, and when Soviet armament on land and sea pointed toward strategic parity to be codified in arms-control agreements and consolidated on the ground.

The internally fractured American response to the Soviet-Cuban success in Angola in the mid-1970s had concealed a newly awakened hesitancy how to act to control change. The furor over Afghanistan hid the revived temptation to withhold after all from the Soviets the recognition of Russia as a world power by indicting their behavior as a regional power. What was rolled back was, however, not so much Soviet global expansion as the political clock, which then approached the zero hour of a possible second cold war. Ambiguity over Angola betokened the need for adjusting policies to a less ambitious post-Vietnam strategy. Agitation over Afghanistan covered up frustration over the consequences of reduced ambition, including the festering Iranian question, and over interlocking past misjudgments about what détente could reasonably mean outside SALT; about what the Soviets could, or could be expected to, contribute to expanding human-rights or public-law morality while being frozen in place geopolitically and out of a positive role diplomatically; and about what America could do within the compass of something once called planetary humanism in order to avoid isolation from the Third World while thwarting a growing Soviet involvement in it.

The near-unanimous outburst of anti-Soviet feeling in the wake of an overt military move that merely ratified a previously unprotested political status quo in Afghanistan was an instance of elevating procedure above substance as a criterion of threat. It set back all prior prospect for dispassionately comparing the Soviet threat with other threats. It meant that neither a public avid for simple foreign-policy nostrums nor a foreign-policy elite divided between those viewing a newly complex world as unmanageable and those yearning for the simplicities of bygone mastery could refuse a seemingly instant remedy to the loss of bearings through a lost war. There was little or no audience for the proposition that the imperial Soviets were not the principal danger to stability; that, having been rejected as potential costabilizers in a critical area, they were bound to set about destabilizing it within widening circles. Thus the stage seemed set for replaying the confusion of signals among the great powers over the issue of influence in political Islam that had preceded the escalation of the cold war-like Anglo-Russian contest into an outright (Crimean) war in the middle of the last century.

The more recent U.S.-Soviet cold war was due both to a vacuum of power that the nearby victors over Germany—other than Russia—were unable to fill, and to a dual western failure: to advance militarily as far as possible (to Berlin and Prague at the very least) *and* to effectively and promptly recognize Soviet control in the eastern-European residuum that was beyond practical reach. With its causes similarly stripped to essentials, a second cold war might originate over the vacuum of power east-of-Suez (created by Britain's final withdrawal from the defense of India against Russia and likewise unfillable by local parties as presently constituted or disposed), and a dual American failure: to advance sufficiently into, or hold onto prior advance in, the evacuated area (such as Iran) *and* to effectively recognize Soviet claim to a share in legitimate access to critical areas and assets in the residuum.

A prolonged refusal to either grasp or avow the elementary, structural causes of the actual cold war gave rise to much surface agitation. A battle of words among spokesmen for the superpowers was followed by one among historians debating the issue in terms of either near-anecdotal facts and events or allegedly fundamental but actually far-fetched "causes." Because Americans in particular ranged all the way from self-assigned blamelessness to *mea-culpa* breast-beating, the debate among them followed the path traced by orthodox and revisionist German historians after World War I. Now the West holds itself once again blameless as its spokesmen weigh responsibilities for the reescalating American-Soviet contention.

Likewise structural is the one key difference between the first cold war and its possible repetition. Conditioning the first conflict was a clear-cut asymmetry between the United States as a world and sea power and the Soviet Union as a regional and land power. It has since become an issue whether this form of structural asymmetry is to continue basically unchanged. Can or will the Soviets be contained in, or pushed back into, their land-bound ghetto? Can or will the West accept that the Soviets, having safeguarded in Europe the continental access route to Russia from the west first militarily and then, at some cost to their ideological impermeability, also diplomatically, have since set about securing their ethnically soft underbelly in the south and expanding their maritime exits for long-term economic security outside Europe?

Soviet pursuit of world power has replicated, updated, and in some respects expanded the foreign-policy goals of the tsars. Soviet ambition has grown less since the end of World War II than has ability, as Brezhnev gave substance to Stalin's perfunctory claims (to a share of Italian colonies and a revision of the Straits regime) on the ruins of Khrushchev's premature forays into *Weltpolitik.* The Brezhnev group drew the correct conclusions from the later stages of the Congo crisis in Africa and the first missile crisis in the Caribbean while deciding on the kind of needed military capabilities; it then deduced from the repulse of its own initiative (in the second so-called missile crisis, in 1973, over the Middle East) where and how to use the new capabilities. American policymakers have failed to give substance to *their* succession to the role of imperial Britain in containing Russian power in ways that might also harness it to the defense of shared interests. They have been more adept at reproducing the India-centered Russophobia of the Britishers in a superficially ideologized garb. They were ready to inflate the stakes, but reluctant to reduce imaginary options to a repugnant choice: between restoring nuclear-strategic (and other military) superiority and merely regulating progress toward geopolitical parity. If common prudence forbade repudiation of strategic-nuclear parity, a sense of providential entitlement anchored in moral superiority and rank seniority ruled out consent to reapportioning either world power or role in the maintenance of world order.

A delayed risk arose from forgetting the condition of public endurance. The "common man" endured the rigors of the "first" cold war because he believed that the West had made a fair try at conciliating Soviet interests and satisfying their legitimate needs. It matters little whether the attempt was perceived in positive terms or was part of a negative image, was read into the invitation to Russia to be one of three postwar "comfortable policemen" or was impugned as a false rationale for western "sell-outs" at the several end-of-war summits. It is not certain that, were stresses to grow into the need for real sacrifices, any of the latest U.S. administrations could have supplied a similar demonstration of prior forbearance.

The testing calamity may or may not arise and, if it arises, push matters beyond a renewed cold war. But it is already possible to conclude—even if not yet easy to convince many—that it was impertinent to invite and was unreasonable to expect a power aspiring to a world role to uphold an order manifestly tailored to keep it in regional confines. It was, for the same reasons, improvident to go on clinging to a doctrine and a strategy that condemned any U.S. policy, of any administration, to at the least the appearance of inconsistency and drift, because it was unable to bar all Soviet expansion for lack of either means or support and had to conceal this inability behind changing rationales.

Not all would be a loss if improvidence pushed matters beyond impertinence. More library shelves would be filled with dissertations about who made the first mistake, committed the first misdeed, or took the first misstep toward another cold, or a worse, war.

Neither changing rationales now, nor retrospective ratiocinations then, could conceal the fact that peevishly denouncing every seeming or actual increase in strength of the Soviet empire, while hailing its every real or apparent political and economic weakness, is not an adequate substitute for a steadied will to resume and reaffirm America's abandoned imperial role. The design for a revitalized, if restricted, American empire has remained as foreign to the crabbed world view of the socio-culturally "new," post-Vietnam foreign policy elites, as the willingness to bear the cost alongside the hidden fruits of empire has remained lacking in the general public.* Attitudinizing by the fading Carter administration has been only questionably improved upon by the posturings of the still ebullient early Reagan administration; neither technique for concealing the atrophy of creative ambition did justice to a fermenting world's need for the constraining or ordering influence of either controlling or countervailing rational power, or powers, if there is to be an orderly retreat of conquering power. The fresh, conservative administration did not begin to supply an answer to the question of how to relate the infinitely extensible scope of a rigidly anti-(Soviet) imperialist policy to the strict limitations of a nonimperial (American) polity, any more than its tired liberal predecessors had known how to replace a genuinely imperial policy with something better than moralizing ersatz imperialism. Both sought sooner or later to escape, one way or another, the horns of the empire-equilibrium dilemma that impale the superpowers into actually still more perplexing efforts to balance the claims of human rights

*I left open the possibility of a different evolution in the otherwise pessimistic conclusions of *Career of Empire* (Baltimore: Johns Hopkins University Press, 1978), pp. 190–97, 319–20, 328–29, 349.

against the demands of interstate rivalry internationally, and to accord advances toward social justice with economic growth as well as stability internally—or also internationally.

The fate of an eventual combination of the but falsely alternative approaches in an American foreign policy for both reordered and orderly world politics hinges on the outcome—and the outcome on the conduct—of the contest with the "other" empire. As a contest, it is clearly larger, and is destined to be longer, than was America's first (and last?) peripheral war of empire in Asia; it is even more truly "political" than "military." Its peaceable conduct and peaceful outcome hinge in turn on more than the possibility to harmonize the requirements of social justice in and beyond the West with the economic costs and prerequisites of such justice; a farsighted policy must also live up to the high challenge of incurring and surmounting the politico-military risks implicit in a long-term effort (outlasting the span on any one administration) to satisfy, within contemporary limits, the eastern nation's intuition of what constitutes historic justice. Such a policy is more fitting—and, properly understood and implemented, can be (when needed) more forceful—than is the proliferation of doomsday scenarios regarding force trends and consequent events as if under way or impending, in defense of measures or strategies apt to reset the West and Russia on the path to mutual catastrophe in a future still remote, but not indefinitely deferrable.

A premature desertion of imperial mission is not made good overnight by overzealous devotion to balance-of-power mechanics. Nor will ominous prognostications about nuclear threat and imbalance erase the obligation to probe beyond the enigmas of a rival empire to the mystifying, organic and normative, constituents of equilibrium between disparate empires. To go on clinging meanwhile to America's eroding near-monopoly in geopolitical access overseas will not prove more lastingly feasible or widely beneficial than did the earlier attachment to atomic monopoly. Nor will a major war—if, for one or the other reason, it becomes (from the Russian viewpoint) necessary—be prevented by a nuclear war having become impossible.

Actually, the way out of necessity's frustrating encounter with impossibility is being cleared by every new weapons generation, as its contribution to the certainty of mutual nuclear destruction makes it more likely that even a major war can and will be confined to its conventional dimension. Indeed, in a reversal of current assumptions and practices, a major-power conflict may become more immune to the ultimate in escalation as lesser-power conflicts become less so. The sole—both sufficient and feasible—condition is that the conventionally winning side persuasively limit its objectives to restructuring the diplomatic-strategic environment to its advantage rather than aim at the political or physical destruction of the conventionally losing party. As this happens—becomes more plausible with every passing decade of nuclear-obsessed arms competition and either less operationally infeasible or more humanly tempting with every day of combat that has passed without actual recourse to the "ultimate" weapon—traditional "high" international politics becomes more than provisionally credible as something other than a gradually discredited simulation of the real thing; the price of misguided policies comes to match, and begins to exceed, the penalty of a mismanaged mix of nuclear and conventional armaments; and a cold war ceases to be a safe halfway house between formal peace and a real war.

If, in the meantime, the present state of morale, manpower, and matériel in the opposing military organizations has remained substantially unchanged, such a war could have only one immediate outcome. Reversing the setback in due course would require the henceforth isolated Anglo-American insular allies to first reverse any prior trend away from nuclear way by propelling China's vast manpower either into the nuclear age or toward the heart of Russia—thus placing Europe and the West at large in extreme jeopardy or lastingly within the penumbra of a great Asian power center.*

Let it be granted for once that it was prudent moderation that arrested America's imperial expansion, at the cost of turning a partial military victory in the late Asian "limited war" into political defeat, inviting economic aggression and civil demoralization. To thus commingle war and peace with their foster parents, empire and equilibrium, in a debatable proposition is useful chiefly if it points to a query critical for the future. Can the United States use the wider contest so as to rehabilitate its dearly won claim to historically rare sagacity from all suspicion, not least that of having been moved to stop advancing by a less instructive inner force and a less freely self-denying instinct. Can it, that is, act now so as to turn a partial military setback—the loss of strategic superiority—into a triumph of the political art on behalf of the more demanding sequel to expansion, consolidation: if not of a nation-enlarging world empire, then of a civilization-sustaining world system of states? So to act may first require managing America's residual sway for some time longer, and better than before, as if it were an empire, after having won and forsworn the larger one as but an instrumental device for waging and ending a cold war. Wresting new self-confidence from the collapse of early arrogance would make it easier to interact confidently with the other, still unabashed empire toward the end of equilibrium, via all-round parity and occasional concert. It would make this easier also because it would make it unnecessary to use alliance—the main policy instrument for balancing rival power—in support of no greater ambition than to force upon the kindred rival one's own degree of abdication before regionally dispersed disorders, to the advantage of either global anarchy or third-power ascendancy.

*For a differently unorthodox nuclear scenario see *Russia and World Order* (Baltimore: Johns Hopkins University Press, 1980), pp. 19–20.

Part One

INTIMATIONS FROM HISTORY

Twice in my lifetime, I have seen the peoples of Europe plunged into the tragedy of war . . . that statesmen proved powerless to prevent, soldiers unable to contain and ordinary citizens unable to escape. And twice in my lifetime, young Americans have bled their lives into the soil of those battlefields—not to enrich or enlarge our domain but to restore the peace and independence of our friends and allies.—Ronald Reagan (address to the National Press Club in Washington, 18 November 1981)

Whoever considers the past and the present will readily observe that all cities and all peoples are and ever have been animated by the same desires and the same passions; . . . But as such considerations are . . . unknown by those who govern, it follows that the same troubles generally recur in all republics.—Machiavelli, *The Discourses,* bk. 1, ch. 39

I

HISTORY AND POLICY.

Perspectives and Problems

An approach to the study of foreign policy drawing on history must be sensitive to what is uniquely constituted, but also must look beyond it to what is comparable; it must look beyond what is specific to what can be systematized. Temporal or cultural differences, changing material technologies or political theologies, will condition particular actions, but configurations of space will be sufficiently persistent and those of power recurrent enough to reduce the impact of such differences on basic patterns of action. To say so much is to affirm a substantial measure of continuity underneath more spectacular diversity. A statecraft committed to this presumption will strive to identify short- or long-term continuities in protagonists, patterns, or processes that can be relevant for policy; it will isolate precedents that are operationally significant, even though (and sometimes because) they are schematic, without denying the interest of that which is peculiar when viewed for its own sake in isolation.

In the search for relevant patterns, the evolution of state systems and of major powers—their rise, maturity, and decline—competes for attention with the development of civilizations. One does not replace the other, however. There is a link among all three: state, state system, civilization. As they evolve and mature, all three are characterized by a growing capacity (and necessity) to act rationally and to innovate creatively, before the process of growth slows down and is reversed into decline.

The rationality in question has a mundane function. It involves relating the most efficacious means to inherently feasible goals. It has little, and need have nothing, in common with the Hegelian postulate of a transcendental Reason that unfolds within and through a particular state or civilization. However, just as the exalted claims of systematizing metahistory can be thus sidestepped, so must the opposing limitations of a strict historicism be relaxed, when it narrows its perspective to unique individuality. Uniqueness or individuality cannot be treated as absolute for purposes of policy so long as the means-end rationality that is necessary to insure the minimum goal of survival is deployed within wider structures of power and interests. These structures are sufficiently determinate to be constraining, and sufficiently constraining to compel adaptation; the same structures are sufficiently broad and inclusive to entail the partial submersion of any one individuality into the dynamic of the larger setting.

The need to behave rationally—or "functionally"—within a determinate setting makes for a variable but definite measure of necessity in interstate relations. This alone reinforces the tendency for basic patterns and structures to recur. Freedom for individual initiative is restricted as a result. It is not abolished. A likewise varying residue of leeway remains, as does some scope for revising interstate norms and practices. Nor does necessity exclude uniformities being modified by the agency of values peculiar to a particular civilization. Historically generated or ratified patterns and trends combine and compete with both the fact of uniqueness and the potential for innovation and initiative within broad patterns. To be aware of this is to marry the caveats of historicism to the ambitions of systematizing (meta-) history.* It will enable history-conscious statecraft to save an inquiry into politics among states from two pitfalls: one, merely recording drearily repetitious interactions among culturally or otherwise neutral and unevolving units of power; another, thinking or acting as if good will, skill, or resolution alone could transform the world at any one point in the cycles of crisis and conflict.

Continuity is compatible with evolutionary changes that do not negate the persistence of basic patterns. It is not nullified by growth in the complexity of factors and forces within recurrent structures or configurations. Heightened complexity may even coincide with increased determinateness of the basic patterns when stripped bare of the dross of institutional accretions and normative or other concealments. Thus, interstate relations in the twentieth century are more complex than they were in the sixteenth century. But the triangular land- and sea-power pattern (crucial to this study) has been gradually clarified in regard to both the identity of the roles involved and the role-determined attitudes and responses on the part of the same or successive parties to the triangle.

*On this distinction see Hans Meyerhoff, ed., *The Philosophy of History in Our Time* (Garden City, N.Y.: Doubleday, 1955), and R. G. Collingwood, *The Idea of History* (London: Oxford University Press, 1946). See also Leon Pompa, *Vico: A Study of the "New Science"* (Cambridge: Cambridge University Press, 1975).

It is tempting to mistake progressive differentiation and multiplication of factors for progress and to identify progress with suspending the harsher features of traditional interstate relations. Yielding to this inclination will conceal or obscure persisting patterns and propensities. Ahistoricity is then the source of conceptual anachronism: where Vico's "conceit of scholars" once projected contemporaneous rationalism into a prerational past, it now often grafts onto the perception of the political present a putatively future-dominating rationality purged of atavistic preoccupation with power and prestige.

Perspectives on actors: the historico-evolutionary dimension

In one or two cases it would be meaningless to view policy toward Soviet Russia in the perspective of a repetitious dynamic or continuous evolution of the state system in general or of the western system in particular: if Russia as such were regarded as a power *sui generis,* or if *Soviet* Russia were viewed as discontinuous with traditional or tsarist Russia. Conversely, the historical perspective becomes relevant when it is shown that the external behavior of Russia and Soviet Russia can be assessed in terms permitting comparisons with the conduct of other major powers. At this point, the basis for such comparisons will be laid by analyzing a critical aspect of external behavior: Russian expansion, in terms of distinctions and categories that can be applied to other major powers, including the United States. Russia must be stripped of the stigma of exceptionality, just as America of its aura, if the hypothesis of overall continuity and comparability is to help conceptualize interstate relations in ways significant for even the most pragmatically inclined of foreign-policy makers.

Russian expansion as nation and empire. It is not uncommon to indict Russia as a nation and power that is both peculiarly and insatiably expansionist and to condemn her as an empire that is endemically unstable. In the first respect, she appears as a country that alternates erratically between spells of apparently irresistible expansionism and apparently irreversible collapse; in the second respect, she is perceived as a power that suffers from a cleavage between a strong military front and a weak socioeconomic rear. If the cleavage may vary in form, it does not in kind; and if the military strength is often fictitious, the socioeconomic weakness is fundamental and incurable. In such a view, no long-term evolution can be meaningful. What then matters for the western powers is only to decide whether to excoriate Russia's obtrusive strength in words or exploit her useful strength for intrawestern needs, and when to take advantage of her weakness in the hopes of perpetuating them.

Only a more balanced view of Russia will eschew inordinate fluctuations in moods and sidestep the perceptual pitfalls of treating Russia's malignant exceptionalism as the obverse of America's benign one. The Russian state is viewed then—as it will be here—as one more often pulled into a role in the central system by intrawestern or peripheral disorders than forcing itself upon that system. Moreover, it is viewed as one that not only has expanded in ways and for reasons common to most or all great powers, but has also grown at rates rarely if ever inconsistent with the prior or simultaneous expansion of other states and the system itself—inconsistent, that is, because manifestly superior.

Just as Spain or England or France (or, in reality or national mythology, America) expanded from a core in a series of responses to life-threatening intrusions from the outside, so too did Russia. The differences only reinforced the comparability. Thus, the inroads from the outside into England were few, feeble, and far between since the last formative one by the assimilable Normans; the one powerfully backed was from the gale-dispersed Spaniards. Only incursions by the Moors into Spain and by the Anglo-Normans into France were comparable in quality or function with the Mongol invasion of Russia.

The later Polish and Swedish (before the French and German) drives for Moscow across the northern or northeastern plain bear comparison with the Spanish (even before the German) drives for Paris from or across the northwestern "low country." But because the Russians had to endure and repel more of such invasions, in greater depth, and with greater frequency, they finally gained more of either territory or control area on the embattled land frontier. Likewise, the tendency of the Russian state to seek nurture in water for its material roots is not any different from the tendency of other states, including those initially more favored in this respect. The early drive for Italy and the Mediterranean of a France restored from her "time of troubles" is the equivalent of a similarly recovering Russia's later drive for the Baltic and Black seas, and toward the eastern Mediterranean. And Russia's own drive to gain a foothold in the northern seas was matched by even the Holy Roman Empire, that least seaworthy of states.

Much the same applies to the size of Russian expansion. By the close of the age of Peter the Great, it was certainly more than matched in the north by Britain's expansion into her first empire in the Atlantic. By the time of the great Catherine, the expansion southward was more than equaled by Britain's into her second empire in India. As Russia's horizons had expanded from the Crimea and the Caucasus to Korea, the same was true for Russia's and England's drives eastward: toward the more northern parts of China by the former and southern by the latter. No different conclusion would flow from comparing the rates of American and Russian expansion, first overland and then overseas, any more than from measuring Russia's growth against the first multiplying and then shrinking number of major power centers in the system at large.

On the whole, method differed more than did matter, and even that only in degree. Warfare was more barbarous and civilization more backward in the east than in the west, also because much of the soil was more barren and the climate brutal. And the strain of Russia's role as buffer between Europe and Asia was of some account in a part of the world where space became more tempting as it grew dear in the west.

Thus qualified, essentially "European" standards can be applied to Russian expansion's thrust and scope. Is this also the case for the temporally articulated phases of its evolution? One related question for present policy is whether the evolutionary trajectory of Russian foreign policy under the tsars intersects with its so far partial if accelerated replication under the Soviets. And, if it does, at what phase have the Soviets caught up with the tsarist sequence in Russia's essentially national foreign policy and chiefly overland-military expansiveness? A related question is whether that particular national-continental policy phase can be somehow interlocked analytically and functionally with a stage in Russia's imperial expansion, also or potentially overseas.

In the foreign policies of most or all major powers, greater inclination to expand tends to alternate with periods of greater concern with consolidation and conservation. Moreover—a less trivial point—the two basic dispositions vary discernibly in motivation and execution at the several stages of a major power's evolution, all the way from its emergence to withdrawal from an active role. One possibility is then to view the present Soviet foreign policy as poised at an evolutionary midpoint. As such, the policy is essentially conservative and oriented toward a global balance of power. Moreover, it rejoins the overall Russian trajectory at the point of the tsarist regime's conservative policy of and for balance of power within Europe only, traceable to the middle-to-late nineteenth century before the regime's decline.

The usual array of phases preceded the conservative one in the tsarist era. In succession, first came an early unfocused expansiveness, directed at the areas of least resistance during an initial formative phase; here belong the pre-Mongol Kiev period with north- and eastward expansion, and post-Mongol Muscovy's primarily eastward expansion, for chiefly economic stakes. It was followed by more systematic efforts to consolidate a viable and sustainable national habitat around the vital core; the two outstanding Ivans (III and IV) and Peter the Great were the main architects. And then, from a basis thus assured, came an explosion of exuberant expansionism, territorial and other, spearheaded by Catherine the Great and still alive in the early reign of the first of the nineteenth-century Alexanders. Whereas next was the aforementioned conservative phase typified by Nicholas I within an enlarged balance-of-power theater, terminal expansion took place in a compulsive-defensive reaction to decay and decline. It saw its finis in east Asia under Nicholas II.

The last stage sets in when a power gradually withdraws into passive dependence on the environing power balance. Russia did not reach the stage of self-isolation in a normal progression, but approximated it artificially and for a time during her revolution. The Soviets began their career with an unfocused expansionism that was motivated ideologically rather than economically; it occupied the formative phase of Trotsky-type world revolution. The race to catch up with the predecline tsarist trajectory continued by reenacting an Ivan- and Peter-like consolidation, culminating under Stalin. Logically and actually next was the expansive exuberance of Khrushchev's world policy, more Catherine- than Peter-like because more Europeanist in diplomacy as well as westernizing in technics. And setbacks in the exuberance period prepared the ground for the latest posture: one of a measured pursuit of balanced parity that extends internal conservatism into the world at large. Accordingly, the length and constructiveness of this phase, and when and how it might be followed by a near-terminal lapse into defensively compulsive self-assertion, will hinge on the success or failure of Brezhnev and his successors.

If Russia's current foreign-policy phase is identified as relatively benign, it can give rise to relatively benevolent conclusions. They will be confirmed true if a similar finding emerges along a different, if complementary, line of sequential analysis, focusing on Russia's status as an empire rather than, as before, a historic nation evolving into a great power. For the positive findings to be mutually reinforcing, the Soviet-Russian empire must be perceivable as approaching a less military and a more civilian phase. In that phase, the regime responds expansively abroad to a substantial advance in the society's or economy's internal evolution. But the dynamic source and quality of the external response meshes easily with conservative reaction to bids for, or trends to, revolutionary change—within or without, in the forms of socio-ethnic or religious upheavals or of strategic-military transformations.

A society that has evolved a substantial industrial or commercial sector typically directs its expansion overseas. It does so in function of an intricate internal dynamic marked by transactions—reciprocal concessions and compensations—between the so-far ruling elite and the rising class or group. The dynamic occupies the midterm of an empire's growth and life path, and supplements earlier stimuli to expansion that are more strictly external or more primitively acquisitive. A crudely acquisitive, predatory pursuit of material payoffs directed enterprising Russians mainly eastward, toward and across Siberia. Begun before, the drive continued after the era of Mongol dominance—itself a threat to existence, the successful overcoming of which typically provides the single most important impetus to empire-type expansion. Such expansion continues when the stimulus from simple predation has veered toward one from preclusion, perceived as defensive, of actual or hypothetical threats from major rival powers. Such threats, we either have seen or still will see, originated for post-Mongol Russia at different times in or across eastern Europe but also in and from Asia. Throughout, but with increasing relative importance, marginal additions materialize when the imperial power expansively defends a widening imperial frontier against disturbances by smaller local powers or anarchic forces. Afghanistan is this incentive's latest illustration in the area.

Historically, it was the rise of a commercial middle class that signaled an intensified role for domestic or societal inter–group dynamic in continuing expansion. A Soviet equivalent of such a dynamic cannot but be constituted and organized in a special way. Still, it may not only restimulate expansion but also redirect it overseas and toward the pursuit of mere influence. The prerequisite is an even but initial trend to diversify the policy-influencing, and civilianize the policy-executing, personnel and instruments away from the military; the likely consequence is to make the methods of imperial expansion, as well as management, more basically civilized by the use of more indirect and less coercive means. This can happen even if the narrowly economic determinant of expansion remains for a time tied to the military dimension, as it tends to be in early-imperial expansion before the economy is liberalized. Whereas the historically recurrent connection is with wars, it can be currently represented, next to warlike local events, by Soviet military-matériel sales or grants abroad.

Russia's lapses into conservatism were due in the late 1840s, as they have been more recently, to recoil from forces and influences that her leaders perceived to be intruding subversively from the outside into the state's social inside. It matters little whether this intruding force was decried as revolutionary by the defenders of tsarist legitimism or anathemized as counter-revolutionary in behalf of Soviet-type socialism. The more important difference between tsarist and Soviet Russia is in the relatively inferior Soviet position in the global balance of power compared to tsarist Russia's supremacy in the east–central European power field. In the contemporary setting, the difference has prompted a more exploitative than repressive foreign-policy approach to external upheavals outside the immediate Soviet orbit. But again, from Napoleon to Hitler and beyond, both Russian regimes were alike in one respect. The tsarist regime was, and the Soviet is, most reliably and acutely aroused to an expansive defense of the empire by the thrust of a westward-lying power southeastward, toward Russia's either strategically or ethnically soft underbelly.*

*See the author's *War and Order* (Baltimore: Johns Hopkins Press, 1968), pp. 4–11, for wider illustration of categories applied to Russia's expansion as nation, and *Career of Empire* (Baltimore: Johns Hopkins University Press, 1978), for more extensive discussion of categories relevant to Russia's expansion as empire.

Distortions in the perceptions of Russia and Russian policies. One way of viewing matters is to regard Russia and Soviet Russia as a continuous entity in foreign policy. Then, much about U.S.-Soviet relations can be inferred from earlier Anglo-Russian relations. Another way is to postulate a radical discontinuity between the two Russias and their external attitudes and relations. The discontinuity hypothesis rests on a particular way of ordering the supposed determinants of attitudes and relations. The change of ideology from regime to regime is rated over geopolitical and cultural constants; domestic political institutions and practices are ascribed greater influence over foreign policy than are the recurrent structures and pervasive dynamics of power internationally.

Another supposition lies behind perceiving both Russias, tsarist or Soviet, as radically different from other major powers, in general or during comparable stages of development. Russia is then viewed as an essentially non-European power, oriental or *sui generis,* and the inner-European state system as also unique—governed by historically evolved conventions peculiar to it rather than by more universally manifest laws of, or tendencies in, interstate dynamics. Such laws or tendencies, along with the associated constraints and stimuli, are then not seen as largely responsible for the basic patterns of the interstate dynamic, while inordinate emphasis is placed on the dynamic's routinized subliminations, self-deluding concealments, or near-ceremonial institutional overlays.

Being about equally commonplace, the essentially untheoretical views of Russian polity and policy and of European interstate politics have been responsible for a radically unstable perception of Russia that extends well into the present. The manifestations of this instability have been the contrary extremes of Russophobia and Russomania, responding to changing events at different junctures. They have been especially marked in the English-speaking section of the West ever since Russia emerged as a significant power early in the eighteenth century. The more favorable attitude prevailed whenever Russia appeared to be of possible use in contests bearing directly on the distribution of power within the West itself. This was the case, beginning with the War of the Spanish Succession, against France, only to apply eventually against Germany. The more hostile attitude resulted when Russia acted on her own. Such diverse and separated events included, in the British imperial period, Russia's advance overland into the Baltic region or into the Baltic Sea navally, and her real or seeming breakthroughs toward first the Black Sea and, at a later stage extending into the American era, the eastern Mediterranean and the Persian Gulf–Indian Ocean and Pacific Ocean areas. In the absence of other reasons, ever since Poland's second partition, periodic troubles there again and again injected the tinder of romantic Polonophilia into the dying fires of Russophobia.

Suspicions had developed in Britain even before convergence of British and Russian expansive drives and interests supplied, from the end of the eighteenth century on, a geopolitical basis for overt conflict in the nearer East and central and eastern Asia.* Conflict over eastern Europe came earlier in the American case and was direct even before extending to the traditional haunts outside Europe. But, in both instances, close to abstract geopolitical stakes were concretized whenever Russia seemed to offer a threat to the western power's access to a critical resource. The spectrum extended all the way from hemp and other naval stores from the Baltic in the early phase to oil from the Persian Gulf in the latest. In changing economic and technological conditions, unconditionally free access to one or another resource was regarded as essential for the western party's survival as a great power and, by extension, a functioning society.

Alarms gave way to equally unbounded admiration for Russia's feats of arms as ally, most notably against Napoleon's France in 1812 and Hitler's Germany in the 1940s. But, again, the admiration was as high-vaulting as any temporary or conditional acquiescence in the geopolitical consequences of the military performance was shallow. Restored peace in the west or renewed East-West tension made it soon appear desirable to push Russia back into her "natural" habitat on the margins of Europe and Asia. Even when Russia seemed a friend, or was a formal ally, resentments ran high when she refused to help implement a western conception of order. This tendency, lately co-responsible for cold-war spells, had an early beginning when the great Catherine refused to supply Russian troops against North American rebels and instead defied Britannia's rule of the waves with armed neutrality.

Fluctuations in moods will always reflect changing configurations in the balances of power and interests. They could not but make it difficult to keep the intermittent Anglo-Saxon view of Russia as a natural ally against a nearer-western threat at an even keel. But the normal changes in attitudes have been accentuated in regard to Russia by emotional excesses implicit in cultural distance. The distance is compounded by deformations peculiar to a pluralistic policymaking arena when the formulation of policy in relation to a relatively closed-off arena such as Russia's is surrendered to the two extremes of ideological generalities and technical or tactical specifics. The first deformation—pan-humanitarianism English-style one day, anti-Communism American-style another day—reflects assumptions of the elective statesman. He perceives the vast public as needing to see issues starkly polarized in ways that are easy to grasp intellectually, are gratifying or at least not offending emotionally, and are neutral in terms of whatever social or ethnic cleavages may beset his own political system internally. The second

*Later Anglo-Russian conflicts and related attitudes are discussed in Chapter 2. British attitudes in the later period are described in John H. Gleason, *The Genesis of Russophobia in Great Britain,* and the earlier period is covered in M. S. Anderson, *Britain's Discovery of Russia 1553–1815.*

deformation—most recently energy- and arms-related—reflects the operational code and requirements of the middle-to-upper-level policy professionals or experts. They have a stake in segregating issues into either technically or tactically definable and manageable slices of space, time, or function. Their assumption is that such issues are separable and, when separated, can be mechanically reassembled into a coherent grand strategy.

Perspectives on systems:
the historico-evolutionary dimension

The opposite to either ideological rationalization or technocratic rationalism is the solicitation of history with the goal of gaining a perspective on contemporary foreign-policy problems and of extracting clues for dealing with them. Historically informed and oriented statecraft has a commitment that is at variance with ideologically biased affirmations rooted in dogmatic certainty; and it is as different from assessments based on current technology or technique and recommended by their apparent rigor as it is from both futuristic anticipations and mere antiquarianism—the first advanced in the name of progress, the second looking back to paradise lost. Disclosing continuities will entail making comparisons between actors and systems at comparable stages of development. Such comparisons will span distances across time, whereas focusing on a shared time frame will highlight disparities among actors or segments of actors unequally matured or integrated into the international system.

The quest for regularities must not overwhelm relativity any more than relativity blot out regularities. Nor must the search for ordering sequence or structure stand in the way of insight if only an ad hoc, or random, comparison of past with present events or conditions can illuminate the path to correct policy by illustrating specific aspects relevant for policy. However, regardless of what past trend, cycle, or event is solicited as an avenue to insight—and how—to ignore perspectives drawing on the past when inquiring into the present problems is possible only at the price of postulating a fundamental change in the nature of international politics. Adopting that assumption is a risky expedient. Instead of adopting it, this inquiry will draw on several ranges of antecedents, from the relatively short- to the very long-term, on the theory that each is significant for a different span of present and future policy.

Short-span perspectives on continuities within and across systems. The critical questions within the shortest time perspective, from about the middle to the end of this century, are these: Will the essentially two-power, U.S.-Soviet, competition repeatedly heat up or will it be gradually relaxed? Will the international system tend toward restoration out of the multistage revolution that helped fire the interstate conflicts surrounding the rise and maturity of liberal capitalism as it spanned the seas and invaded continents? Or will order collapse, or the center of power shift decisively, under pressure from the next wave of revolution or rebellion originating in the extra-European world?

What about, first, a prolonged conflict enfeebling both of the rivals, one a relatively more western and maritime power and the other a more eastern and continental one? An early example of such a conflict is that between Byzantium and Persia up to and including the early seventh century. The eventual attrition of both rivals helped raise the curtain on the expansion of Islam, to the detriment of the relatively victorious eastern Rome as well. A two-power conflict ultimately tends to favor a third party. This does not mean that third-party threat will automatically produce or reliably consolidate détente between two principals or that concern about such a party will convert détente into entente.

A case in point is an epoch-making European peace (of Cateau-Cambrésis, in the mid-sixteenth century) between France and Spain over Italy. Both were Catholic powers with rulers equally antagonistic to revolutionary Protestantism. Ideological consensus on the subject of religious innovation and accompanying social upheavals made the secular rivals essay a common front, but without substantial or lasting success. The outcome of the prior contest had been too favorable for one party (Spain), whereas external appeasement caused greater internal division and weakness in the other party (France), for the desire for détente to long compensate for the disparities in the arena of power politics. The obverse can also apply, and ideologically biased perceptions defeat a promising attempt at accommodation undertaken on the strength of balanced military power that is deployed but held in reserve unused. Such a situation arose early in the thirteenth century when a Sicilian-based western emperor and his Moslem counterpart in Egypt tried to resolve the conflict over access to the Holy Land at the tail end of the crusades. The effort was thwarted in the West by the radically anti-Islam, clerical enemies of détente, no more willing to appease the territorially focused political conflict between pope and emperor within Christianity than they were to forgo in that contest the tactical assets stemming from the failure to attenuate the religio-ideological cleavage between Christianity and Islam in the world at large.

Some kind of third party was present in both instances: the Protestant party in the first, the pre-Reformation papacy in the second. No obvious third party influenced Britain's and Napoleonic France's attempt to reach accommodation at mid-conflict (the Peace of Amiens, in 1802)—unlike in the later Franco-Russian effort at Tilsit, when England was the ultimately insufficient common enemy. While wartime exhaustion or frustrations deputized for a third party as incentive in the first-named effort, the inhibitions included a tactical dilemma in both. Either party sought to safeguard itself against the possibility that a tenuous peace would yield to renewed hostilities. This uncertainty encouraged either party to cling to the contested positions renounced contractually or otherwise as part of the effort at accommodation. As one party's safeguard became provocation for the other party, the possibility of a renewed conflict grew more probable; the tactical dilemma triggered renewed hostilities in a protracted conflict. Instrumental in precipitating the resumption of Franco-Russian hostilities, the dilemma was sharpened in the Anglo-French case by an underlying incompatibility between the dominant land power and the preeminent maritime state. The former's urge toward overseas outlets from a secure continental base was, in the latter's perception, a threat to its geostrategic and economic arteries and thus to its very heartbeat in the home base; France's claim to equality spelled England's fear of abridged freedom.

When this happens, the polemic over who defeated the appeasement effort is futile and can be settled only by invoking fatality; the structural incompatibilities can be overcome, if at all, only by a strategic concept correctly weighing the risks from too many or too few timely concessions to the forward party.

What are the suggested conditions of effective détente pointing to entente? They include some kind of parity in arms deployments and in outcomes of contests over stakes focused territorially, underpinned by a clear identification of a shared threat, as well as supporting it. Moreover, all such conditions must be sustained by the erosion of nonpragmatic ideologies; tactical fears be subordinated to strategic vision; and the structurally induced ambitions or fears not be wholly incompatible. Whether any or all of these conditions are present in the U.S.-Soviet relationship, or are likely to materialize in the near future, is a question to which one clue may lie in the evolutionary perspective on the international system. A possible such perspective is supplied by first the Italian and then the all-European state system.

Suppose that a typical (occidental? near modern?) state system is, after some false starts, conceived in the defensive reaction of relatively lesser parties to the "first" strongest state (Milan in the Italian system, France or Spain in the European one). It crystallizes as a conflict or succession of conflicts between two major states fosters the rise of a growing number of comparably strong states capable of contending over a balanced distribution of power. It is consolidated when a major realignment involving principal member states confirms the system as flexibly responsive to fluctuations in power and related interests (a critical realignment in the Italian system occurred in 1451, when Florence shifted her alliance tie from Venice to Milan; in Europe in 1756 when France, after a brief and tentative postwar rapprochement with Britain, exchanged the Prussian alliance for one with

Austria in the resumed Anglo-French contest). The system reaches maturity when several satiated powers make a more or less serious attempt at peacefully regulating their interactions in diplomatic concert (thus the Holy League of 1454 in Italy; the Concert of Europe of 1815), much as the effort may be discreetly biased against the most forward or restless party among them. And finally, the system incurs a terminal crisis when its members invite, or intermember conflicts pull, larger outside powers (France and Spain; the United States and Soviet Russia) into active involvement. These powers then supersede both the founding or preeminent members of the system and the autonomy of the system itself as they enlarge it.

Questions arise: Is the contemporary, global system still in the first phase of initial conception, with interested parties reacting to one or the other superpower as the principal threat? Or is the system already visibly moving into the second phase, that of crystallization, when third and fourth politico-military or economic powers stake out shares in access or control in addition to the original two? Or else, are conditions already beginning to take shape that might induce the parties to the original polar rivalry to weigh past sources of conflict against the emergence of new rivals and threats? Such a weighing of new incentives to concord will always precede, often over a too-prolonged period, the event of a dramatic major-power realignment. The release of accumulated policy incoherences then catapults the system over the barrier of "hereditary" enmity (or only inherited rivalry) onto the wider plain of flexible readjustments.

It is easy to see at what stage of system evolution a U.S.-Soviet détente becomes practical; less easy to agree that it is present and ready for appropriate action on both sides. At the still later point of entente, the crisis of succession, often attending major realignment, would not be presently one attending the transition from a defunct dynasty to another. It would involve, in the wake of a miscarried U.S.-Soviet conflict over succession to the European powers, the issue of who would follow in preeminence to the two contemporary Europe-derived successors to traditional Europe, herself hailing from classical Greece and Italy. "Who will succeed to rival candidates for succession?" is no less weighty a question among states or civilizations than is that of "Who will watch over the custodians?" within them. At stake are the chances for resolving the crisis attending all transfers of primacy in a way that leaves open the yet longer path to a world-wide concert of relatively equal powers or politically organized cultures.

Longer-span perspectives on continuities within and across systems. The short-term view is again governed in our time by preoccupation with the most salient conflict between two major powers. What conditions are likely to intensify or attenuate such a conflict within a setting broadly defined by the evolutionary stage of the state system at a particular point in time? When the perspective lengthens beyond the next decade or two and merges with a medium-term perspective (one running well into the next century), attention shifts to a cluster of three major powers, incidentally propelling both analysis and prognosis from a less to a more firmly patterned set of likely events and developments.

The difference can be stated in terms of virtual opposites: the relationship between two salient powers (e.g., presently the United States and Soviet Russia) tends to influence, to the point of determining, the changing distribution of power and the actual or perceived hierarchies of threat; in a well-defined triangular setting, it is the power configuration that will largely control relationships among the three principal (and related or subordinate) parties, unless a deliberate effort counters the inherent tendency or tendencies. The historically frequent three-power configuration appears to be again emerging (between the United States, Soviet Russia, and China) into dominance over the system. The two features—the configuration being recurrent, and its tendency to control relationships—taken together make it possible to project past patterns and outcomes into a hypothetical future.

Also helpful in devising a grand strategy can be insights from longest-term, secular and more or less cyclical, trends and tendencies. As the temporal perspective lengthens both backward and forward, the focus moves beyond power dynamics in the abstract—the reciprocal effect of power structures and conflict relationships in an evolving international system. The longer view can better encompass changes in, and differences between, dominant types of actors and action defined by sociocultural norms and politico-economic practices.

The cycles in "international" history that are easy to trace across the longest time are not necessarily the easiest ones to articulate precisely. A foremost phenomenon of this kind is the alternating predominance of so-called civilized societies, first manifest in agricultural-sedentary groups, and of likewise vaguely defined barbarian, initially pastoral-nomadic, groups. "Barbarians" can be seen as only alien or also inferior. They came from the east, beginning in Mesopotamia, only to trickle back from west to east in more modern times. In either case, they invariably injected some kind of crisis into the center of the penetrated culture. However, it matters whether theirs was a sudden conquest or, as often happened, only a gradual, even peaceable, infiltration. Most barbarian conquests owed more to mobility than to mass, in the form of vastly superior numbers, along with some advantage in weapons technology. Typical among the infiltrators were the "Germans" who migrated into the Roman Empire before and after the fifth century. But much the same applies to the Indo-European charioteers intruding into the Middle East in the second millennium B.C., the Normans or Saracens into western Europe in the ninth century A.D., and the Mongol horsemen into thirteenth-century Russia (and into the higher, farther-eastern civilizations of China, India, and the Middle East).

Barbarian intrusion will cause unavoidable disruption in the overwhelmed community. Its costs will be offset when irruption regenerates the community's social base while generating a novel, hybrid blend of political organization and intercommunity statecraft. Hybridization of this kind was conspicuous in the post–Roman Empire "barbarian West" during the period from about 400 to about 900 A.D. It fused Germanic war-band practices with Roman-law precepts whereas, at the opposite extreme, the looseness of the rule by the Golden Horde made for a less pronounced effect in post-Mongol Russia.

In a class by themselves as "barbarians" are outsider powers invited by one or more of the key actors into a conflict-ridden arena. They do not suddenly or gradually irrupt as either hordes or settlers into an unformed or decaying social or political system; they are not the Goths or the Franks moving into Romania. They include: the Wu state, which was called into the ancient Chinese state system;* the Persians or Romans invited into Greece; the French or Spaniards summoned into Italy—and the Americans into Europe. A wider system then supersedes a conflict area that has shown itself to be insufficiently self-sustaining. However, the powerful outsiders, rather than contribute significantly to a new mode of statecraft, will gradually assimilate the older system's arcana after being initially repelled by them and then only reluctantly initiated into them. As for the political culture of the members of the self-destroyed system of states, it will not have much of a prospect to be regenerated. It will adopt more of the newcomers' vices than of their virtues.

In the category of "civilized" states, three types that set the tone for the exercise of power have tended to succeed one another: first, sacral (administrative or military) territorial monarchies or empires; then, largely secularized maritime-mercantile states; and finally, a somewhat corrupt synthesis of the two: that is, continental powers with overseas ambitions. To a degree that climaxed in the Third (German) Reich, and is not absent from the Soviet adaptation of an older Russia's Third Rome vocation, the third-generation powers were unlike the religiously inspired first-generation regimes in that their dominant ideologies had only falsely inspirational, or pseudo-sacral, overtones. But they had these, and they also fused the military culture of the first type and the maritime one of the second type into a compound of militarism and navalism that, as both reaction and revolutionary challenge, were armed bids for place within an all-absorbing system restoration.

Viewed on a grand scale, the archetypal temple communities and the

*In the sixth century B.C., to be distinguished from the still more "outer" barbarian Ch'in that "unified" the system in 212 B.C. See Richard S. Walker, *The Multi-state System of Ancient China* (Hamden, Conn.: Shoe String Press, 1953), ch. 4.

larger, variably sacral and military monarchies and empires in ancient Mesopotamia and Middle East (in the main Akkad, Babylonia, Egypt, and Assyria) were eventually replaced by the maritime Greek city-states as the leading type of political organization. In turn, these city-states were themselves superseded by the amphibious Roman Empire in the aftermath of abortive bids for a like achievement by the Persian-Phoenician and the Hellenistic continental-maritime power aggregations. Similar sequences can be traced in the post-Roman phase within the Mediterranean area (from Byzantium to the Italian city-states and on to Spain or the Ottoman Empire) and in the all-European arena (from the medieval feudal monarchies to the northwestern Atlantic states and on to Germany or Russia).

The sequence in each cycle reflected the changes—first for the better, then for the worse—in both economic and political organization within the particular culture circle or geographic area. But only once was the cycle closed by land- and sea-based power coalescing in a mixed empire, the Roman, that also unified the preexisting multistate system. In other instances, actually or potentially amphibious powers found it hard, if not impossible, to overthrow the maritime states from a larger territorial and stronger military base. Frustration and failure was the lot of Persia relative to the Greeks; the medieval Germans (before, initially, the French and the Aragonese) relative to the Italians; Spain and France relative to the Dutch; France and modern Germany relative to the English. Only after the maritime state or state system had gone into decline did it become vulnerable to overland drives from the rear: thus the Greeks to Macedonia, the Italians to Spain and France, and the European Atlantic powers to Germany or Russia. Moreover, the bids of the would-be amphibious powers to subdue sea powers tended to resolve themselves into conflicts between at least two of them, to third-power advantage. Thus, conflicts between Macedonia and Syria over the Greeks were resolved to the advantage of Rome, conflicts between Spain and France over the Dutch to the profit of the English. And, to some extent at least, the struggle between Imperial Germany and tsarist Russia over British assets in the Middle and Far East ended to the eventual advantage of the United States. Within this scheme, to whose ultimate advantage would redound a Russo-Chinese contest over waning American positions off Eurasia?

The tripartite conflicts involving a dominant maritime power and two unequally amphibious continental challengers spread from inchoate beginnings in the Mediterranean to northwest Atlantic Europe at the beginning of the modern-capitalist era. At first, the conflicts typically profited the sea powers, and ended in their formal victories. They contributed nonetheless to their decline. Compounding growing war costs, war-induced attrition, and war-attending diffusion abroad of skills or assets, was the eventual disappearance of the material conditions that had originally lifted the western maritime over the surrounding world. Advantages became liabilities when the initial concentration of trade- or industry-promoting political power within the maritime states flagged; when the early advantage in economic specialization between the northwest and Europe's and the world's other regions was nullified by the loss or dispersion of preferential access to markets, key minerals, and sea or other communication routes; and when the headstart in such varied domains as technological innovation, transportation and managerial techniques, and entrepreneurial drive was also greatly diminished.

In the wake of northern Italy and southern Germany, decline followed initial advantage first in the Netherlands and in due course also in England. If the trend continues, it will bode ill for the dominance of the expanded northwest Atlantic system around the United States. The consequent migration of preeminent power might again coincide with the critical maritime areas and peninsular or insular actors being outmaneuvered by land. Thus Alexander circumvented by land the overseas Greeks and the Phoenicians, setting the stage for the Hellenistic successor states in the Aegean and the eastern Mediterranean, and the Venetians were shut out by the Ottomans over land in the Black Sea. The West might one day find itself outmaneuvered, and its power center in the Atlantic bypassed, by the Russians (or the Chinese) in the Arabian Sea region or elsewhere.

Yet at least as significant as the geoeconomic and strategic causes of sea power decline have been the psychopolitical ones. The decline of the Greek maritime world had much to do with calling in the Persians to arbitrate divisions among the Greeks; the decline of the Italians, with calling in the French (and the Spaniards against the French); and the old European northwest finally faded when those claiming responsibility for preserving its culture felt the necessity to call in the New World in order to avoid reshaping the structure of the old. Could the same fate befall the West if, refusing to think in terms of its largest possible compass relinking the Baltic with the Atlantic to include Russia (as it had predecline Poland-Lithuania), it should draw the farther East, in the form of China in particular, ever deeper into the quarrel internal to the Occident?

In the end, the invited power is liable to suffer almost as much as the inviting powers. The latter degenerated as short-term concerns of domestic politics rose to primacy. However, ever since Persia squandered her gold in Greece, and either the German emperors or the French kings destroyed their credit in Italy, the greater power invited to master the unmanageable complexities of others either wasted its own material substance or neglected other more straightforward or significant strategic tasks. Instead of looking northward toward the Greeks, the Persians could have been profitably preoccupied to the south and east, whereas the Holy Roman Emperors could have usefully attended to internal consolidation and the rulers of France to the vulnerable northeastern frontier when yielding to the lure of the southern sea. There are contemporary parallels as the Europeans are mired ever deeper in the economics of domesticism, and involvement in an indefinitely prolonged intra-European East-West conflict diverts the United States from attention to either internal or global-peripheral weak spots (while China pauses before plunging into a more than token engagement in intraoccidental conflicts). The long-term impact of the different kinds of misguided or one-sided west European and American involvements upon Atlantic dominance in the world at large is still obscure. But it might be as damaging as would be any further deterioration in unfavorable material factors, be these economic or narrowly military-strategic.

So long as the maritime Atlantic world retains its inherent strengths, it ought to be able to hold off even an intensified drive by would-be amphibian Soviet Russia. It would not then matter whether the drive is directed (Macedon-like) from the continental rear or (Ottoman-like) laterally by way of critical marginal seas. But the price of a too inflexible opposition to finite Russian ambitions might eventually be one more major war between the West and Russia in a triangular land-sea power setting comprising China. An Atlantic northwest that is visibly declining might become instead the object of a contest between two would-be amphibian powers, Russia and China. Such a contest would encompass the Atlantic world's maritime rear in the Pacific. It would displace eastward either only the focus of world politics or also the center of gravity in world power, depending on which one if either of the two extra-Atlantic powers could decisively win. One possible outcome of conflict, or alternative to conflict, between Russia and China is their recoalescence into a system-wide land- cum sea-power complex on the Roman model. The Atlantic world would then be hard pressed from Eurasia, as Carthage and Greece had been subdued from Italy and as Italy was from premaritime western Europe; an overshadowed western Europe would drift toward a role similar to eastern Europe's today, as Russia's economic and racial counterweight to Asia.

Were war to supervene between the West and Russia, it might re-create for the Atlantic-centered universe the situation of the Mediterranean world after the collapse of its comanagement by the western and eastern branches of the Roman Empire. Outer "barbarians" would then flow in, propelled into economically distressed and partially depopulated areas by demographic pressures from behind; or, at least, alien values would infiltrate a different kind of vacuum. Even if the environment has been only partially devastated by war, it would be long before fresh civilization revitalized the West, and before a hybrid statecraft, blending old ways and rules of conduct with new, came into being to restore something like an international system world-wide.

Were Soviet Russia to be peaceably brought into full partnership instead in the European concert and, by extension, the western one, she would match the already more fully acclimatized American "inner-barbarian" outsider of yesteryear. An entry by invitation is apt to diffuse the mores and techniques of the maturer system to the newcomer; importing Russia's cultural idiosyncrasies into the West by this route could offset America's impact on western mores and blend the two "vices" into an original virtue, possibly for all. Progression toward an all-occidental land and seapower concert would not necessarily entail an early start on a new sociopolitical synthesis. But the attendant major realignment would signal a new flexibility in the global system and, thus, a critical advance in system evolution toward conditions favoring a multi-cultural, genuinely hybrid, global statecraft.

Advance toward a sociopolitical synthesis—of capitalist productivity and socialist ideals of distributive justice, of checks on both libertarian and authoritarian excesses—might only follow movement toward a new synthesis of spiritual and secular factors. Just as within a long-lived political civilization such as that of ancient Egypt, emphases from one to the other factor tended to shift within a long-lived state system such as the European. The gradual early fading of the sacral element in medieval monarchies, such as France and the Empire, was accelerated when their conflicts with the ostensibly most spiritual of powers, the papacy, became focused ever more on territorial and economic stakes in either Italy or the Levant. If spiritual powers had thus been secularized, the seeds of an eventual reversal in the trend were sown by the maritime powers, which followed the feudal monarchies as tone-setting, being progressively territorialized. The latter trend gained in momentum as an ever larger land base was needed in order to prevail in the world at large or to compensate for losing out in contests with local adversaries. Thus, if Holland, England, and America were each more of a territorial power, the prototype of the maritime republic, Venice, shifted to the terra firma after being expelled from the Black Sea, whereas England moved ever deeper into the Indian subcontinent and beyond after being expelled from the coastal fringes of the better part of North America. In a contrary movement, the military land powers beginning with Spain have become maritime in intent, even if not ever fully in reality.

The spiritual powers turning secular fostered institutional and other separation of the two world views or principles, pending a late trend toward reconvergence. The converging movements of the sea and the land powers tended in turn toward a degree of symmetry between them in kind, punctuated by frequent reciprocal subversion in action. The dialectic did not stop there whenever the would-be amphibian land powers set out to combine a drive toward the sea with a tendency to respiritualize their value or legitimacy base—as a way of dealing with the stresses occasioned by their late entry into the interstate system.

There is a parallel between one kind of reformation and a different kind of revolution, which casts some light on the ensuing—and continuing—problems. Early secularization was temporarily reversed in the religious wars, triggered by opposition to the corruptions of the papal prototype of the sacral monarchy in an economically depressed setting. Thereafter, secularization was completed by the calculating pragmatism in thinking congenial to even the most religiously reformist maritime powers and the privately most pietist mercantile societies. The pattern repeated itself when the continental latecomers rationalized their challenge to the primacy of the maritime powers by attacking the corruptions allegedly inherent in the mercantile culture—one impugned as "plutocratic" by the political right and as "capitalist" by the political left. The similarity with the reformation continued whenever either peacetime or war-induced economic depression intensified the drive behind the proposed revolution. The revolt against mercantile secularism was commonly attended by either decline or repression of private pieties. But even then, or especially then, it fostered a pseudo-spiritual kind of millennial state ideology. Past its beginnings in Imperial Germany and tsarist Russia, the reaction climaxed in Nazi and Soviet totalitarianisms, both of them initially if unequally revolutionary.

Resistance to the second German "reformation" (from Luther to Hitler, by way of Bismarck and William?) in quasi-religious total wars failed to leave behind a spiritually leavening effect on the West. It instead increased the spiritual vacuum precariously filled by materialism, not least in the western portion of defeated Germany. This leaves open the question as to the effects of an encounter with a Soviet Russia that is decreasingly Soviet and increasingly Russian, an encounter keyed to accommodation with a settled regime that would continue being less totalitarian and more dependent on the core nation's spirit. Might not such an encounter reinforce the maritime West's moral bases and strengthen it for contacts with the other forms of politically manifest spirituality or religiosity coming back to life in the world at large? If it does not, the effort to somehow remerge power with spirit in the political realm would be set back. The failure would make it all the more difficult to cut through the vicious circle of land-sea power conflicts externalizing a protracted intrawestern revolution. And it would be harder to restructure, in a manageable way, the East-West polarity in both its narrower (or European) and wider (or global) circumferences.*

Varieties of historical phase: systematic and selective comparisons

Although the ideal is a systematic comparison between the structures of

*For a full appreciation of many of the preceding points, and for a complementary historico-evolutionary scheme, I refer the interested reader to the "Coda" ("The System: Patterns of Persistence and Revolutions within Evolution") in *Russia and World Order* (Baltimore: Johns Hopkins University Press, 1980). Following works by Fernand Braudel, a major source on the politico-economic aspects of the rise of the Atlantic West is Immanuel Wallerstein, *The Modern World System,* vols. 1 and 2 (New York: Academic Press, 1974 and 1980).

power within the dynamic, and the stages of growth and decline in the development, of international systems or actors that are intrinsically comparable, the contemplative analyst in search of a perspective will often have to adopt the stance of the policymaker facing a problem and searching for an operational precedent. He will make comparisons that are random and inquire into relationships that are located outside an ordering set of comparable structures or orderly sequences, in the belief that selective comparisons can usefully supplement the more systematic ones, so long as they do not replace them.

Limitations and advantages of recent and remote phases. In the foregoing discussion, the object was to situate the contemporary state—or evolutionary stage—of the global system; comparisons were made between and with stages in the Italian and the European state systems in particular. A similar procedure was adopted in situating the present stage in the development of Soviet Russian foreign policy. By contrast, relatively haphazard comparisons were made when exploring the conditions of détente between rival powers over time. Throughout, the main stress has been—and will continue to be—on periods preceding that between the two world wars. Although, in what follows, occasional references will be made to the interwar situation culminating in the late 1930s, this approach differs from one invoking the so-called Munich analogy as the basis for addressing the key contemporary issue: that of East-West "appeasement." The simplest assumption behind that analogy has been: what is more recent is or must be more relevant. It is not—as it is here—that the prelude to World War II would become increasingly pertinent for events at the center of the system only if the "lessons" from more significantly comparable pre–World War I and still earlier conditions were not heeded or were misapplied.

Only under certain conditions could the U.S.-Soviet relationship—or the East-West relationship as confined to Soviet Russia and the West—be systematically compared with the pre-1939 interwar period. A major condition is that the contemporary and the interwar state of the international system are structurally close to identical. This would mean that the contemporary system, too, is characterized by lopsided multipolarity while the defensive powers (decadent or civilian-spirited) and the offensive ones (self-styled dynamic or militaristic) are inconclusively polarized along changing axes by ideologically determined affinities (anti-Communist or anti-Fascist), lacking a solid support in geopolitical considerations.

Such a configuration—modeled on that of the 1930s—would have to be more suggestive for the present and immediate future than is the reappearance of the recurring triangular configuration of continental and maritime great powers, along with the turn-of-the-century combination of conventional multipower diplomacy and world-wide late-stage imperialisms. And it would be necessary to disown the new relevance of the still earlier, ideologically colored (if not necessarily determined) near-bipolar relations between Christendom and Islam in general or, say, the Habsburg and Ottoman empires in particular. Moreover, for the 1930s to supply a surer guide than they do, Soviet Russia as one of the key actors would have to be as clearly committed as was Nazi Germany to continental expansion by massive military means, to the neglect of overseas expansion by various means. And the United States would have to resemble, in more respects than is conveyed by superficial behavior, the Britain of the late 1930s rather than the Britain of the turn of the century.

The impression of only very partial comparability of the present with the interwar period persists when the criteria of overall system structure and the development stage of system or actor are replaced by the yardstick of salient functional areas or issues, the military and the economic.

In the military sphere, a very general aspect and a more particular one are at stake. In the general realm, where military technology influences basic sociopolitical trends and organization, the events immediately before and during World War II marked the climax of the gunpowder revolution in its principal effect. The effect was to accelerate sociopolitical transformations, first toward the centralization of territorial states out of feudal "anarchy," later toward the consolidation of colonial western empires overseas and the multi-ethnic continental empires in eastern Europe. Since then, the nuclear revolution has had the opposite effect. It has decelerated the political transformations that the major states especially were able to effectuate internationally; and, not least in the lesser powers, it has promoted disruptions intranationally by virtue of its second major, depressant, effect. Nuclear weaponry and stalemate have not only lowered the level of usable and effective force to one readily available to nonstate actors, but also undermined or downgraded more generally the claim of governments to authority insofar as that claim was based on role and efficacy in guaranteeing external security.

All of these consequences are reminiscent of earlier, premodern, statecraft at both the center of the international system and in its relation to its periphery. So too are the efforts to compensate for diminished external efficacy or internal authority by other means, often devious in method and likewise uncertain in terminal effect.

As regards the more specialized issue, that of armaments competition, it establishes only a superficial similarity between the present and the interwar periods. The competition has been a critical object of diplomacy in both eras. But the earlier arms race was something of a one-round race and was keenly perceived as being such for policy purposes. At least one side (Nazi Germany), and perhaps both sides, were economically unable to perpetuate the arms competition's quantitative or qualitative side indefinitely. Hence, once the German headstart began to erode, the issue of fluctuating armaments advantage was almost inevitably converted into the battlefield issue of whether the German conquests were irreversible. The situation was not such when the prior American arms advantage over Soviet Russia began to fade, any more than it had been such fully in the pre-World War I Anglo-German naval race. As for the issue of larger equality or parity beyond armaments, it was not unknown to the 1930s. But it, too, is reminiscent more of the period before the first global conflict than before the second one. One consequence is that whereas the contemporary competition in strategic armaments is undeniably significant, in a long-range historical perspective it can be demoted from the dramatic salience it occupies within a foreshortened one.

In regard to the other functional area, that of economics, recent conditions have seemingly moved toward some similarity with the interwar period. At least for a time, the almost exclusively politico-military and strategic emphases of the cold war era have yielded to raw-material dependence and economic interdependence as objects of concerns surrounding national power and international stability or order. However, there has been a significant difference so long as contemporary international politics in general, and Soviet-western relations in particular, revolves around a single prominent material resource: oil. Dependence for national power on a single material asset that comes to determine much of policy differs from a multi-resource situation. The interwar era was oriented toward a range of resources, as distinct from some remoter periods. From earliest antiquity on, the supply of and access to a single resource—be it copper or iron or silver, timber or grain or coal—constituted at various times the focal point not only for the economy but also for the politics and external strategies of organized communities. It does so again, raising the question as to whether the one-resource focus, instead of actually simplifying stakes and relationships, has not increasingly supplied a pretext or rationale for simplistic approaches to complex relationships.

Finally, when the cultural aspect is included along with the two functional ones, other differences from the 1930s emerge. Thus the interwar conflict was confined to the narrow, intra-European compass of the East-West cleavage, with Germany's degree of eastern-ness relative to the so-called western democracies being a function of the role she did or would agree to play relative to more clearly eastern Soviet Russia. By contrast, the current East-West cleavage has both a narrower dimension confined to European or European-derived powers and a wider global dimension that involves these powers with the politically reactivated third-world societies or civilizations, including China. Now it is Russia that can be propelled further eastward or newly westward by actions of the latter and western transactions with them.

Any world policy that would encompass this enlargement and be sensitive to guidelines or analogies from history will have to absorb patterns and conditions preceding the onset of Europe's global dominance. Questions arise. Is the contemporary global East-West issue significantly illuminated when it is viewed as merely globalizing the conditions of, and political responses to, the economic inferiority of eastern Europe to western Europe, and the consequent quasi-colonial "exploitation" of the former by the latter? Or is it more relevant to focus on the world-wide resurgence of religio-cultural polarities and conflicts between the West and the wider East? Those go back to medieval "holy wars"—crusades and jihads—if no farther, whereas the early patterns may have been only superficially modified by the intervening acculturation of global East to the West's legal-institutional norms and diplomatic modalities.

Furthermore, is the most significant key to either analysis or just intuitive understanding the notion of conflict among major civilizations? If so, what is the relevance of the Chinese ways of empire and empire disintegrations and, say, of the African ways of peaceable interunit accommodation alongside systemic stagnation? Or else, is it equally or more instructive to revive the notion of a decreasingly dominant central civilization, exposed to infiltrations and pressures from outside forces that can be described as functionally if not otherwise barbarian? If so, is this notion instructive for policy responses or does it only reveal the underlying psychological or moral issues?

What is, residually, the essential "nature" of contemporary international politics? Is it a but somewhat moderated analogue of interwar relations among essentially consolidated great powers, contending over mutually understood stakes and, without exception, "rational" in the last resort? It is certainly not so analogous in all of the key respects. One may treat as novel and profound the impact on contemporary high policy of *trans*national phenomena and *intra*national organizational-bureaucratic routines; or one may minimize their novelty and importance. But all the more significance will then attach to a source of qualitative difference located in conventional *inter*national politics. The full range of that politics now comprises two marginal phenomena qualitatively distinct from the adequately resource-supported core of rational transactions among still or again active major powers. One concerns, at either the peaks of their policymaking or in the periodically erupting mass base, the new third-world actors. These can be viewed—with admittedly arguable plausibility—as displaying modes of (prerational) perception and (primitively institutionalized) practice that are characteristic of early civilizations. The other extreme is simultaneously occupied by the west European nations in particular. They can be seen with equal validity as disclosing in international statecraft a tendency typical of late civilizations: to withdrawal from self-assertion, into a merely derivative or only simulated perpetuation of traits from the high-culture period.

A world picture so constituted in variety and complexity is not reducible to the cleavage between powers satisfied with the status quo and powers intent on revising it, basic to the interwar period, much as it does encompass this difference. The tendency of the satisfied powers in the interwar period was to cling to the thesis, and to try less persistently to apply the theory, of a qualitative change in postwar over prewar rules and norms of international politics; the reverse tendency of the dissatisfied states was to affirm in both doctrine and practice the continuing validity of traditional statecraft in regard to goals and, in key respects, means. Whereas the revisionists as to means were traditionalists as to prior outcomes, for the revisionists as to outcomes (and traditionalists as to means) the averred changes in legitimate methods of statecraft were only nominal or opportunistic; they were merely declaratory rather than actually and invariably conduct-determining also for their proponents. This particular difference in basic outlooks has reemerged in both dimensions of the East-West cleavage as the key—if rarely considered—link between then and now. It would be difficult for an approach to statecraft that substitutes the hypothesis of evolutionary variety for the idea of all-encompassing progress not to side with the interwar revisionists' skeptical view of the degree of actually transpired basic change in interstate relations.

An uncertain balance sheet of continuity and change in tendencies and transformations. The present can be compared and contrasted with the past on many levels. The present is not in all respects more like the 1930s than the nineteenth century, or the seventeenth A.D. than the fifth B.C. It may be possible to abstract straightforward continuities in the evolution of any one international system, differentiate them from discontinuities, and compare both with those of another system. However, when addressing foreign policy, it is less easy to confidently return and nicely order answers to questions about the present: To which earlier period, in relation to what key issues, is the present continuous with, or comparable to? In relation to which salient modalities of dealing with them? On what levels and over what time spans? Under what supposition as to continuity, change, or alternation in the basic "nature" of key powers, international politics, or key military and economic functions and cultural norms? One extreme result of being deterred by such complexity is to ignore the historical perspective altogether; another and middling, to ransack episodic history for convenient support of momentary preconceptions; yet another and in a different way extreme, to affirm radical across-the-board discontinuity and change on the basis of changes mainly in material or tangible factors.

Ignoring a crucial part of history, or mistaking its warnings for warrants, will deliver the instruments of destruction and self-destruction into the hands of policymakers who, determined to change a status quo, are insensitive to historically evidenced costs of seeking to overthrow it quickly by force; positing instead a kind of antihistory is tempting for policymakers of a status quo–defending power, anxious to cling indefinitely to past gains by abruptly changing the rules of the game. Whereas the defending power then subverts the possibility of achieving valid outcomes that improve on history, the overly assertive one deforms and betrays its valid ambition to leave an imprint on history. The dichotomy is in full force when a falsely conservative (American) statecraft treats the rival's superficially radical goals as illegitimate on the strength of a modernist theory of legitimate means, while the increasingly conservative (Soviet) rival conceals conventional goals behind a supposedly legitimating revolutionary rationale; when one nation's ultra-liberal or differently illusionist urge to transcend the actual for an ideal reality cuts across another nation's travail to realize itself at long last in the world as it is.

It is arguable that the major discontinuity in interstate relations has been a progressive shrinkage of the "real thing" into mere approximations or functional substitutions, of substance via semblance into mere simulation. The mutation was completed as to both means and ends in formerly central or self-sustaining state systems that had been superseded and lapsed into subordination (e.g., post–Renaissance Italy and post–World War II Europe); it is only at the halfway point for the international system as a whole when once accomplished transformations subside into mere tendencies, backed by variably forceful but finally unsuccessful temptations or trial runs aiming at such transformations. However, so long as international politics is conducted as if all-out transformations are sought and could be achieved by the deliberate agency of states, the mere tendencies will have qualitatively the impact of accomplished transactions.

Two illustrations must suffice. Although successfully invaded several times before, Britain was not actually conquered from the European mainland during the dominance of seapower in modern times. But the continuation of European and world politics in a competitive mold generated the view that ultimate and enduring success for Britain's rivals reposed on the possibility of accomplishing her conquest across the channel or finding an alternative pathway overland to its equivalent. The eventual result of thwarting all attempts to accomplish either was a more broadly based, continent-wide state superseding Britain nonetheless as the preeminent maritime power, if through peaceful "conquest." The other illustration is more hypothetical. For the Soviets to close off either the eastern Mediterranean or the Persian Gulf by an accomplished enveloping movement overland is probably impossible; they certainly could not do so without unacceptable risk. The operation is one that would replicate the lightning achievement of Alexander in one respect and the end result of the more gradual British penetrations in the area in another. This inability will not impede Russia from seeking localized implantations in the area in order to enhance her bargaining position. She will wish to create the presumption that, unless compensated by access to role and resource there or elsewhere, she might push beyond mere tendency to actually trying to complete a fundamental transformation of the existing order of things. Yet to treat Russian statecraft from the outset as if it were unqualifiedly committed to the extreme achievement, as well as capable of it, is to promote the undesired result at some later time and, perhaps, at other hands.

Intellectually self-disciplined makers or students of policy will probe assumptions behind alternative strategies; making such assumptions explicit enters into the range of attributes of either a usable theory or a coherent doctrine of foreign policy. Such assumptions are all the more useful the more specific and determinate they are; we shall narrow them down to formulations meeting this requirement in due course. Conversely, there has been some, if less manifest, merit in visualizing the problem of even the most practical strategist against the grandest of backdrops, one sketched by the external manifestations in history of the barely varying predicaments incurred by men both within political communities and in relations between them. Such is the philosophical ideal. It is less commonly practiced, and may be of less ready-made utility, than is the breakdown of secular trends or long-range cycles into more limited antecedents. These are the particular events and tendencies that offer the possibility of relating present to past policy quandaries with the aid of direct analogy. They will be explored in the chapter that follows. Whatever questions may attach to analogy as a method or instrument of theory are offset by the method's well-tested practicality. Appropriate analogy will be an aid to the practicing statesman's creative awareness even where it cannot be his sure guide to realizing a particular purpose.

II

PAST HISTORY.

Antecedents and Analogies

Scanning past constellations of one-time great powers is not the same as composing a horoscope for living states. But neither is the effort to gain from consulting the past an insight into the character of the present and into the pitfalls and promises of the future a merely antiquarian exercise.

The historically evidenced background that can be most revealingly projected into the immediate future includes one two-power and one three-power conflict relationship. Tsarist Russia and imperial Britain figured in both configurations of power and are currently replicated by Soviet Russia and the United States. China replaces tsarist Russia in the triangular setting. Concern with configuration of power is the first step toward, but is not sufficient for, either understanding or shaping critical relationships of world politics. These are also subject to a range of beliefs and dispositions that reflect the culture of men in society at least as much as they react to the necessities of states in an international system.

Both doctrine (as a set of premises) and strategy (as a set of precepts) are at stake in the East-West relationship focused upon the U.S.-Soviet contention; it is the supreme challenge for grand strategy to interlock, in the formulation of both premises and precepts, the rationally propelled dynamics of power keyed to interests with the passion and the will that reflect the spirit of a nation or culture engaged on ascent or decline. So long as the contention is viewed only in geopolitical terms, it is one between a (receding?) sea power with a major continental base and a (ascending?) land power with debatable naval capabilities and overseas aspirations. In influencing that relationship, the special kind of perspective and prejudice secreted by the existential differences between the two kinds of power will gradually predominate over sociopolitical or other belief systems originating in other conditions and aspirations. And still other moods and myths, rooted in still deeper differences of historical experience and culture, will modify the dispassionate rationality of *Realpolitik* when the relationship is also subject to the rift between East and West. That relationship has been as persistent as it has been varied over time in the identity of key parties to it and in its practically significant compass. For our purposes it has been defined most critically by the West's confrontations with Islam and with Russia.

Sources of conflicts and confrontations: structural and accidental

A triangular configuration repeatedly consisted of a sea power, a land power with such naval ambitions as to make it potentially amphibious, and a power almost wholly continental. Between 1900 and 1914, Britain, Imperial Germany, and tsarist Russia occupied these respective roles in what was so far the most perfect of such triangles. Typically enough, the arena and the implications of the attendant rivalry were world-wide; so was the ensuing military conflagration. By contrast, the bilaterial Anglo-Russian rivalry that continued up to the accommodation of 1907 was more specific in scope. It was geographically limited from the Near to the Far East via central Asia, and it erupted into a more restricted military conflict. What are the reasons for such developments? And are they part of a more general historical pattern that might be of consequence to contemporary circumstances?

Wars as guilt, fatality, and accident. The triangular interplay gets underway when the would-be amphibious state challenges the defending sea power over the issue of parity on the seas and overseas. A major, system-wide conflict becomes unavoidable if the land power has a more substantial territorial and material base than the sea power. Understandably enough, the latter then feels unable to concede maritime parity to the former: adding major sea-based to greater land-based strength would propel the amphibian beyond continental preeminence or paramountcy to global supremacy. The twofold jeopardy of the maritime power is matched by the aspiring land power's exposure to a twofold incentive to expand toward the oceans. The would-be amphibian is anxious to protect his rear against the potentially stronger continental background state (or coalition of states), and he is determined to safeguard his expanding economic needs and interests from dependence on the revocable tolerance of the dominant sea power. Whereas the latter objective requires assured access to positions overseas, the former requires concert or successfully conducted competition with the dominant sea power. But it is the third, continental rear, power that precipitates the issue by either growing too fast or aligning itself too closely with the maritime power.

So viewed, the Anglo-French global conflicts of the eighteenth century enacted against the continental background of the Germanic powers (chiefly Habsburg Austria and subsequently Prussia) had been as unavoidable as was World War I once the nineteenth century ended on the note of a growing Anglo-German rivalry. These, and still earlier, antecedents (involving Spain and the Netherlands by the end of the sixteenth century) suggest a recurrent pattern. And the recurrence downgrades the significance of changing specific factors in explaining this kind of conflict; rather, it demotes such factors from a determining to a merely conditioning role.

Thus, explaining German fleet-building in terms of socioeconomic and domestic-political considerations can only refine and supplement the primacy of interstate structure. Similarly discounted can be the retrospective regrets or criticisms of those who faulted German statecraft for having alienated Britain by building a navy that was too big or of the wrong kind at a time when rapports with Russia were becoming hostile. Actually, the policymakers in Berlin and Potsdam understood only too well that if she was to remain a great power, Germany had to seek world-power status promptly, with or without British approval. Otherwise, Germany's global access could be foreclosed by a Britain all the more jealous for being in decline, and her independence as a great power foreshortened by a Russia no more tolerant of German greatness because she, too, was exhibiting economic and demographic growth. If not held down by the British, Germany risked being outgrown by America and Japan as alternative successors to Britain overseas.

As to Russia, she feared being isolated diplomatically with Germany's cooperation even before the estrangement between the two countries was aggravated by economic grievances and consolidated by changes in popular and dynastic sentiments. Increased German agricultural tariffs against Russian grain and decreased readiness to float Russian bonds played a role. But this mattered less than the role German statesmen (beginning with Bismarck) felt compelled to play as Austria's partially captive and Britain's partially covert accomplices in imposing the check of diplomatic isolation on Russia's "imperialism" in the Near East. The resulting Russian setbacks imparted an anti-German twist to Russian nationalism, always eager for a free hand from interdynastic solidarity in foreign policy.

As in the earlier triangles, the "laws" of power prevailed gradually over prudent strategic "choices." The portents began to gather when fortunes of war and accidents of longevity shifted the balance of authority from the

Russian tsars to the new German emperor (William I). They were solidified when the balance of sentiment later veered from personal affection for the old to antipathy for the young emperor (William II), well before Germany's nonrenewal of the Reinsurance Treaty with Russia made the rift official. With the ties between the Prussian and the Russian dynasts weakened, the geopolitically determined and passionally reinforced imperatives of conflict between two henceforth too-equal continental neighbors ceased being neutralized. The die was cast when the British, shunning parity with Germany, preferred Japan and America (as a prelude to preferring France and Russia) to the navally newly ambitious land power. They would not defray the growing cost of leaning on the premier continental power for diplomatic support, as they did during much of the Bismarck regime, in order better to manage Russia (and France, while keeping their options open with regard to the United States) overseas—and, as later events showed, defer thus Britain's unavoidable slippage from preeminence.

Quite different from World War I was the local war in the Crimea. It was not only unintended but also unnecessary. The war grew out of Anglo-Russian rivalry in a land-bound regional theater: the European Near East and central Asia. It was conditioned by the dynamics of a triangle: the Anglo-French-Russian one in the eastern Mediterranean. But that triangle could no longer dominate world politics any more than it could cause a world war. The France of the lesser of the two Napoleons was more revisionist than resurgent; she was insulated from Russia by the German powers (Austria and Prussia), and she was to need Russia against both in succession.

Because the power structure was too diffuse to be clearly determinant it allowed for complex factors to cause the war as well as merely precipitate its onset. They ranged from ideological pretexts or aggravators (the moral revulsion of Christians against the Turks or Islam and the Britons' Russophobia), through domestic calculations and compulsions (of the yet unstable Napoleon III), to misleading or confusing personal summitry (the tsar's in England) and inept or intriguing diplomacy (by Russian and British envoys in Constantinople). They included substantial economic concerns (Russian, over grain exports to western Europe; British, over trade in and beyond the Black Sea) and serious diplomatic misjudgments by all parties (by the western allies and Austria as to possible Russian concessions, and the earlier one by the Russians as to whether the Anglo-French alliance was possible).

Everyone agreed on one thing only: the necessity to "act." Action had to be taken to comply with the British perception of Russia as a rising amphibious power in the Mediterranean (threatening the Straits and Constantinople) and an expanding land power in central Asia (threatening India). And action was deemed necessary to adjudicate the Russian claim to offset the western naval threat to Russia's underbelly (in the Straits and the Black Sea). In the end, the supposed need to act precipitated a war no power desired and no power configuration imposed. But the lack of valid cause did not lessen the gravity of the long-term consequences of Russia's defeat: in the heart of Europe, Russia's diplomatic reprisals against a traitorous Austria in connection with German unification; inside Russia, a domestic reaction in the form of resentment, reform, and railway-building. Both classes of consequences fed directly into the making of the ultimately fatal triangle.

Were the so far only latent status of the latest, and in spatial terms seemingly terminal, American-Russian-Chinese triangle to change into an acute one, impulses rooted in structure of power could be expected to propel nations toward a global conflict. Only comparable configurations make big history repeat itself, not facile similarities spawning factual analogies between, say, the Serbia of 1914 and the Yugoslavia of 1984(?), between the deaths of a Franz Ferdinand in Sarajevo and of a Tito in Ljubljana. But most or all of the specific "causes" of the war in Crimea could be easily interchanged with reasons or rationales for a revived U.S.-Soviet cold war, over roughly the same stakes and area, and act as irritants or stimulants within the more fateful scenario.

Statics and dynamics of two-power conflict and equilibrium. The possibility of history repeating itself imparts interest to those features of the Anglo-Russian rivalry that are still significant. They combine both land- and sea-power features and dilemmas. As land powers, Britain-in-India (and Egypt) and Russia-in-central-Asia (and the Balkans) had to delimit a boundary that would reliably secure the Russian empire's "Achilles' heel" in central Asia, as well as the Indian empire's penetration point at the Khyber Pass. They had to consolidate that boundary with the aid of unevenly controlled and intermittently contested buffers (Afghanistan and Persia), variably inclining to and recoiling from one or the other greater power as momentarily more threatening—before and after both 1907 and 1917. The seapower issue was located in the eastern Mediterranean and the Red Sea–Persian Gulf–Indian Ocean area and ramified into the Balkans.

According to then-familiar tenets of geopolitics supportable by historical evidence, the seapower issue implied a dependence and a drive: the dependence of insular Britain as the dominant sea power on remote bases, prompting the effort to control all relevant coasts; the drive of heartland Russia to eliminate at least some such bases overland from the rear. A successful envelopment would convert the critical body of water into a closed sea, immune to remote seapower and securable by even inferior local seapower. Such theoretical absolutes (to be articulated by Halford Mackinder) were fraught with dilemmas for policy. On the one hand, actually operative policies had to be projected against the absolutes without precipitating worst-case scenarios. On the other hand, the worst-case scenarios, while only overhanging the practically less far-reaching policies, kept the underlying issue of basic rights and fundamental requirements alive.

Thus, the British were not always and wholly opposed to Russia having access to the Persian Gulf by means of a port facility serving only economic needs, even as they continued to fear and oppose Russian penetration into southern Persia generally; they could not but make light of an aborted Russian foray overseas into Abyssinia (today's Ethiopia) and Siam. On the Russian side, the military craved a secure port on the Persian Gulf (as part of the 1907 accommodation). But the naval men deemed it undefendable (also because the only friendly coaling station near enough was the French one in Djibouti), and the managers of Russia's public finances were opposed to costly adventures in the Persian Gulf and in Persia herself.

The issue of specific requirements involved the contested right of the heartland power. Is it entitled to access to and beyond the near seas, in addition to a secure political and economic orbit? The British acknowledged at least part of the second entitlement in 1907 when conceding some of Persia; they also guaranteed that Afghanistan—already feared by Russia as a center of Pan-Islamic agitation—would not be used for anti-Russian activities. The likewise disputable right of the sea power is to deny maritime access to the land power for like reasons of national security, equated in its case with naval-military and economic preeminence, bordering on monopoly, worldwide.

The validity of the conflicting rights depended then, before, and since, on the relationship of these rights to the requirements of equilibrium. Whether or not there is a balance of power between the differently endowed and unequally favored heartland and insular states will depend on the distribution of either side's preferential access to secondary heartlands (e.g., India for insular Britain), rimlands, and offshore islands. Assessments will vary with existing technologies and techniques for projecting differential material assets along each power's peculiar combination of interior and exterior lines of communication. And a critical question for even a tactically inclined statecraft is whether the momentary or intrinsic advantage of either the insular power or the heartland power is sufficiently great to tip, in the interest of world equilibrium, the balance of to-be-conceded controversial "rights" toward the power that is at a disadvantage in its geostrategic or material endowments.

In the late nineteenth century, the fragile equilibrium between Russia and Britain had both a static and a dynamic element. By the 1880s, static equilibrium was well underway by virtue of agreement on reciprocally acceptable land frontiers between spheres of influence in central Asia and, to an extent, the Balkans. The dynamic equilibrium depended on each party's ability to exert leverage over the other. That capacity existed on both sides. It was exercised as part of a tactical interlock between the two most critical zones: central Asian and eastern Mediterranean. Thus, when the British aversion for Russia's expansion in central-Asian Transcaucasia had helped escalate frictions in the European "Near East" to the point of (the Crimean) war, the Russians made ready (with inadequate forces) to relieve their stance in Europe by marching through one of the buffers against British India. During a later Balkan crisis, in 1878, the same recourse was envisaged as an offset to Britain's occupation of Cyprus, itself a supposed counterpoise to Russian overland pressures against the Ottomans. When, yet later, the Russians pushed into Manchuria and Korea, northeast Asia completed the unified multiregional field of pressure and conflict. The Russians viewed the advance as preemptive, given Britain's (and possibly Germany's) economic headstart and trading advantage and Japan's geostrategic initiatives in Asia. On their part, the British saw the Russian push as extending the overland threat to India all the way to the Chinese theater. They proceeded to counter it with the Japanese alliance. Since then, specifics have changed more than has either the general pattern or the areas at issue for both static and dynamic equilibrium; while the U.S.-Soviet land frontier in eastern Europe has been delimited, the process of delimitation in the Middle East and in Asia goes on.

The unplanned linkage of two-power and three-power conflicts. Although the two-power structure and conflict are distinct from the triangular configuration, the two kinds overlap. Not only do all the powers regard themselves as only preclusively, and thus defensively, expansive in both instances. The tendency of two of the powers toward either conflict or concord determines the position in the triangle of the third, itself able to influence the relations between the two. But the two situations also differ, next to the magnitude of stakes, in the stringency of time limits.

Leading Russians judged expansion into the Far East to be necessary at the end of the nineteenth century, before the English and the Japanese took all. The rapid rise of Japan, in particular, seemed to place a time limit on effective Russian advance, with the result of a misguided precipitation in Korea leading to a mismanaged war. With that war over, Russia's resurgence and accommodations with both Britain and Japan set a similar and still more pressing time limit for Germany within the Anglo-German-Russian triangle. The stakes were soon more substantial for Germany than they had been for Russia, extending as they did beyond access to secondary markets (Asian, thought important for a Russia that was not competitive in Europe), or a single port facility in warm-water latitudes (Russia's in southern Korea or in China). The reason is that the later German attempt to preempt Russia in east-central Europe did more than follow Russia's expansive attempt to preclude Britain and Japan in the Far East. The two attempts were actually linked together. England's entente over one part of Asia with a Russia defeated in another part of Asia made Germany's exclusion from an accord with Britain irreversible. Such an accord had been possible only if directed at

Russia in both Europe and Asia. Once the German Reich was identified as the threat common to both Britain and Russia, relaxing the rivalry between the latter two meant their tying the noose all the more tightly around the former.

Had instead an Anglo-German accord taken place at the turn of the century, much else would have changed. Russia (not Germany) would have been forced into the position of the key would-be amphibious rival of the preeminent sea power. With France as questionable ally, the United States as no more reliable sympathizer, and Japan indeterminate, Russia would have faced a dominant Anglo-German (cum Austro-Hungarian and Italian) coalition, with Germany acting initially as a naval auxiliary to Britain while seconding British interests in Asia from a safeguarded continental position. Instead of being first defused and then superseded, the two-power Anglo-Russian conflict would have matured into a full-scale confrontation with an altogether different kind of resolution.

Thus only a completed triangle imposes strict limits on strategic options; two-power structures and conflicts enjoy a greater latitude. Significant projections can be made from both configurations into the future-as-history, defined by U.S.-Soviet bipolarity and U.S.-Soviet-Chinese triangularity. But more reliable than positive forecasts are negative predictions concerning the results of policies that ignore the projections altogether.

It is only one of two main possibilities that the U.S.-Soviet conflict might be defused by common concern over a third party. At one point, before the threat from Germany finally resolved the Anglo-Russian conflict, the reactivation of France as a Near Eastern irritant in the 1830s and 1840s (in the Mehmet Ali Egyptian crisis) loosened up briefly the post-1815 Anglo-Russian polarity and converted rivalry into a spell of diplomatic cooperation; but the détente was only temporary. Similarly, beginning as early as the 1880s, even a doctrinally antiwestern pan-Slav Russian—and less dogmatically Russophobe Britons?—could begin to sense the need for a common Anglo-Russian front in Asia against local forces of anarchy and fanaticism.* But, for the diplomatic convergence process to culuminate in entente, the southeastward German thrust into Turkey and toward the Persian Gulf had finally to provoke not only Russia qua land power with ethnic and economic weaknesses, but also Britain dependent on safe maritime approaches to India and beyond.

The more recent situation has been less promising so long as third parties aggravated the superpower conflict instead of helping defuse it. Whereas a rising China has replaced Germany as a source of threat to Russia, when extending her political influence or pressure southwestward—via Bangladesh, Pakistan, or (briefly under the Desai regime) India, and Sinkiang—a weakened United States perceived her as an all the more helpful counterpoise

*Cf. Otto Hoetzsch, *Russland in Asien: Geschichte einer Expansion*, pp. 102–22.

to Russia's strategic threat to the West, real or imagined; and the Soviets sought to exploit sociopolitical anarchy and economic aspirations in the Third World against the West for a similar mix of reasons.

Cyclical recurrences in conflict escalation. The logic of structures and configurations of power is reinforced by evidence from events that occur in sequences or cycles. The most striking sequence involves the land power that seeks amphibious status and parity with the dominant sea power in the combined continental-maritime sphere. When its initially moderate bid has been thwarted, the sequence is from finite initiatives in the continental (European) and overseas theaters to an all-out drive for dominance on the continent alone as a basis for a second, more forceful, bid for a correspondingly increased prize.

Adumbrated by Spain in the transition from Philip II to Philip IV, the sequence reached maturity with Napoleon. His expansionism in Europe (or, taking into account his designs on Egypt and India, in Eurasia) followed upon the prior failure of the *ancien régime* to coordinate its continental and oceanic initiatives in the face of British hostility in both theaters. Bonapartist expansionism was in large part the external consequence of the Bourbon failure, just as the Revolution and Napoleon had been its consequences internally. Similarly, the domestic regime and the politico-military strategy of the Third Reich resulted from the frustration of of the Second German Empire's simultaneous probings in middle Europe and, say, middle Africa or central America. It might consequently become a matter of grave interest to both western Europe and China if the first stage of Soviet expansionism were to be drastically set back outside the mainland before it had reached a stable point in terms of status satisfaction and material saturation.

Moreover, just as the simplest structure becomes a more complex configuration with the addition of a third power, so the sequence of two phases becomes a cycle when the second phase is but a transition to a third that resumes the sequence. So far, the sequence was resumed each time by a state more potent than the preceding and defeated one, after a period of turbulence. Accordingly, if the French emperor's defeat in the wake of the *ancien régime's* paved the way for the German emperor's attempt and failure, and the still more crushing defeat for the second German bid in the guise of Nazi Germany set the stage for Soviet Russia's so-far comparatively moderate continental-maritime quest, the obvious question is: Who will follow Russia, if she is first thwarted and then finally defeated? With whose aid, if anyone's? And, inasmuch as the area of fragmentation between west and east has expanded with each conflict since the decomposition of the Ottoman Empire in the Balkans, with what consequences?

Sources of expansion and integration among powers: patterns and problems

A well-ordered state, which Soviet Russia has become, does not set out on a career of expansion whenever it has the military capability or an ideology that invites it to do so. The more inclusive structures or configurations of power are at least as important, and some crucial sequences and cycles, while not determining, are suggestive. The historical record reveals yet other conditions, events, and processes that, when properly adjusted to contemporary conditions, are of interest when the issue is the thrust and tempo of future Soviet expansion.

Motives, manifestations, and momentum in Russian imperial expansion. Ever since Russia's growth beyond Muscovy into empire received its impetus from the initial rollback of the Golden Horde in the late fourteenth century, it conformed to many of the patterns typical for major-power expansion. A key sequence was from a predatory drive to increasingly defensive, but expansive, preclusion of outside threats to the physical security or economic access of an emergent empire. Chiefly trappers and tradesmen manned the initial predatory drive against weaker forces along river and portage routes; they were later joined by peasants in search of fertile soil. It took ever stronger and more official agents to deal expansively with changing threats from Turkoman nomads, the Swedes and the Poles, and, in the final phase, the British and Japanese (replacing the weakened Chinese) while the imperial frontier was being pushed forward by subimperial predators (the Cossacks) or proconsuls (chiefly military men). With the originally strong impetus from the trading "middle class" weakening progressively until late in the nineteenth century, when it seemed to regain some independent strength, the role of the central government grew steadily. The early close connection between political economy and military conflicts was not unusual. However, it did not give way at a later stage to conditions permitting freer trade or more informal imperialism, either before or after the collapse of the tsarist regime.

From the very beginnings of Muscovite supremacy, the main direction of expansion was determined by the need to protect the geostrategic, economic, and racially vital core against threats from south, north, and west—to wit, to the steppes from marauding Tartars, to approaches to the sea from militaristic Swedes, and to the seat of national faith and power from Catholic Poles. Generally, the impulse behind the either sequential or near-simultaneous thrusts northward (toward the Baltic Sea) and southward (toward the Caspian and Black seas) was on balance defensive, while the drive eastward (toward the Pacific Ocean) was more acquisitive. But whether the Russians expanded in response to threat or to temptation, the core never ceased to feel vulnerable to hostile invasion or isolation. Invasions came alternately from west and east, but isolation was invariably initiated from the west when the purpose was to bar Russian action in the Near or the Far East.

At least three features of possible significance for the future emerge from the historical record of Russia's growth into a position of sufficient power to permit further aggrandizement in alternative directions. First, there is the oft-noted alternation in Russia's thrusts into Europe and Asia. Advances into Asia occasionally dissipated energies needed internally or in Europe. They never implied the abandonment, even temporary, of Europe. The more the Russians were perceived as Tartars in Europe, the more they saw themselves as Europeans in Asia, while attempts from within or without to make a separate Eurasian identity meaningful invariably failed. The orientation toward Europe, recommended by geography (there is no equivalent in the west to the mountainous barrier against at least part of Asia in the south), was ratified by the uneven makeups of the actually or potentially threatening Asian and European powers. The disparity made Russia's defensive and offensive involvements vis-à-vis Europe alternate relatively frequently when compared with the longer time spans in regard to Asia. Thus, after centuries of defense against Asia, Russia's counteroffensive began around 1500, whereas China might replace late nineteenth-century Japan only in the twenty-first century as the counter-counterattacker.

One "lesson" from the past is clear. Neither the defense of the vital core against China nor offensive forays into peripheries of Afro-Asia were likely to disinterest the Russian government in western Europe. Strategic involvement outside Europe may even promote an intensified cultural engagement within Europe as an antidote and a diplomatic one as a reinsurance.

The second feature of continuing interest is that Russia's overland thrusts—including those toward more or less land- or ice-bound seas—were significantly more sustained and successful in the past than were forays across or toward open bodies of water. This was true for nineteenth-century probings in the direction of Alaska, the then Abyssinia (now Ethiopia), and even the Amur River. More recent drives in altered conditions toward Angola, Ethiopia again, and Aden, might not engender full-scale analogues of earlier shortcomings. But thwarting all such forays would boomerang if frustrated expansionist energy surged back into traditionally more successful—overland—directions and environments.

The major official economic effort in tsarist Russia, tenuously linking the "feudal" elements and the newer middle class, went into building continental railways. It did not go, as did the comparable politico-economic undertaking in Imperial Germany, into building an ocean-going navy. Next to topography, one reason for the difference was in the at least partially inverted relationship of industrialization to war in the two eastern monarchies. In post-1890 Germany, the needs of advanced industrialism increased pressures behind a world-wide Anglo-German competition. In Russia by contrast—and this is the third relevant feature from the past—it took especially mismanaged wars to trigger spurts of economic and sociopolitical modernization as part or sequel of major internal upheavals. The modernization itself served then in due course as a basis for the next thrust forward. In modern times, the cycles of advance-defeat-reform-advance and so on began with the sixteenth- and seventeenth-century wars with Poland and Sweden. They impelled the initial militarization. The pattern continued through the Napoleonic Wars, when the Continental blockade following defeat fostered initial industrialization. And the rhythm was perpetuated by the Crimean War, the Balkan War of 1878, the war with Japan, World War I, and, via near-defeat, by World War II.

The latest instance was the setback in the 1962 Cuban missile crisis, aggravating the earlier one in the Congo. The experience launched the Soviet regime on the latest spell of technological borrowing and military self-strengthening, toward a substantial capacity to project power by air and sea over long distances. Also worth noting is that Russia's doggedness in compensating for setbacks more than carried over into the invariable tendency to avenge all defeats suffered in Asia. Such workings of the "spirit" are of little comfort to a western strategy that would overrely on an Asian alliance for thwarting Russian ambitions abroad.

Parallels and peculiarities in Russia's integration into the state system. Russia's expansion had been neither quite like nor quite unlike America's before defeat in World War I had suspended the external determinants of tsarist imperialism and the ensuing revolution had transformed the domestic—political and socioeconomic—stimuli. To be sure, much of the Russian setting displayed the most salient feature of the American expansion: an underpopulated continent open to a predatory drive. Yet, in such matters as the role of the state and the military, Russian expansion was closer to the Roman antecedent than to the American pattern. It even resembled British expansion of the seventeenth and eighteenth centuries insofar as the landed ruling class predominated over the commercial middle class in the actually completed phase of Russia's expansion, much as it was itself subject to the state. Moreover, if in both the Russian and the American cases a vast continent invited expansion from the settled center outward, the essentially predatory drive was attended at least initially by sharper threats to colonists in Russia's south than in America's west. Later, the locally motivated drives against inferior social organizations were replaced by the pulls that the outer system of more fully crystallized states exerted on both Russia and the United States. But again, the pulls were more stressful for Russia than for America, and the responses less voluntary and less rewarding.

The several interacting pulls from the west that drew historic Russia into late entry and partial integration into the European state system can, when reduced to power terms, be found in the advantages, needs, and failures of the West-centered complex of states. The pulls constituted in their full range both threats and opportunities for Russian statecraft.

To begin with, the technological and organizational superiority of the West relative to Russia's own backwardness caused the Russians to feel insecure vis-à-vis their closest western neighbors, compelling them repeatedly to imitate the West in order to develop locally matching strength. Thus, an early instance of the functional or technological revolutions that made the modern West, the military revolution associated with gunpowder, was relayed to Russia in the seventeenth century. The industrial and transportation revolutions, notably in railways, reached her only toward the end of the nineteenth century, whereas the accelerating process of transmission has climaxed only lately in regard to the technological revolutions in nuclear energy, electronics, and other fields. The gunpowder revolution made Russia insecure vis-à-vis Sweden and Poland, and dependent on farther western (including English) mercenaries. The revolutions in industry and transport enhanced Russia's insecurity relative to Imperial Germany, making her depend on French financial markets for means to construct railways too often of greater strategic interest for France than economic utility for Russia proper. It remains to be seen how the balance of threat from, dependence on, and imitation of, the more progressive West will concretely evolve and manifest itself in the future.

Repeatedly, imitation not only modernized but also distorted sociopolitical development. Thus the peasantry was fully enserfed to the benefit of lower nobility when the gunpowder revolution had phased out the nobility's lucrative service in the cavalry. Next, a feebly reemergent middle class was infeodated to the authoritarian state when it proved unable to handle on its own the commercial-industrial and transportation revolutions, while the noxious dialectic culminated under the auspices of a totalitarian political party bent upon accelerating the exploitation of the subsequent technological revolutions.

However, noxious or beneficial, dependence was not wholly one way. It was first in the west that material and technological progress outstripped the development of individual states into coherent social and administrative entities, and the crystallization of the entire European state system into a stable or stabilizable one. Thus deranged, the West needed Russia for coping with its instabilities by means of legitimist reactions or diplomatic revolutions. The politico-diplomatic need in the face of sociopolitical revolutions came to match Russia's needs and dilemmas fostered by the West's technological revolutions. At first, Russian rulers rejected requests for aid against both the expanding Ottomans in early sixteenth century (despite the precedent-setting western offer of Constantinople) and the Holy Roman Empire in the early seventeenth century. The later intermittent, but often decisive, Russian engagement took place first in the Germanic balance of power (the Seven Years' War) and then in the all-European balance of power (the Napoleonic Wars). An earlier defensive thrust to the sea (against Sweden, under Peter the Great) had compelled a radical speed-up in Russia's functional westernization; involvement in old-regime and postrevolutionary continental warfare and diplomacy drew social elites ever deeper into cultural Europeanization. The engagement escalated as Russia evolved through the eighteenth century from an auxiliary into a patron of older states or dynasties; a full European identity was won in the mid-nineteenth century when the eastern power was called upon to repress the socioethnic upheavals that filtered from the west into central Europe.

When, in the twentieth century, the revolutionary current was reversed, from a west-to-east into an east-to-west flow, the exertions that had brought about the Communist revolution were tied to the last in the series of Russia's outflanking alliances with remote western powers against overassertive western powers. Before the series ended in an alliance with France and Britain, and, eventually, with the United States against Germany, an early connection with Austria against France's allies in eastern Europe had been replaced by partnerships with old-regime France against Prussia and with Britain against Napoleonic France-in-Poland. Barring Germany's resurgence and a consequent merger of American and Soviet concerns about such resurgence, there now appears to be no ready prospect for an outflanking alliance with the farther West against the nearer one, and, therefore, no likely extension of technological westernization into updated "Europeanization" in sociocultural depth by the traditional route. Therefore, for the foreseeable future, the "socializing" or "acculturating" function of diplomatic strategies is confined to an alliance against powers or threats more genuinely "eastern" than is even a communized Russia—with the United States, or first, against its rigidities, with the west Europeans.

Features in Russia's acquisition of status and role. The West's technological and other progress rivaled its political problems in pulling Russia into the international system. The political problems included an occasional vacuum of power or vacancy of mission to the west of Russia, as well as the over-assertion of national power and ambition. First to wane was the might and the mission of Poland vis-à-vis the East in general. Next to fade, after the decline of the Ottoman Empire had ended Austria's mission in relation to Islam, was the capacity of the Habsburgs to check French imperialism. Russian might had to replace the Austrian one for a time, before the rise of the German empire rendered both unnecessary against France, but not Russia's weight against Germany. The still later wastage of a mission, Britain's imperial one in Asia, has since been followed by the erosion of America's position world-wide. The fluctuations made for only diplomatic or also territorial Russian gains, as did, beginning with the contention over colonial possessions in North America, continuing upheavals and divisions in the west.

Not all of Russia's expansion, spelling integration into the state system, can be reduced to pulls originated in the west (or east). But the pulls predominated on balance over predatory thrusts in the crystallized parts of the system even as preclusive thrusts blended with more unequivocally predatory ones elsewhere. All considered, tsarist Russia was functionally predisposed toward late entry into the European state system by her early and continuing material needs. She was favorably positioned for such entry structurally as well, because of western failures and instabilities. And she was strategically incited into implementing the entry expansively by western needs for political and social stabilization. In addition, when entry meant expansion, and integration could be equated with imperialism, Russian response was exacerbated by alarmist reactions in the West and adamant opposition to even limited Russian gains. These reactions did not sufficiently discriminate between cause and effect when the enlargements were commensurate with the very instability that had made Russia's intervention necessary and her consequent expansion possible; and the same reactions discriminated against Russia when her gains are measured against other expansionists' in comparable stages of development and settings.

Finally, as a late entrant into the system, Russia by and large proved to be doctrinally flexible. This was the case first in the religio-ideological dimension, such as in relations between Orthodoxy and either Catholicism or Islam; it continued to be the case later in regard to sociopolitical values and ideologies. Thus, different embodiments of Russian autocracy allied or were ready to ally with French republicanism and with Anglo-Saxon liberal democracy against more cognate systems, be they dynastic-German, totalitarian-Nazi, or Marxist-Chinese.

Hindered by asymmetries and disparities, Russia's functional integration into the international system has not neatly meshed with cultural integration. And her politico-military methods have lagged behind the widely prevailing diplomatic norms. But if Russia's westernization and her Europeanization were not synchronized, neither were the benefits accruing to her and to the West congruent. Rates of progress in the several areas varied. By the end of the tsarist regime, Russia's integration into the system as a coequal power and full-fledged strategic player had outstripped her functional and cultural integration as a "modernized" society. By contrast, in the Soviet area, the latter types of integration seem to have forged ahead of the former one, which imparts next to formal status also a corresponding role in the management of world order.

By the time tsarist Russia became an imperial defender of legitimism within states, as well as a key factor in concert-type legitimacy among them, she had evolved far beyond the mere status integration of pre-Mongol ducal Russia. Although part of the western dynastic-marriage market, the latter was effectively linked to Europe only by trade. The progression from status to role has once again only begun for post-Stalinist Russia. This condition will prevail so long as essential military-strategic equivalence in mutual deterrence remains unmatched by an equal part in bilateral deliberations on central issues of global and regional politics. In earlier circumstances, the first tsar, Ivan III, rejected western offers of spurious status-integration (kingship from the Holy Roman Emperor in return for joining the fight against the Ottomans). The latest among the Soviet successors to the last tsar have likewise refused to be satisfied with mere status symbols of an auxiliary association in upholding western-style world order. The tsar had declined to acknowledge the western empire as *the* most authentically Christian by accepting from it formal dignity; the commissars would not certify western-style world order as immutably legitimate in exchange for comparable symbolisms.

Who has benefited most from the accomplished extent of Russia's integration into the state system? So far, Russia's chief benefit has consisted of the technological and institutional innovations that flowed eastward out of the western functional or social revolutions, while the West has benefited from Russia's contributions to an evolution of the international system that remained free of hegemony and was thus, in a special sense, immune to the ultimate in systemic revolution. The specifically Russian input into the state system entailed smaller costs to the West than were the social costs to Russia of the West-originated innovations, which the state-system dynamic accelerated and the diffusion and reception of which it in large part imposed—a disparity, moreover, made all the more irksome by the gap between Russia and the West being narrowed only sporadically, as well as on most occasions painfully.

Because the needs of elementary security dictated Russia's technological-cum-institutional reception, and the needs of others prompted her integration into the system, Russia can be said to have been drawn into the latter. So was the United States, although under conditions vastly less traumatic and with results that are so far globally more aggrandizing. By contrast, the other late entrant, Imperial Germany, forced herself by and large upon the international system in the act of unification. Only at a later stage was Germany also in part at least drawn into a premature bid for aggrandizement by the decay of the western European powers when, having grown while the system itself took shape, these powers set about to shield their decline and avert competition over succession by reformulating the system's constituent ground norms.

Varieties of assimilation and alienation among ideologies and cultures: cycles and continuities

The ways and circumstances in which a late-entering power claims an enlarged role and status may turn the international system into a revolutionary one. The mere possibility will create a problem for the policies of more conventional, mature, or conservative older great powers. These powers have not only to identify the stage and extent of the late entrant's self-assertion, but also to decide how to deal with the attendant interplays of different value systems and cultural norms. How deep, the question then is, is the past outsider's alienation and how promising are attempts at genuine assimilation and co-optation? Because cultural diversity has predominated over affinity in East-West relations, added tensions, first within Europe, aggravated the strains and stresses that late entry always causes within the social order of the late-developing state, as well as in the international order.

One side of the circular interplay between internal and external orders is best illustrated by Germany. That side predominates when the stresses are projected outward from within a body politic caught up in the travail of belated adaptation. Another side is illustrated by tsarist Russia—and by the United States as a likewise late entrant. It is in evidence when stresses are injected at least as much or more into the body politic from an outside that is unbalanced and either constraining or exacting. The growing inability of late-tsarist Russia to deal with external constraints and exactions helped propel a traditional-orthodox order into a revolutionary-socialist one. However, Russia's transition has been less certain and complete culturally and even ideologically than institutionally. As a result, an increasingly complex mix of eroding Soviet Communism (as ideology) and reascendant Russian nationalism (as culture) may yet accentuate the first-mentioned problem, the outward projection of internal stress. In the wider East-West relationship, the third-world political cultures will also combine assimilation with alienation in regard to western culture. The predominance of either and its manifestations will depend on whether the material necessity to adapt to the dominant western economy, or the psychological need to differentiate the collective self from still-obtrusive western values, while being attracted to them, is more pressing—and with what ultimate effect.

In both dimensions of the East-West dynamic, the medium term between possibly very different short- and long-term outcomes will be the critical one for politically relevant conduct. It will reflect the comparative strengths of three factors: belief systems or ideologies that are only rationally apprehended; more deeply ingrained cultural norms and mores; and still deeper, instinctual power drives keyed to either political exigencies or social grievances. It is, therefore, hazardous to make a priori judgments leading either to a dogmatic affirmation (to wit, as to the unchanging ideological commitment of a major power such as Russia) or to a self-consciously pragmatic belief (namely, in the facile acculturation of third-world societies).

The crusades and coexistence between Christianity and Islam. Lessons for relations with both the nearer (Russian) and the farther (third-world) East can be found in the long-lasting interplay of Christian West with Islamic East, begun in the seventh century and rebounding in the present. The historical record shows that differences in ideology—including religious beliefs—will not rule out alliance or détente between ideological antagonists as a way of adjusting to political exigencies. Ideology will be periodically reemphasized, but each time around will be weakened in its force and transformed in its function, even if it is officially and formally upheld against change or infraction.

The collision between Christianity and expanding Islam reached its first plateau of pragmatism in late eighth century, when each side was divided or fragmented from within: the Arabs in Spain and the Christians in Sicily and Italy. Alliances across cultural and ideological divides then made for an equilibrium that was dynamic because it was plural, and stable because it rested on the approximate parity in the organic power of the main camps or camp leaders. The situation changed when the crusades of Europe against Islam caused the resurgence of ideology in a repolarized relationship, aggravated by the fundamental similarity of the contending beliefs (as monotheistic, Old Testament-derived religions). But significant occasions for détente and accommodation, reflecting a momentary power stalemate, continued to punctuate the cycle of ideologism-pragmatism-revived ideologism; for example, when, in the thirteenth century, the crusaders' previously conquered Latin kingdoms in the Near East were being rolled back as had been the Arabs in Spain and Sicily, or when, in the seventeenth century, problems of distance and logistics made Ottoman campaigns and sieges too brief to bring further gains westward while Habsburg power was growing in the east.

Alternately, protracted competitive coexistence, such as that of the Ottoman and the Habsburg empires, could best be relieved by geostrategic diversions, when the Austrian Habsburgs looked westward toward the Atlantic (as part of the Spanish succession issue) and the Ottomans toward Asia. Whereas the Viennese court's ambition was only a late and secondary feature in comparison with the world-wide diversion of the farther, maritime West, its growing advantage in technological progress and organizational efficiency over Constantinople was a key factor in the power reversal from east to west. The reversal, prepared while western Europe had withdrawn into herself after the repulse of her farthest-eastern crusading advance, set the stage for an East-West coexistence that became less competitive as it became unequal.

However, the limits of voluntary accommodation had been repeatedly either stipulated or demonstrated in practice by that time. Thus ideological peculiarities were formally reserved in the mixed Franco-Ottoman alliance against the Habsburg emperor in the sixteenth century. Nor was an in-depth cultural assimilation achieved between Christians and Moslems as a result of either a power stalemate or the close social intermingling of individuals within the conquering Latin kingdoms in the east—any more than it was to be much later in the western commercial and administrative strongholds in the lands of Islam or any other overseas possessions.

Coexistence versus conciliation between capitalism, Communism, and Russian nationalism. Contacts between Russia and the West had points of similarity with those between Christianity and Islam. Once again, collision was made worse by fundamental similarities, first between Orthodox and Catholic Christianity and, later, between Marxist socialism and socially concerned rationalistic liberalism. Likewise following precedent in the later era was the ample Soviet capacity to pragmatically adjust to the dictates of political necessities and to the impulses of power drives. Defense could alternate with expansive offense on both sides, but accommodation was easier when mere deployments substituted for direct clashes of military forces; diplomatic détente short of intimate accord was again possible even if parties disowned all equation between unholy alliance and infraction of secular dogma—or if a faction within one or the other party set out to block rapprochement. Cleavages within the Communist camp were alike with divisions within the western one in helping the long-term process of pragmatization, either jointly or separately.

However, especially within the Soviet bloc, defensive reactions made certain that an effort to protect essential interests would not invariably relax dogmatic fixations. After suffering setbacks in premature expansionism, medieval Europe closed herself off to protect the integrity of her religion. So too did Russia under Stalin isolate herself once the initial crusade of Communism against the capitalist infidel had been repulsed. Since then, again as in the earlier case of Europe, the strength the Soviets gathered in self-isolation has been directed outward, challenging western vital or vested interests overseas. If the consequence is repolarization, it will tend to resurface ideological hostility in the midst of a growing array of either influential or insurgent parties in the international system at large.

Since powers more eastern than Soviet Russia are also on the rise, one fact has become significant. Islam has always stood for, and, say, China may again come to stand for, the integral fusion of ideology and culture. But the very term *Soviet Russia* denotes a duality and suggests a possible cleavage between surface creed and ingrained norms. Accordingly, any erosion of Soviet ideology is likely to release Russia's cultural values for resuming convergence and promoting accommodation with the West so long as the

West does not compound anti-Sovietism with Russophobia, and does not reconcile Russian nationalism with either Communism or Soviet patriotism by equating it with wilfully expansionist aggression or virulent racism.

Whether ideology is social or religious—and, when the latter, engaging Christianity against Islam, Catholicism against Protestantism, Orthodoxy against Catholicism—it becomes politically more significant the closer it is tied to the defense of a concrete group interest. If, for Communism, this was initially a class interest, it has increasingly become in the Soviet Union the Russian national interest. Conversely, ideology is at its purest before it has acquired a power base. It will decay when the need arises to defend a power base through pragmatic or expedient adjustments and compromises: defending "socialism in one country" is not the sole example of postponing pristine ideological goals, hopefully until disposing of the next threat on the horizon and actually to the Greek calends. The paradox is most acute when either a sociopolitical or a religious ideology keyed to transcending the particular in the universal gains a cutting edge by association with a mundane bid for supremacy—and is either only deformed on the way to ascendency or also finally blunted in defeat. One way or another, the salience of the hegemony issue will frustrate the ideology's link to transcendence: Russianism will triumph over Communism.

While the balance between them was changing, Russianism and Communism may have been complementary in some respects. Thus, the latter has not so much blighted the innate character traits of the ethnic Russians as it has exposed them to rationalized disciplines more spontaneously present in the West. Less disputable than any ideal complementarity is the fundamental continuity between traditional Russia and Communism when it comes to equality with the West. That basic identity also transcends all differences between Russia and east-central Europe, including Germany. Like the late German, Russian ambivalence toward the West reflected lopsided assimilation into the West-dominated value and state systems, produced fitful self-assertion as a last-resort bid for full acceptance, and was more deeply rooted in an inner tornness. Under varied doctrinal guises, the desire to retain the prized inner richness and freedom, deemed superior to the westerner's, was indecisively at war with the desire to acquire the accoutrements of western-type economic progress and political freedom without attendant western corruptions. The elusive task has been to steer reception (of material or cultural goods and institutional devices) clear of the irreparable rejection—of self by self as a mere imitator; of the West as a model conclusively shown up as flawed.

The split between inner and outer riches and freedom compounds the difficulty of synthesizing spirit and power, the two sides of integral politics. The resulting stress for the society and its elites has been most acute under the impact of defeats or setbacks, beginning with the Crimean War in Russia and following World War I in Germany. It will be projected outward all the more intensely if the West meets the more eastern nation's sense of contributing to the human spirit with denials in the realm of national power—including, not least, liberating (if, the Greeks thought, eventually corrupting) seapower.

The feeling of having contributed will aggravate the sense of being forcefully or unjustly denied. The dissonance between contribution and denial will turn a frustrated desire for acceptance into overcompensatory assertion of power and will. Even if the self-assertion is initiated within the confines of criteria for legitimate entitlement as repeatedly modified by the West to suit itself, it will eventually defy those criteria. For a Pan-Slav, a Pan-German, or the successors of either, the interplay of power and spirit becomes a philosophically romanticized (or historicized) tug of war between relativistic *Realpolitik* and absolutist politics; expediency ceases to constrain defiance if, in a politics of despair, courting catastrophe has become the only remaining form of struggle against submission to denials or surrender to the consequences of defeat.

When a Pan-Slav Russian nationalist stressed ruthless *Realpolitik,* he reacted to what he saw as Russian receptivity to unreal chimeras, invented or applied for the benefit of more western parties. The chimera could be the government's monarchical legitimism, prompting a Nicholas I to suppress rather than exploit the 1848 revolution against Austria, or it might be the powerless (Slavophile) thinker's penchant for philosophical idealism and romanticism made-in-Germany. The Pan-German and later the Nazi rebels sought instead to transcend "mere" *Realpolitik* of the Bismarckian kind in a throw of dice that would either give Germany world power on the quick or banish light from the world forever. Not quite wrongly, the late entrants saw in shutting themselves off from counsels of moderation the only course open to them for pursuing equality with late western positions by early western means. Both stakes and tensions will rise when heroic politics is propounded by men who, self-perceived as the sociopolitical elite and actually marginal, have to build emotional bridges to disaffected masses if intranational integration is to be the first step to the nation's integration into the world system on ego-satisfying terms.

Whereas power is what it is, and its constituents change but slowly, "spirit" can have many meanings and be moved by more than one stimulus. Marxism-Leninism may be less effective in this regard than was Orthodox—or (in Germany) Lutheran—Christianity, but its totalitarian bias may be no more lasting and no less subject to secularist erosion. The Third Internationale went the way of the Third Rome when, aborted in both center and periphery, world revolution gave way to the substitute task of safeguarding socialism for a chance to evolve into last-stage communism. Confined to one country, so that it could be both the first and the foremost of its kind, the ideal goal was vitiated as ineluctably as had earlier been the summons to safeguard orthodox Christianity in Russia as, then, the supposedly both latest and last country to be called to the task. The vision of Russia as the most spiritual of Romes was blurred by the mundane quest for the second Rome, Constantinople, across the Balkans. The more recent myth faded when priority shifted from saving the world to surviving at home, and from the conquest of social iniquity to the reconstitution of military empire. As the nature of man once more censored his idea of society, the secular residues of the Tartar khanate and the more exalted residues of the Byzantine basileus fused for the second time in the Soviet neotsardom, only gradually moderated as it became collective. However, any Soviet leadership could be counted upon, when facing an outside threat or challenge, to follow the westernized Petrogradian emperors just as they had imitated the Muscovite tsar of integral Communist-type terror, and to appeal, at whatever ideological cost, to the myth of Russia's holiness, all the more unalterable because superficially endlessly corruptible.

Soviet East and the West in a rebellious world. Western statecraft may stand aloof while the Europe-Asia balance oscillates as uncertainly within Soviet Russia as that between the attractions of Europe and opportunities in the Third World does in the determination of Soviet foreign policy. The West may wait and see what happens if either a sociocultural miracle or a sleight of hand gives life to a "Eurasian" neuter. The West may awaken to alarm only when, expediency having made Soviet statecraft court "Afro-Asia," necessity will make it beware of the European rear before violently confronting Asia. Or else a western strategy can aim at restoring the early tie between Europe and ancient Kievan Ruś, worn thin as it may have been by thirteenth-century Asian and later western invasions. The strategy can aim at giving a political meaning to the functional links between the West and Russia that began in the late fifteenth century and were, historically, either too "pragmatic" because opportunist, or not pragmatic enough because ideologically rigid; it can foster initial convergence between the West's self-conscious secularism and Russia's self-attributed spirituality as the underpinning for reapportionment of sea- and land-based power on the geopolitical surface—and can tolerate that reapportionment as an impetus to continuing convergence.

In the real world, Russia's sense of ultimate identity with the West, and the West's with Russia, is bound to grow or decay according to conditions in the world enclosing both. Thus, whereas Russia has always felt most western when oppressed by or frustrated in Asia, the West was ready to accept Russia as part of Europe for the first time when the eighteenth-century Enlightenment discovered the yet stranger cultures of Asia. The equation changed when the end of the anti-Bonaparte honeymoon coincided with the surge of critical supplies from overseas ending dependence on Russia's grain and timber conjointly with dependence on her men and guns. With Russia thus once more less allied than alien, she became for a time more casually alienable and freely indictable—for instance, over Poland and the Balkans.

A different way of integrating an assertive power into the international system, one avoiding the concession of equality and the communication of a sense of acceptance, is the German route. It is marked off by a catastrophic series of wars concluded by the precipitate integration of the westernmost parts of a partitioned country into the West within a state system threatened by imbalance. The contemporary West might be unable to travel such a costly course to the finish in relations with Russia without rousing a China no less nationalist-imperialist than is Russia and without prematurely raising China, at the other side of an immense power vacuum, to a position exceeding Russia's in either 1815 or 1945. Nor could the West effectively pursue the "German" strategy without avoiding the costs and risks of indiscriminately courting the countries of the Third World—including those whose alienation from the West has been gathering new strength.

While the completion of formal decolonization has made the Third World take a second look at western materialism, incipient de-Sovietization has set the Russian "soul" free to once again weigh the rival attractions and penalties of renewed links with a West that is something more than a mass-producing industrial machine. Alienation will have an edge over assimilation when the parties' cultural norms differ more than do their respective ideological beliefs. The same is true when the interacting cultures are highly unequal in material power or immaterial potency and either ideologically or culturally motivated animosities are not kept in check by cross-cutting conflicts over prosaic stakes, immune to appeals of transcendent—for example, pan-cultural—solidarities. When alienation rules between cultures, alliances of states either become impossible or are indicted by purists as treasonable; politics tends toward fanaticism rather than pragmatism; erosion of ideology is replaced with explosions of idiosyncrasies. All this suggests that the cleavage between the West and some or much of the third-world "East" is still harder to bridge than that with the Soviet-Russian state and society.*

Alienation is at its most acute when slave rebellion predominates over, or

*It is in the assimilation-alienation perspective that must be seen—and condemned—the boycott of the 1980 Moscow Olympics by the U.S. administration. The sanction was intended to administer a rebuff to the Soviet regime as the offensive aggressor. The implication of the censor's moral superiority was instead an offense to the Russian people, a reminder of their subjection to ostracism at the first pretext and the least provocation. The boycott was also supposed to make good the West's failure to boycott the Berlin Olympics in 1936. But exactly because the West had allowed the Nazi-organized Olympics to proceed on schedule in the more western and civilized Germany, it had to think twice before again discriminating against Russia. The episode denoted once more the inability of the "pragmatic" western—or, more precisely, insensitive American—public mind to have empathy with the eastern Europeans' sensitivity to anything that smacks of western depreciation. In this as in other respects, America's notorious absence of collective tragedy dulls insight into the inner workings of other peoples' responses and adaptations to theirs.

succeeds, social revolution. From Spartacus in the Roman empire to Pugachev in the Russian empire, dispossessed slaves or peasants ignite rebellions; revolutions are set off by possessing if dissatisfied social classes or on their behalf, from the Gracchi in Rome to the Girondins in France. Rebellions rise from unappeasable psychological resentments, whereas genuine revolutions reveal socioeconomic conditions that are ready for melioration. Most grand-scale upheavals, including the Soviet revolution, are variably proportioned compounds or both. The object of the revolted slave is to recover elementary dignity; to this end, he must reverse the existing relationship of psychic dominance or physical mastery, even at the risk of material self-destruction. The revolutionary's task is merely to redistribute material goods and political power as alternate means and ends. Revolution can be led or appeased from above by timely concessions; it evolves near spontaneously over a predictable path toward the restoration of a stable regime and reequilibration of the social system. Rebels can be only overawed into renewed submission by acts of terror, or rebellion debouches into chaos as a way station to restructured tyranny. A success short of triumph for the revolutionary is to be co-opted among the social elites; the sufficient victory for the rebellious slave is to demoralize the adults in the master group and corrupt or win over its young.

Reactions in the decolonized Third World to the West—and to its local allies and imitators—have combined revolution and rebellion, heavily favoring the latter. The form and intensity of the visceral revolt of self-perceived former "slaves" against former "masters" and their local satellites or surrogates varies across the range of third-world societies that either possess or lack the psychic supports of an authentic historical culture (e.g., Islam and India versus some others), and either possess or lack the physical supports and institutional disciplines deriving from real prospects of significant power (e.g., China versus most others). Irrespective of such differences, however, the apparent trend has been toward revolt over revolution: the three major early-twentieth-century upheavals in China, Persia, and Turkey may have had a larger component of social revolution and a lesser component of racial rebellion than their mid- and late-twentieth-century successors in (so far) China and Iran. Over shorter timespans, within Islam alone, the late-nineteenth-century sequence was from Arabi Pasha to the Mahdi—from a would-be sociopolitical reformer anxious to imitate the West in not-yet-occupied Egypt to a religious revivalist revolting against all things western in the Sudan. The more recent sequence has been from Nasser to Khomeini, the first still battling reactionary Islam in behalf of not-quite-red "socialism" and the second restaging in Teheran the Mahdi's seizure of the white devils in Khartoum.

Culturally xenophobic religious fanaticism—or religiously colored fanatical nationalism—either replaced or relabeled in such cases the mass aspirations unappeased by defeated or deficient social reformism. When the Third World reached out expansively toward modernity in the initial postcolonial phase, its articulate objective was to subjugate the West morally in the name of values adopted from it. From Burma to Iran via (tentatively) India, and in different ways in Africa, that reaching out has since been succeeded by an urge toward self-isolation in religio-cultural orthodoxy confining "revolution" to one form or another of repudiation of the West.

Similarly, the roughly two-hundred-year first superficial implantation of the West in the then Near East was followed by Islamic counter-crusades and about four hundred years of near separation, with the West pushed back to trading with the East in ways it could neither militarily enforce nor forcefully protect. The more recent spell of western ascendancy in the Middle East again lasted two hundred years or so, ending in the mid-twentieth century and apparently followed by counter-colonizing Arab-Islamic resurgence. The stage is thus not necessarily set for another four centuries of reciprocal near-isolation. But a milder form of temporary divorce would functionally replace the buffers that at one time shielded the Islamic East from both the strengths and the foibles of the West, and the West from either the force or the faith of the Islamic East. The gradual thinning out of the buffers was begun by the removal of the Ottoman empire and continued with the decay of the more trust-conscious among the western imperial administrations. Replacing the cushions with contacts, western-inspired and -directed economic developmentalism (misnamed neocolonialism) multiplied frictions and intensified them into more serious antagonisms. Mere frictions or outright antagonisms have obscured the fundamental similarity of the overtly or covertly controlling concern, with only mundane well-being, on the part of foreign agents and local beneficiaries of modernity. They also dramatized an either only initial or merely ephemeral shift in power—presently away from the post-Latin West and back toward the neo- (and some would say pseudo-) Islamic East.

In such a setting it is at best officious for western, and specifically American, statecraft to busy itself avoiding isolation from third-world cultures that seek isolation from the West as the first step out of alienation toward rehabilitation. Nor can the West ignore the need occasionally to inspire awe after losing authority, if it is to remain able to rein in the anarchic bias in slave rebellions and discipline progress toward whatever reparation may be just—or simply politic. The need can be ignored least of all in favor of mistaking rebellion for revolution and then setting out to mastermind its supposed evolutionary potential. Social revolution does have an advantage over rebellion in the economy of appeasement by material means. This advantage and related rewards, however, have to be weighed against the liabilities and risks of allowing an abrupt shift in the balances of economic power to follow from one in moral will. This is true even where condoning the more material of the shifts might make it easier to negotiate the transition from revolt to revolution as the high road to equality, at the end of which the psychic boon of restored dignity becomes one with the material good of an unprecedented prosperity.

Gushing gold and gravitating power between South and North. The Arabs may or may not be borne to more than shallow resurgence on the stream of oil on which the Entente powers are said to have swum to brief victory in the first of the world wars. It is yet less certain whether a merely oil-based resurgence can consolidate for any length of time the position of economic superiority over, or main threat to, the (European) West, which would restore the relationship of forces prevailing at the outset of common Arab-western history. Much will depend on whether a newly introduced outside—now Soviet—military power will, as did the Turks, first check Arab Islam and then become a yet greater, if less volatile, threat to the West; or whether, reversing the sequence, an initial military threat will become an "objective" if no other ally for the West.

The material source of Islam's resurgence raises the question of long-term power gravitation across a wider field. Preeminent power moved from southern to more northern latitudes, both locally (e.g., in Mesopotamia and Greece as well as Italy) and—in a generally northwestward direction—globally (from Mesopotamia); and it moved thus as changes in the main sources of energy in both fuel and food favored larger-scale, and eventually industrial, organization. A shorter-term subcurrent flowed eastward in modern times on the European continent. Henceforth, the main direction may be reversed or the issue of power be revised in kind. If power again flows south- or southeast-ward for either past or present energy reasons, the trend would ultimately favor China, regardless of whether the global northwestward and continental-European eastward power trajectories had previously converged and intersected in Russia.

While the issue remains in abeyance, a new kind of relations among states and cultures might revise the whole problem of power instead of only reversing or inflecting its flow. The material factors either causing or attending the so far completed power migration would then have to be diffused ever more widely, as well as more gradually and noncoercively, with consequences for the way and sequence in which the latest entrants (including third-world) affected an international system engaged in successive stages of globalization. For such impacts to follow upon one another at an accelerated rate and still slow down power gravitation as a means to muting the disruptive concomitants thereof, the successive new entrants would have to differ crucially from the old. They would have to either bypass the travail of (nation-) state formation and maturation, or pass through and beyond it with a minimum of externally projected internal stress. Such maturation is a highly political process.

It, too, may be accelerated, but may even then have to precede the kind of depoliticization that has been spreading from the European to the entire Atlantic West and has rendered it philosophically receptive to the lure of a post-power political "world community."

As lateral entrant, Soviet Russia has followed upon the successive entries of tsarist Russia, Imperial Germany, Japan, and the United States. Each entered into a more matured, fully crystallized or already decomposing, Eurocentric state system. By contrast, today's incipient global system has only begun to take shape as U.S.-Soviet bipolarity fragments and its determinative core factor, American primacy, fades. In consequence, Soviet Russian strategy makers do not face the pressure felt by Imperial Germany's leaders to extend power and influence before all peripheral positions were occupied; to act soon or give up forever.

The Soviets need not succumb to anything like *Torschlusspanik,* because the gates to either the outer periphery or the inner city of world power are not about to be shut for the long night of well-policed peace and quiet. The global system is volatile in temper, brittle at the center, and fluid in both regional and global power distribution. This also means, however, that the norms of "legitimate" or habitual great-power behavior and the shape of feasible great-power goals are being defined by action alone for an indeterminate future. Nor is it certain that the continuing erosion of western power would not exert an ever stronger pull on many other actors to join the system on their terms, and thus set off a general crisis of succession. There is, therefore, ample incentive for the Soviets, the chief late entrants of the moment, to adjust their sense of future possibilities to the need of codifying the ensuing necessities for others. This prudential need can be construed as a form of systemic constraint on Soviet Russia. But the complementary challenge for the West in general and the United States in particular is to move away from a denial-oriented doctrine and strategy toward Russia—or endure the consequences of a structure that has eroded at random or crystallized too fast and adversely.

Next to other changes (e.g., from naval to nuclear weapons as the ultimate ones), the greater volatility of the system and the more open-ended time scale without doubt modify the lessons to be drawn from the Anglo-German-Russian triangle and the ensuing two Germanic wars. But they do not reliably nullify those lessons. This is all the more true because at least some of the seemingly new features only restore some of the latitudes that surrounded both the bilateral and the triangular land-sea power interplays in the three to four centuries preceding the twentieth. Now as then, the stark simplicity of major-power structure will withstand for some time longer the most tumultuous winds of change and the most turbulent human desires from within or outside that structure before conceding a partial or perverse fulfillment of anyone's present ambition.

Analogies from past events and particular tendencies help bring vast historical perspectives from secular trends and long-range cycles down to earth. They help situate policymaking at a level where such analogizing from history can fruitfully complement self-consciousness about presently operative assumptions. However, particularization is really useful only if it serves an effort at generalization, at abstracting from scattered analogies key structures and processes sufficiently determinate to serve as a policy-relevant focus—a focus more immediately and directly relevant than the grand evolutionary perspectives on past policies that can better elevate reflection on present policy than guide its implementation. When all the different operations have been performed on the historical record with an eye to reasoning out or rationalizing preferred strategy, history and reflection have done all they can to assist in shaping the main contours and filling in the particulars of a grand strategy.

Part Two

ELEMENTS OF DOCTRINE

When World War II ended, . . . [o]ur military might was at its peak, and we alone had the ultimate weapon—the nuclear weapon—with the unquestioned ability to deliver it anywhere in the world. If we had sought world domination, then who could have opposed us?

Consider the facts: over the past decade, . . . [t]he Soviets steadily increased the number of men under arms—they now number more than double those of the United States . . . Historically a land power, they transformed their navy from a coastal defense force to an open ocean fleet; while the United States, a sea power with transoceanic alliances, cut its fleet in half.—Ronald Reagan (address to the National Press Club in Washington, 18 November 1981)

Inner dialogue must tend to sketch its own structures of thought, to condense, regulate, and discover latent meaning in events and words that formerly seemed random. What other form of command remains to an exile?—John H. Finley, Jr., *Three Essays on Thucydides*

III

THE FUTURE AS HISTORY.

Projections and Prophecy

A doctrine comprises premises and projections. Premises underlie what is believed to be true and what is intended to happen; projections denote what might happen under various assumptions and as a result of different courses of action—or strategies. For both purposes, the historical record will have to be broken down into constituents—that is, structures and processes—that have direct operative significance. The object is to proceed from a general, philosophical perspective to a particularized, pragmatic purpose. There can be no intellectually respectable and more than fortuitously successful strategy without a coherent doctrine. The precept of how to act is contingent on the premises behind the decision of why to act in one way rather than another; it may incorporate the projection of past trends into a prophecy of future calamity if wrong premises were to stake out the path to an erroneous strategic precept.

Any attempt to derive "lessons" for strategy from history, if it is to be more than casual, must draw on both structural and temporal dimensions of reality. The structural dimension refers to recurrent, or repeatable, structures or configurations of power among comparable parties as to the place they occupy or the role they play. The temporal dimension concerns the points in future time at which the antecedents may again become significant for strategy in view of past sequences and cycles of events. Structure and time are both at issue in the problems created by new major powers entering late into a more or less open and receptive international system. Applying a common yardstick will be a way to isolate the possibly significant difference or differences between past and present incumbents in continuing roles. Even if only tentative, the findings will affect the prospects of alternative strategies.

Varieties of projection from historical antecedents: structural and temporal

When using analogies from history as a basis for policy analysis and advocacy, it is necessary to keep in mind one caveat: however disciplined they may be, the transpositions from past to present and future can be only relative. Thus, it is not the actual time spans that can or will be reproduced, but only the relative lengths of time; it is not necessarily the past forms or means of projecting power or enacting conflict that will repeat, but only their updated functional equivalents across the full spectrum from military hardware to procedural mores. Just as the different techniques of competition that developed as part of the cold war were the functional equivalents of a shooting war, so a World War III could readily take a form quite unlike the spasms of total violence in the two preceding blood baths—and be no less cathartic or catastrophic. All this means that even an approach to grand strategy that systematically incorporates "lessons" from patterned historical antecedents can be at best only quasi-scientific. It can be only a handmaid to statecraft as an art employing intuitive judgment of current tangibles and intangibles to bridge two extreme poles: disciplined retrospection and inspired prophecy.

Past dates and possible future developments in the power triangle. Structures of power will take less time to change than such major processes as assimilation among cultures, a definitive erosion of ideology, or the integration of a major power into the international system. One reason is that "process" will have to prepare changes in "structure" as well as help consolidate them. It took a limited amount of time for Russia to shift from being Britain's chief rival within the two-power structure to being her ally in the triangular configuration. Yet most of the critical processes affecting Russia had begun prior to the two-power conflict; while progressing, they eased the transition from two-power to triangular conflict; and even now, they have not yet been wholly completed—if Marxism is seen as continuing Orthodoxy in differentiating Russia from an either repelling or repellent West.

When we turn from the preliminary question to particular structures of power and related conflicts, various possible dates and time spans come into play. Thus, after centuries of a variably amicable and antagonistic relationship gradually rising from one of only trade to a political one, the system-wide two-power Anglo-Russian conflict lasted from 1815 (or the early 1820s or the mid-1850s) to 1907—that is, somewhat less than one hundred years at the longest. By contrast, the subsequent Anglo-German-Russian triangle unfolded over a much shorter time, at the most liberal reckoning over half a century (from approximately 1895 to 1945), in two acute phases. Its climactic and decisive phase occupied still less time (to 1914 from either 1901, the date of Anglo-German failure to agree on alliance, or 1907, the date of the Anglo-Russian agreement). If the rhythm continues, the U.S.-Soviet conflict could go on for several decades before it begins to be resolved in earnest in the triangular setting. The estimated period of incubation becomes even longer if China is expected to grow into a serious threat to Soviet Russia only as slowly as "Germany" did within the Anglo-French-"German" triangle. Then the critical time span was from about 1700 to 1870, from the real start of both the Anglo-French maritime conflict and the initial ascent of newly royal Prussia to the point at which France began to relinquish the role of the would-be amphibious challenger to Germany.

The acceleration of history makes it hard to believe that the current triangle would match such century- or centuries-long time spans, even if the so far decelerating effect of nuclear weaponry is taken into account. But the *relative* lengths of time taken up by past crystallizations and actual confrontations are suggestive. They suggest that the bilateral U.S.-Soviet conflict that has been under way since 1945 will continue to dominate the 1980s at the very least, whereas the triangle comprising China will begin to shape up decisively only in the 1990s, if then. If we assume that the earlier triangle began to take shape before 1907—that is, in 1901, the date of the final failure of the Anglo-German attempt at accommodation—it can be inferred further that mismanaging the 1980s will make the 1990s and beyond all the more critical.

Mismanagement can follow from mistaken timings, including failures to synchronize the pursuit of variably short- and long-term policy objectives. This might mean, within the global East-West compass, poorly timing the steps taken to implement U.S.-Soviet reapportionment and U.S.-Chinese rapprochement. Within the narrower East-West compass, it also might mean failing to match Russia's progression with western regression: Russia's imitative leap forward, meant to reduce her habitual time-lag behind the West, would then be unmatched by a western, and specifically west European, move backward in time, into meaningful repoliticization and remilitarization in external relations past the current absorption with domestic welfare. Western retrogression will have to get under way before Soviet Russia has moved too far in catching up with the West's own past in overseas imperialism—an arena of human endeavor wherein her efforts have been smoother even when not always more effective or continuous than had been tsartist Russia's earlier imitations of western constitutionalism and industrialism.

A tempting alternative has been to address the problems of the 1980s as if they were already those of the 1990s and beyond, and to do so with either the methods or the moods of the 1950s. The Chinese willing, this meant boosting China in addition to the United States' engaging in rigid if largely rhetorical containment of Russia and the Europeans' indulging in mostly U.S.-reprobating passivity. It also meant offsetting the seemingly adventurous Soviets by methods liable to boomerang: on the plane of U.S. reprisals in the short run and on that of U.S.-Chinese rapprochement in the long run. It meant, finally, ignoring a major historical time factor: only brief periods elapsed in the past between the would-be amphibian's first-phase drive (a relatively moderate drive—overland and overseas—which was defeated) and its second-phase all-out drive for continental hegemony first, but not only. Roughly as long as in the earliest and imperfect instance of Spain (from the passing of the second, to the last try under the fourth, Philip), about two decades sufficed in the case of both France (from the last Bourbon effort to Bonaparte) and Germany (from William II to Hitler). Moreover, it did not take much longer for the sequence to be rounded off into a cycle as the would-be amphibian, finally eliminated, was replaced by the next-in-line challenger on land and sea (i.e., Spain eliminated in 1659, France in 1870, and Germany in 1945, replaced, respectively, by France in the 1670s, Germany in the 1890s, and Soviet Russia in the 1960s).

It is possible to discount such tentative projections from history and focus instead on relative weapons technology and degrees of military readiness when projecting periods of greatest danger. Such a period would now be the mid-1980s, when the Soviets are expected to reach the peak of their military superiority over both the United States and China. However, by that standard of judgment the Germans were still more clearly favored in 1906 relative to both Russia (just-defeated and revolutionized) and Britain (post-Boer War). Yet they did not strike out, despite the ample occasion created by the so-called Moroccan crisis and the provocation of the diplomatic defeat they suffered in that same crisis. The reason they did not strike out is as simple as is the flaw in projections from material capabilities only. Even states whom adversaries stigmatize as inherently aggressive or expansionist do not lightly stake their fate on a throw of dice at the supposedly optimum moment. They move in earnest only when they feel the breath of inescapable necessity—meaning, of course, no more than a warrant to act preemptively on the strength of a high improbability that an anticipated adverse shift in the power balance would or could be reversed by a favorable twist of chance in the future.

Secular processes and sequential probabilities in East-West conflict resolution. What is essentially a process—the relations between the West and the third-world

"East"—is likely to unfold in a sequence even longer than the paramount structural East-West issue of U.S.-Soviet-Chinese relations. The perspective is not one of the present decade and the following ones, but one of the remainder of this century and the bulk of the next one. The nearest analogue is the relations between Europe and Islam that were articulated by time cycles spanning centuries. Thus, roughly, the Arab conquest beginning with the seventh century was followed by Europe's counteroffensive in the eleventh century. Thereupon, the rollback of Christianity in the Levant, beginning in the thirteenth century, was carried into Europe herself by Ottoman Islam until it peaked in the sixteenth century. And Islamic advance was replaced in the seventeenth century by Europe's shift from defense to offense, ending only in the twentieth century with signs of western regression and the beginning, perhaps, of yet another cycle.

When facing the earlier Islamic offensives and the related options of mutual assimilation or antagonization, the West was able to stage only a delaying rear-guard action. It may not be able to do any better in its relations with insurgent parts of the Third World. In the apocalyptic vision, the crisis of world order spreading from a periphery in revolt can be seen as succeeding the era of four empires: in ancient tradition, the Assyrian, Babylonian, Persian, and Roman; in an updated modern version, the Spanish, French, British, and either American or Russian empires. However, more likely than a terminal chaos after the last empire is another epoch of empires or equilibrium, if only after the decay of the essentially western or Euro-global system had sufficiently fertilized the soil for the growth of a next one.

There may be a better and more orderly way. The East-West drama could still be played out in three acts, each taken up by a more inclusive or deep-seated conflict. The first conflict to resolve was within what has become the contemporary West, including West Germany. It was a socioeconomic conflict among classes, with ideological overtones. It was appeased even where not fully resolved through the welfare-state formula with the initially indispensable aid of nationalisms, themselves fostered by interstate conflicts. Interclass appeasement was thus forthcoming only after the cleavage within societies—between city and country and between incipient capitalism and fading feudalism—had expanded into a schism between powers primarily maritime and, originally, only continental. However fragile, a social peace emerged at the end of cycles of fleet-building and fighting that was chiefly on land, of material destruction and reconstructions, in countries supposedly made "fit for heroes" to live in at long last.

Advances in assuaging the intrawestern conflict merely shifted the main locus of contention to the ideologically slanted cultural cleavage between East and West, running through Europe even if no longer confined to Europe. The cleavage, originally focused on Germandom, continued as the ebbing of the early confrontation made the remaining one, between the West and Russia, loom all the larger. Still deep, this split has ceased to be beyond healing once the predominantly Slavic East in Europe began to be integrated with the West on the socioeconomic plane. Many of the profound traditional differences have lingered and new surface disparities have been added. But the eastern area has begun to be assimilated to the western rationalist-industrial mode by way of the state-socialist alternative to the welfare state. Assimilation has gotten under way even though it is no less riddled with conflicts than has been—in function of an eastward-shifting land-sea power schism—the process of fitting Soviet Russia as the last remaining European great power into rational world politics. As the strands in the antagonistic integration of Soviet Russia and eastern Europe into the essentially still western system multiplied to include also the cultural strand, it was more strenuous than ever for all concerned to hold their own in each of the arenas. But, as so often happens, a protracted competition also had a beneficial side. It served as a mechanism for absorbing a confrontation between ideologies and cultures into a sobering struggle over world power and a race for survival against global chaos. In the ordeal of healing a long-standing rift, the diversity of preferred means has been an advance over single-minded fixation on either fundamental or fictitious differences in valuations and motivations, even when the discord over means was provisionally sharpened by the basic identity of national goals.

The conflict between the European East and the West has become both salient and ripe for appeasement only when resolving its social-class conflicts made the West both strong and weak enough to tackle the external issue. Its socioeconomic compromises made the West sufficiently stable internally to address the yet unresolved issue seriously. But the delayed social consequences of the welfare-state formula have also sufficiently eroded the West's politico-military dispositions and its moral fiber vis-à-vis the outside to make what had become possible into a necessity. Supposing that the sequential principle remains in force, it will be necessary to first integrate Soviet Russia more fully into both the global system and an enlarged West before it will be possible to substantially advance the resolution of the next, third-in-line conflict. This is a conflict that resides in a yet deeper cultural cleavage, with ideological and racial overtones, between the global "East" and the West—or, as currently phrased, between South and North.

A serious approach to an equitable South-North relationship has been impossible so long as the underlying conflict has been imprisoned in contentious economic issues and unbalanced economic structures. Both issues and structures were inherently intractable so long as the North (or, more precisely, Northwest) was in disarray economically as well as psychologically. With initiatives toward resolving the conflict thus fundamentally stalemated, a range of asymmetries and disparities has complicated matters further. Inside most of the Third World, the criteria for defining the needs and interests of a country as a whole (including the masses) and those of its elites have not been identical. Moreover, the South and the North have developed very disparate views on what constitutes a legitimate basis and a proper leverage for apportioning influence over the terms of accommodation. Reducing competition within the industrial North (or the larger West), including Russia, should set the stage for achieving greater unison with the South on, among other things, the meaning and implications of the (colonial) past and the permissible use of material assets in readjusting the relationship for the (community?) future. At issue is the use of high technology by the North and of underground resources by the South as either common inheritance of mankind, or source of unilateral leverage by one of its constituent parts—or something in between. When movement toward greater harmony within the integral North makes a South-North accommodation in depth possible, the attendant realignment will also make it necessary, if only to avoid polarizing world-wide interest blocs along strict (white versus nonwhite) color lines.

The unevenly tractable character of the different conflicts can set only an approximate timetable for their phased resolution. Regressions within the several acts of the drama, as well as derangements between subplots, are more than possible before it has become practical to reconstruct a genuinely global system, or reform it into a true world community. To will, therefore, an overleap of the second-in-line in favor of the third-in-line conflict on either expedient or ethical grounds will not advance the latter's resolution in the remainder of the twentieth century. A rush for shortcuts that has little or no foundation in either past experience or present evidence might instead delay genuine South-North accommodation into and beyond the twenty-first century.

Similarities and differences between past and present: states and state system

Fostering an orderly evolution in world affairs is a task arduous enough to encourage utopian scenarios with a fair chance to produce apocalyptic outcome. The difficulty inherent in the search for order is not lessened when the strategist considers, as he must, specific differences and similarities among past and present incumbents of the various roles, including their ways of relating to an evolving international system. What effects, individual and in the aggregate, do such differences and similarities have upon the significance of recurring basic structures of power and the sequences of events for grand strategy? Does the medley of similarities and differences invalidate projections, or does it merely increase the need to introduce judgment into the makeup of a valid precept or prescription? Does the balance of favorable and unfavorable, positive and negative, impact from the differences and the similarities increase or decrease the prospects of usefully referring back to the past for a suitably adjusted strategy?

Russia versus Germany and America versus Britain as role-holders. The first thing to consider are the differences between the two would-be amphibian late comers: tsarist Russia and Imperial Germany. Unlike Russia, Germany represented a highly developed material power in the geopolitical center of Europe even before being unified. When it came, unification may or may not have been strictly necessary for insuring the nation's growing sense of identity. But basic security had been unquestionably less at stake for the Germans before the 1860s than it had been for Russia in sixteenth- and seventeenth-century Europe before *her* consolidation. What was, in these circumstances, the wider role of unified Germany after 1871? A possible answer is that her overweight was neither as much needed for sytemic stability, nor as easy to integrate into it, as was, from the mid-eighteenth century on, Russia's more limited as well as more peripheral weight. Moreover, because Germany had always remained an integral part of Europe, she did not have to join the European system of states via a protracted process of graduated attraction and revulsion, as did Russia. But this fact merely exacerbated her sense of being unjustly left behind for too long in the race for preeminence among Europe's constituent nations, inspiring an inclination to reshape the system forcefully. Germany's abrupt coalescence thus readily turned into a bid for conquest when national unity failed to be rewarded quickly enough by equality world-wide.

As already noted, whereas Russia was drawn into the system, Germany forced herself upon it initially. She did so by virtue of strengths that, developed in preunification latency, created a growing need for an expansive overseas policy that would reequilibrate the old rural sources of military strength with the new sources of industrial-commercial vigor and popular-nationalistic vitality. A result was a difference in the "casual" relationship between industrialization and war: the former "leading" to the latter in the German case, the latter to the former in the Russian. Moreover, if Germany's eventually military revolt was against the power distribution generated by the British-originated socioeconomic revolution in the international system, her immediate impact was due to system-revolutionizing innovations in the critical arenas of military organization—the advance planning by a general staff and the instant use of railways for military deployments—and technology, such as the needle gun and highly superior artillery. Conversely, a chief source of Russia's unease with the extant power distribution was the geographically conditioned issue of military security (her inability to bar hostile—meaning chiefly British—naval access to her Black Sea underbelly via the straits), much more than the issue of economic prosperity (via a free commercial egress through the straits). And, far from innovating in the military sphere except perhaps in deployed numbers, Russia proceeded by delayed imitation of the principal military threat or rival of the day, beginning with the Tartars and ending so far with the Americans.

Thus, Germany chiefly tested the capacity of the system to absorb and assimilate the internal strains that an insurgent new member was externally projecting. Russia offers primarily the contrary example of a society on trial as to its capacity to withstand strains injected into it from the outside. Or, to state the contrast differently, the international system had to come to terms with Germany's social dynamism, whereas Russia's society had to come to terms with systemic determinism.

The differences between Germany and Russia in national power and international effect were substantial and remain pertinent. Yet they do not nullify a shared identity and a basic similarity. As to identity, they were both not only late but also eastern entrants, with comparable politico-cultural reactions toward the maritime West. However unevenly, both revolted at some point against the West's previously acquired preeminence and its continuing denials of meaningful parity. It is a minor point that in both the cultural and political realms Russia was, once again, lagging behind and imitating the more westward-located originator when it came to phrasing the protest and rationalizing the insurgence in the age of romantic-to-religious nationalisms and ideologies. As to similarity, both powers reacted expansively to the fact or threat of isolation: Russia regionally in the Balkans before the French replaced the gradually eroded German connection; Germany at first more globally when she had to settle for an increasingly precarious Austro-Hungarian alliance.

Nor are the differences insignificant for being only relative and for raising an intriguing issue of cause-and-effect circularity for the two powers historically. Whereas Germany's more primary social dynamics projected her fairly quickly into the force field of systemic determinism, pressures originating in the system exacerbated Russian social dynamism—slower, but then also explosively. And finally, the significance of the differences and similarities is not wholly eroded because they are only partially transferable from tsarist to Soviet Russia. Whatever the qualifications, the larger pattern remains valid. The comparison can be summed up as suggesting that, even if not equally in form and degree, the old and the new Russia have been less assertive abroad and less impelled from within, and thus more readily integrable into the system, than was Germany. And that conclusion, if accepted, can be interpreted as meaning that, instead of invalidating the larger analogy, the differences impart credibility to a prospect. They suggest that a strategy designed to relax the logic of the land-sea power triangle—or even to simply bypass that logic in the passional East-West context—has a better chance for success in the present than in the preceding case.

In offering that prospect, the differences between Russia and Germany complement two others. One is the longer time fuse of China's explosion into a full-scale threat to the "central" power (Soviet Russia) than was tsarist Russia's (against Imperial Germany). Another is the spatially larger home base, which is near-continental rather than small and insular, of the United States when compared with Great Britain's in the role of sea-power defender The first difference makes it easier for Soviet Russia to hesitate before staking all on a continental assault; the second, possible for America to remain watchfully aloof or ambivalent while Russia adds overseas assets to continental ones—to reserve final judgment before concluding that such additions automatically subvert the overall land- and sea-power parity between the two differently situated states.

Yet however much the advantage of the United States over Great Britain in size and home-grown resources may strengthen the argument in favor of a strategy for overall parity, this will not automatically prompt its adoption. For the strategy to be put into effect, less favorable differences and similarities in situation and style between the two Anglo-Saxon powers must be overcome. To safeguard access to raw materials and commercial outlets Britain was, and the United States is, dependent, if perhaps unequally, on ever less secure, remote bases—a disadvantage apt to also become one for the heartland power as it expands farther overseas. At least as important is a less tangible factor. Insularity of either the British or the American kind breeds a common pragmatism that produces inconsistencies in policy, along with a bias toward alarmism and compensating moralism. Thus, the British were inconsistent when they deplored the Kaiser's navalism after they had condoned the half-hearted inroad into Africa by the Iron Chancellor as an offset to French (and, possibly, incipient American) imperialism. They failed to appreciate that colonial expansion would logically lead to naval ambition. The makers of American foreign policy were similarly muddled when they took the Soviets to task for inversely deducing geopolitical ambitions from the increased military (including naval) capabilities the Americans had freely or frivolously conceded at an earlier stage.

An absence of consistent doctrine gave rise to alarm when the logic of the situation began to belie earlier expectations and run counter to ingrained pretensions. One result was for policymakers in both insular states to oscillate between over- and under-estimating the internal and external capabilities of the eastern-continental power; another, to overreact militarily or only rhetorically from typically inadequate military and overinflated "moral" positions of strength. The moment to overreact came when the maritime power had ceased to be immune to continent-based resistance to its ascendancy. The wider economic benefits flowing from that ascendancy were valued by all or most continentals other than the foremost (and thus locally feared) land power. As a result, it was the latter who offered first or foremost resistance to the curtailments unavoidably entailed in the benefits. While the leading sea power overreacted in one way or another to the opposition, the preeminent continental state was cumulatively provoked by the one-sided advantages actually or supposedly possessed by the leading sea power. The specific advantages reinforced a major and basic one: the ascendancy of each of the Anglo-Saxon islanders unfolded within an international system whose norms they shaped in keeping with their interests more than any other power.

Late-entering America and Russia and the international system. Side by side with similarities, there are crucial differences between British Albion and the American Union. For one thing, America's hold on the system is easier to relax than was Britain's. The consequent provocation to the Soviets and the pressure on their response have been less compelling. And if the economic as well as political world system has become less easy to dominate, the new dominant sea power proved less able to do the dominating that is still possible. Eighteenth- to nineteenth-century imperial Britain had been trained and tempered through many earlier spells of involvement and isolation. Not so America, whose two short and comparatively stress-free skirmishes with Germany (over the succession to the British empire) prepared the United States as poorly for a late entry into the Euro-global system as for giving an initial shape to the expanded proto-global system in confrontation with Soviet Russia. The ease of America's entry opened a gap between a preeminent role outside and a politically parochial and psychologically untempered inside, while the unaccustomed impact of the international system in its initially tightly bipolar structure offered little leeway for gradually and, therefore, more than superficially adjusting the internal value-and-authority system to the new role.

In relation to the emerging global system, the United States was the latest of the late entrants who helped to supersede a failing system of states, and sometimes helped to reinvigorate the expanded system, thanks to resources of strength gathered previously in relatively secluded or marginal positions. Just as Wu or Ch'in in the early Chinese system, so Macedonia was such a marginal power in the Greek, and Rome in relation to the Hellenistic, state system; similarly, the northern monarchies occupied the position vis-à-vis the Italian system, and the so-called eastern courts (or autocratic powers) aimed at it vis-à-vis the all-European system.

Although the United States seemed to be suitably placed to perform the role that fell to it by European default, an entry that was premature for America internally may also have come too soon and too abruptly to benefit the system itself. A negotiated early peace in World War I was required if preeminent power was to follow its by-then natural course and go on gravitating eastward on the continent—from Spain via France first to Germany—while continuing to move more slowly northwestward on the cross-cutting world-wide trajectory. Only such a peace would have let Russia leave the war before she succumbed to radical revolution; it would also have spared the west European powers from total exhaustion, deferring global decolonization to mutual long-term benefit. Unless, however, the Imperial German regime had the internal strength to abide by the verdict of a miscarried Schlieffen Plan (and sued for peace in a henceforth theoretically unwinnable war), peace could be had early enough only on the basis of the German military advantage that survived the opening setback. The Anglo-Saxon elite in America may or may not be judged to have played a noxious role in the drift toward the war as the not-too-discreet opponent of Anglo-German accommodation earlier in the century and as still more patently Britain's preferred alternative to a deal with the Germans. Yet the American social and political elite's moral sympathy with Britain from the start of the war and the growing American material aid to the Entente was unquestionably first instrumental and then decisive in foreclosing an early military outcome immediately favorable to the Central Powers and by indirection to Europe as a seat of preeminent power.

On this premise, contemporary disorder in the world is in part at least the delayed consequence of American interference with a more organically evolving process in Europe. Current world politics might yet become the means for partially correcting the derangement, depending on which way deliberate strategies will tip the uncertain balance of similarities and dissimilarities between the United States and Russia.

Similarities include the predatory features of the early transcontinental expansion and, at a later stage, the role of both powers as shapers of the international system in its fluid phase. But while ostensibly pulled, like Russia, into the system as a weight for equilibration, the United States also materially precipitated both its own involvement and system evolution; Russia, on her part, tended to lag not only behind the other key great powers but also behind the stage of consolidation or rationalization the system as a whole had attained at any one time. Potential for conflict is clearly present in the difference. In her unchanging resolve to make up for the time lag and catch up with the chief rival of the day by imitating it, Russia had one advantage that she passed on to the Soviets: she evolved into increasingly important roles in the international system only gradually, even as she incurred repeated internal convulsions. Her progression was, thus, quite the obverse of America's, which, after evolving more organically within, was incited into full external involvement by an escalating series of isolated conjunctures.

It remains difficult to guess which great power was better prepared by the past to face comparable difficulties. Both suffer, as did also tsarist Russia, from the growing disparity between usable national power and the larger arena. The disparity had overstrained France's old regime and precipitated its revolutionary liquidation even before a similar fate overtook Imperial Germany. The penalty has, therefore, been a relatively mild one for the United States when, following an abrupt integration into the world system, internal crisis of purpose attended the gradual dislocation of the initial congruence between the national economy and the economic requirements of a world role and between elite ethos and the role's politico-military requirements. As for the Soviet system, keyed though it is to correcting tsarist Russia's fatal gap between internal means and external goals, deepening international involvement has done little to mitigate a traditionally Russian incongruence: politico-economic ideas and institutions are adapted less efficiently than are military techniques and technologies.

Soviet leaders might hope to deal with their disparity—between values or institutions for civil existence and weapons or incentives for coercive expansion—by bringing about the collapse of an embarrassingly pervasive West. The United States might hope to deal with *its* disparity—between external role and internal resilience or rigor—by devising a domestically cheap way of containing the Soviet Union. Both have their special strengths and weaknesses. Russia's arduous but continuous external career reinforced her armor qua power while she continued, as a society, her traumatic quest for an inner freedom thought to be different and deeper than the West's; the United States was less well-prepared for carrying on with its both discontinuous and hesitant exercise of power abroad while seeming, as a society, better able to act out *its* internal drama of deciding whether and how to relate formal individual freedoms to substantive social disciplines also in conditions short of flagrant national emergency.

As each groped competitively for a way out of its disparity, both powers were under pressure in one way or another to move concurrently toward parallel or concerted actions that would shape a fluid international system into a genuinely global one. To instead shape the world in their nation's individual image was the ambition of the Slavophiles and later of the early Bolsheviks when stressing positive contrasts with the West; it has also been the goal of liberal proponents of the American way of life when advocating its world-wide imitation. This essentially ideological goal is made only superficially pragmatic by either side's desire or effort to injure the other side, directly or indirectly—be it, in Russia, the various "realists" ranging from the Pan-Slavs to neo-Stalinists or, in the United States, the "neorealists" (or "neoconservatives") and old-style cold-warriors.

The initial moves toward more positive goals have to come from the country that, still predominant, is the one qualified to legitimate the other side's lesser role. One such move is to treat the Russian state, even in its Soviet garb, as a normal state. As such, the Soviet state is heir to all the instincts and impulses favoring spontaneous and compulsively defensive increases of power. Another move is to treat the Russian people as one of the last historic peoples in the traditional mold. As such it looks to a form of greatness that would bring new respect from others and fulfill ancient dreams about the self, before also its patriotism fades and the fading merges with an innate absence of civism in integral depoliticization. The third—or actually the very first—step is for Americans to relinquish the presumption of their own uniqueness, and thus look upon themselves as just another group of people on the historical treadmill. They will not truly accept the essential continuity that exists between Soviet Russia and not only tsarist Russia but also all other great powers until they have given up the view of themselves as endowed with both the capacity and the right to save the world from itself—and from history.

The two Russias and a not quite changed world. Basic continuity between tsarist and Soviet Russia blends with surface discontinuities on many levels. In terms of geopolitics, continuity in specific targets and directions of expansion—whether attempted or achieved—is qualified by unequal efficiencies of the tsarist and Soviet national systems as well as by different points of contact with the international system. In this respect like Imperial Germany, late-tsarist Russia faced a settled state system unreceptive to change. Soviet Russia has faced instead a volatile international system, ready for a redistribution of power even as attempts are made to redefine its norms.

Improved internal efficiency and even but provisional reduction of stress from the outside seem to have given Soviet Russia an advantage over tsarist Russia. If so, this would indirectly improve the long-range prospects for the West of coming to terms with her peaceably. However, the easing of external stresses also shifts the balance of concerns to internal, or societal, strains. They are partially lodged in tsarist-Soviet continuity in relating "spirit" and "power." Both regimes interweaved transcendent elements (religio- or socio-ideological) with temporal ones (coercive and managerial) in near fusion, differing thus from the tendency in the west to either militantly oppose the sacral and the secular to one another or separate them altogether. However, Russia's eastern, integralist principle of secular-spiritual fusion at home has also been commonly at variance with external practice whenever she malintegrated the extremes of either absent or superabundant power with the yet more varied manifestations of spirit, in ways likewise different from the West's. The several discrepancies could not but compound otherwise rooted social stresses in Russia and exacerbate the alternate narrowing and widening of the gap between Russia and "Europe."

What Soviet Russia also inherited from the tsars is the similarity in internal structures with pre–World War I Austria-Hungary. The Habsburg monarchy cannot play a principal role in a comparison stressing the international system, but it invites potentially catastrophic analogies with Soviet Russia on the basis of ethnic heterogeneity.

Ethnic heterogeneity can be effectively surmounted only in an ethnically neutral political organization based on a dynastic or an ideological-party principle. When neither is effective enough, and the international system is stressful, "normal" social stresses will worsen. There may then be externally disruptive activity as the governing elites resist internal decomposition. When the resulting crisis potential came to affect Austria-Hungary, tsarist Russia was its external detonator. China could easily assume the role relative to Soviet Russia at some later stage.

There is also a more positive side, or at least possibility, if a delicate interethnic balance inclines elite action toward some kind of restraint. Thus, the German-Austrian and, even more, Hungarian elites were reluctant to incorporate any more Slavs into the Habsburg monarchy. A similar concern would either militate against bringing additional non-Russian or non-Slavic populations into the Soviet system, or favor only a loose, satellite-type, dependency status for them. Moreover, should the dominant Russian element continue to decline in relative numbers, this might foster a movement away from coercing the non-Russian but Slavic populations within the Soviet bloc and toward courting them in an effort to neutralize the more "eastern" minority groups.

The new tilt would accentuate any westward shift in Soviet foreign policy already under way as a means of countervailing the drift toward Asia in the demographic balance. That kind of mechanism was very much on the minds of the leaders of Germany and the German-sponsored dominant ethnic elements inside the Habsburg monarchy when they opposed any increase in autonomy for the Slavic ethnic groups before World War I. Their fear was that more codetermination for the western Slavs would incline Austria-Hungary's foreign policy toward the western powers. Finally, the interethnic situation may foster the desire of the ruling group to diversify the equation as much as possible with the help of ethnically diverse allies, clients, or dependencies from ever farther off. As it proves its competence in doing so, the regime will expect to strengthen not only its de facto authority but also its claim to leadership.

World-wide ethnic diversity brings up the question of the similarity of the present world to the past one. Discontinuity dominates when comparing the relatively settled world of the Anglo-German-Russian triangle and the world of the U.S.-Soviet-Chinese triangle, but is less pronounced when a still earlier era of transition from merely intra-European to world-wide politics is summoned to memory. Transitional fluidity has been again replete with disparate forces, many of them anarchical. They now oppose not only expansion by great powers but also any special role for these powers in upholding a minimum order. Although serious, this is not necessarily a fatal hindrance to reapportioning the measure of U.S. and Soviet access and influence the great powers can still exercise. The impediment can certainly be overcome more effectively in common than in contention. And if spontaneous small-state resistance and recalcitrance are of a kind to stalemate or neutralize entire segments of countries acting locally at cross-purposes, this will reduce the burden of order maintenance while enhancing access to sanctions and interventions for all present or future greater states.

A reemerging continuity with the more conventional (pre–World War I) world is also limiting the effect of discontinuities. It takes shape as the early post–World War II blend of ideologism and nuclearization begins to recede behind the new mix of policy pragmatism and renavalization in relations between the superpowers. At the same time, modernization cum decolonization in the Third World seems likely to be set back in many places by a new traditionalism, inviting degrees of recolonization of the lesser and less developed powers in their rapports with the greater and more fully developed ones.

A tentative balance sheet and projection. The pluses and the minuses, features of similarity and difference between both actors and stages, make the two- and three-power relations and conflicts in the past and present either more or less amenable to adjustment as an alternative to Armageddon. They would seem to produce a net plus for adjustment possibility in the next phase, when the comparison is between the 1890s and the 1980s. They also leave essentially valid, even if not intact, the "lessons" to be derived from recurrent structures and related roles and drives, while they enhance the prospects for strategies that heed those lessons. There is currently a greater leeway than was recently "traditional," in terms of the critical timetables set not only by comparative material resources, be they Soviet Russia's relative to China or the United States' when compared with Britain's, but also by the evolutionary stage of the likewise old-new international system. Just as Spain (and France) competed with Britain over the shape and thrust of world politics at an early stage, so Soviet Russia (before China) has come to share the lead in shaping the system in its latest phase in contention with the United States, and need fear confinement in a settled order less than did Imperial Germany—and even, to some extent, tsarist Russia.

The enlarged latitudes create opportunities for more relaxed and more risk-taking strategies that would introduce, on the American side, concern for lowering pressures within as well as on a rational contender into the concern for keeping the rival's ambitions in check. And, as co-shapers of the evolving system, also the Soviets might be more visibly inclined to make concessions to the emergent need to go back partially on at least some of the premature grants of formal independence in the system's most conspicuous weakspots. There is, however, also an ample margin for mismanagement on both sides. Pitfalls include the antidoctrinal pragmatism that the United States has perpetuated after Britain, the cultural absolutism that Russia shared with

Germany and that the Soviets have reinforced with ideology, and the divergence between the western and eastern, insular and continental, mindsets. There are, furthermore, the different kinds of internal weakness, mainly motivational in the American society and mainly material and institutional in the Soviet system. They reflect each side's peculiar derangement between domestic evolution and foreign involvement, aggravated for America by the requirements of an increasingly burdensome role and for Russia by the increasingly problematic relationship between immediate opportunities and eventual dangers.

Actual or potential maladjustments result from the asymmetries in (greater American) efficiency and (greater Soviet) persistence that the two major powers display both within their domestic arenas and in the international arena. They are made worse by mal-synchronization in the rates of speed at which society, state, and state system evolve in different parts of the world. This is evident when society outbids or outlives the state and undermines its role in the state system in the west at a faster rate than it catches up with even a primitive state and system crystallization in much of the old-new East. Some advantage may flow from the fluidity of the proto-global system. But mal-synchronization may at any time develop a vortex effect, pulling all into disorder, while asymmetries preclude the superpowers from seeing disorder as a threat to both.

Much will in the end depend on how Russia and America come to view the mix of differences and similarities between them, as compared with what divides them from the third powers and forces that they are still free to perceive either as tactical friends or as strategic threats. The prospects for long-term coalescence are as good as, but no better than, those for final confrontation. Movement toward either outcome will continue to parallel convergence, although very different aspects of society, polity, culture and material power will converge toward very different overlap points depending on whether the overall drift is toward entente or toward a terminal "misunderstanding."

Elements from history in conservative doctrine: analogic and prophetic components

Similarity of structures and broadly congruent timespans are essential for a valid historical analogy. Even then, the analogies can be only tentative and equate only basic dispositions and functions rather than specific events and outward forms. This is also true when the object is to extrapolate strategies. But it does not mean that structures similar to past ones necessarily call for strategies similar to those employed in the past. As often as not, to learn from history means to learn from past failures; projections from the past can lead to predictions of future calamity if the policy purpose or method remains unchanged. The caveat certainly applies to the ill-starred containment strategy practiced by Britain vis-à-vis Imperial Germany.* Hence noting an analogy with one-time structure often serves best as the point of departure for a counteranalogy with respect to one-time strategy. When the newly formulated strategy differs fundamentally from an earlier one, the analogico-historical approach issues into historical revisionism, albeit of a constructive kind. It casts a critical look upon what is past recall, though not necessarily beyond partial remedy, with the intention to amend the next time around.

Lawlike tendencies and functional versus radical continuity. As a support for proceeding by analogy in devising policies, are there general laws to be detected, laws that are neither so general as not to be worth stating nor detailed with so many particulars as not to be general? Even were the answer to the question in a strict sense "no," it would not cover recurrences that are neither frequent or regular enough nor sufficiently identical in kind to supply the raw material for general laws, but are sufficient to warrant statements about conditional tendencies suggesting some continuity.

Situations reoccur and tendencies reassert themselves because both the subjective and the objective matrices of statecraft are relatively constant. The first matrix is made up of persistent drives identifiable with "power" (and sustained by "spirit"). The drives are aimed at escape from a two-sided predicament, compounding the contingent and morally ambiguous quality of political action with the materially confining arena of that action. The second matrix is made up of no less ubiquitous constraints on such escape efforts. Identifiable with "geopolitics," the constraints are lodged in replicable configurations of power in physical space (only modified by diversities in political "cultures"), which are sporadically reconditioned by changes in techniques and technologies.

Because the range of possible power configurations and related modes of rational behavior is finite, comparable ones recur; because there *is* such a range, there are also opportunities for choice to relieve an overarching aura of necessity, reducible to lawlike tendencies and the injunctions of the imperative of self-help. However, because the tangible and intangible stakes are contended over by too many, and the contested goods or rewards are scarce, perceiving one's drive behind the competitive quest as an act of defense will be as irresistible as it is to elevate interests into rights. The ensuing little dramas easily obscure the underlying outline of tragedy even as

*But this need not be always the case. Thus, structure could be projected and strategy extrapolated from Bismarck's successful unification of Germany to the unification of Europe without either predicting calamity or prejudging the odds as to consummation. See the author's *Europe Ascendant: The International Politics of Unification* (Baltimore: Johns Hopkins Press, 1964).

feelings of mutual grievance hide the indifferent laws of gravity implementing the contrary pulls of reason and passion from sight. So long as it abides, the tragic nexus will exonerate most indicted villains in interstate relations, while the gravitational side will invariably turn apparent victory into a mere deferral of defeat.

In an environment of this kind, qualified recurrences do not add up to a radical continuity that discloses a transcendent manifest purpose to be distilled from mundane events. A preordained course would make strategic or moral choices into figments of conceit even as it held out the prospect of a permanent release from the two-sided predicament. Valid continuity is neither so radical nor does it run through outward forms. It links together recurrent structures that a continuously operative motivation relates to an unvarying range of essential functions; it is manifest in the efforts that externally changeable agents make and the roles they perform when pursuing persistent ends of statecraft in order to satisfy comparable dispositions.

Slices of comparable reality and meaningful analogizing. Not all historical antecedents become meaningful analogies. It is not enough to identify and assemble random facts or events from the past and suggest they might be repeated in the present or future. Nor do haphazard comparisons necessarily denote substantial comparability of either structure or function. Instead, capable of meaningful comparison are entire clusters of occurrences that stand in significant relationship to repeated or repeatable configurations.

Thus, the Austro-Russian rivalry was of great immediate importance in the decades preceding World War I, as was the matching Franco-German tension in the west. Still, the role of both Austria and France in the critical period is of little moment in a forward-looking analysis. It can be ignored in such an analysis because, so long as the Anglo-Russian conflict was alive and well in the eastern Mediterranean, the Austrian position vis-à-vis Russia can be assimilated constructively to the British (as it was contractually, under then-existing treatylike instruments). When the Anglo-Russian conflict had lapsed, Austria's role and attitude relative to Russia became subordinate to Germany's in the triangular context, both in actual practice and for the purposes of ex post schematic exposition. So too were, on these same grounds, the Franco-German rivalry and the Franco-Russian alliance superseded by the Anglo-German hostility and the Anglo-Russian entente. Whereas France had been a key actor functionally in her own right in an earlier triangle, before being superseded by Germany as the central continental state with naval and overseas ambitions, she was by 1914 functionally significant mainly as Britain's extension into the continental balance of power to be kept stalemated as a means of distracting Germany's resources and ambitions from the global bid. The fears and ambitions of both Austria-Hungary and France are thus of interest only as precipitants that brought the latent structural-systemic Anglo-German conflict to a head, while Russia looms large not as a regional actor in the Balkans but as a growing threat to Germany's world policy from the eastern-continental rear.

The superseded continental powers remain redundant for the main lines of a future policy-oriented analysis even when it is possible to reconstitute their present equivalents as a hypothetical or practical matter. Thus France could be "replaced" by a western European complex that, while in principle revisionist in relation to the lost eastern (German) provinces, is essentially defensive; or else, the same complex could take the place of Austria as one seeking to revise the European status quo farther to the east more actively and assertively. Leaving both historical powers out of the historical account (while assigning a role to western Europe in the present context) illustrates the difference of a discriminating from an all-inclusive analogy, of a structurally conditioned functional analogy from a literal or formal one. Not every, not even every major, actor, relationship, or event need be provided with a plausible analogue to assure verisimilitude for a comparison that reaches across time and past specific differences in order to become all the more relevant for strategy.

What slices of reality can then supply the wherewithal of meaningful analogizing and, thereby, tentative projections from the past onto the future? One such slice of reality consists of recurrent structures or configurations of powers. Whereas two powers and the relationship of conflict and accommodation between them suffice for structure, at least three are needed for a configuration. The two-power structure and conflict are more concrete spatially but also more contingent operationally than is a schematic three-cornered configuration, including that of powers differently situated in relation to continental and maritime theaters.

Another slice consists of recurrent sequences or cycles of variable "events." Two events or stages make up a sequence; a modified replication of the original act or event is the third movement needed for a cycle. There is a sequence if one kind of expansionary drive is followed by a different kind of expansion by the same power; a cycle, if another power takes over where the first power left off, and repeats the sequence. Similarly, more pragmatic valuations and concerns may succeed to more markedly ideological ones in guiding foreign-policy behavior, just as consolidation of power may follow upon its expansion as the main goal. Alternatively, there may be cyclical reversions from a later to the earlier posture in both motives or methods and objectives, while each return can exhibit enough change to do more than restart or reproduce the sequence—for example, change from coercive to consevative function of ideology after a pragmatizing spell; from early-exuberant to late-compulsive expansion after a period of consolidation. The international system itself, finally, may merely shift from the empire to the balance-of-power principle or mechanism as the foremost ordering one, or there may be returns to the first condition after the second dissolves into transitional chaos.

Yet another slice of reality consists of long-term processes that encompass both the structures and configurations of power and the sequences and cycles of event. A critical process can be stated in terms of an opposition between socialization and containment. Socialization is a relatively stress-free integration of a "new" entrant into a larger or preexisting system; its more or less rigid containment elicits more or less rebellious reaction. When assertive politico-military powers are to be integrated, whether they are or are not socialized while being contained greatly depends on whether their external expansion (and outside response to it) has influenced their internal authority toward becoming more concentrated or deconcentrated. The states to be internationally socialized can differ in their cultural norms from the predominant tone set in the larger system by a different culture. Any particular mix of containment and role- and status-integration can then either foster a progressive assimilation of the political elite that acts for the culturally distinct society in the world at large, or it can further alienate or finally antagonize it relative to the dominant culture tone and the tone-setting power or powers.*

As a precipitate of all other events and transactions, the gravitation of preeminent power covers the longest time span and ranges over the largest space. Even when negotiating more than one pathway simultaneously, preeminent power can revert to the starting point in what is then a circular trajectory. Conjointly, the system as a whole is certain to alternate between dissolution and reconstitution, revolution and restoration.

Projections, predictions, and the limits of analogy. When the appropriate recurrences have been identified, and the historical analogies that are significant for policy established, the past can be projected into the future in a disciplined manner, tempering awareness of present peculiarities with sensitivity to pertinent past patterns and tendencies. One inferior alternative to the golden mean is to repeat the follies of the forefathers without knowing what they were; another, to read elementary do's and don'ts into a very recent salient event or two without testing the apparent lesson against a larger setting of constraints and latitudes.

Wise strateg*ies* can inflect the thrust of lawlike tendencies, but wise strateg*ists* will discern and take into account the regularities relevant to their quandary. The path to wisdom is full of twists. Recurrent patterns externalize the

*It serves as an aid to memory to decompose the slices of reality lending themselves to analogy along an s/c axis: structure-configuration; sequence-cycle; and socialization-containment (although *integration,* interdependent with *decompression* and *liberalization,* is the term more commonly used in the text in regard to socialization).

working of drives for power and other deep-seated beliefs and aspirations that change little and operate within material or geographical settings that are both unchanging in fundamental identity and changeable by man's ingenuity in the influence they exert. Recurrences have to be initially formulated in a schematic fashion if thus abstracted and broadly defined situations or events are to be significantly comparable; but before concluding from precedent to policy, similarities have to be qualified by differences between past and present individualities. However, many of the differences will be shown to be secondary or inoperative if similar patterns of significant relations and behavior recur despite them. This does not mean, finally, that projecting past trends is the same as predicting future events. Accidents, innovations, and unprecedented initiatives will make the future unpredictable even if the variegated historical flow can be abstracted into regular or recurrent patterns. But disciplined analogies from the past can make the unpredictable future more manageable, by making the present less startlingly novel. Making the future more manageable is at once the outer limit of strategic statecraft and the first duty of the maker of strategy.

Whereas projection from the past does not secrete reliable prediction of the future, it does consciously or unconsciously underlie statements about the future partaking of prophecy. An element of prophecy is an integral part of any truly "grand" strategy. Such strategy does more than coordinate a range of instruments (politico-military, economic, cultural, and so forth) in pursuit of an aim; it also defines the aim and, being a set of precepts to guide future action, incorporates a doctrine that in turn specifies the premises and presuppositions warranted by past events and tendencies. A grand strategy that leans on doctrine for basic assumptions, that depends on projection for awareness of the main problem, and that draws on prophecy for a sense of the stakes and the price of wrong direction will be rooted in history. It is so rooted even when it is intended to transcend history by altering previous outcomes. Likewise rooted in history and intended to transcend it, although in unequal proportions, are doctrine and prophecy. Only projection altogether lacks the urge toward transcension. Because it is in consequence tied to empirical reality more closely and less ambiguously, projection constitutes the sole potentially "scientific" effort. But for the same reason, though essential, it is only a preliminary or auxiliary constituent of a grand strategy that is at least equally dependent on the partially intuitive doctrinal components and the almost wholly intuitive prophetic ones.

Prophecy versus projection and kinds of strategy. As an imaginative complement to projection, prophecy is less useful as an intimation of positive future events liable to result from unchecked play of inborn *drives* of-and-for power than as a warning. It dramatizes the calamitous consequences of action that would ignore lessons from past outcomes conditioned by recurrent *structures* of power. When the full-fledged prophet speaks on foreign policy without making it, he will typically be the gloomy Cassandra flirting with apocalypse in order to shock the prince into forsaking perilous routines for amending policies. But if prophecy is to contribute to a veritably grand strategy from within policymaking, as it were, it will have to grope for the vital middle ground between utopia and nemesis, between, on the one hand, the egotistic bliss of indulging in the urge to break fully with the drives and the laws of power in the pursuit of an ideal state and, on the other hand, the collective doom certain to ensue from wholly surrendering to the drives in the belief of being unconditionally served by the laws of power.

If prophecy is to occupy the middle ground, it must deal with international politics as it is, an either high or low drama with an undercurrent of tragedy. And even when it aims at muting the play of power drives that easily escalate competition into catastrophe, it must not propose canceling the creative minimum of tension between rival powers and interests.

Because the catastrophe that is not to be repeated is commonly prepared by the mutual enfeeblement of rivals in a "wrong" cause, and because intrinsic to the tragedy is the conflict of entitlements viewed on both sides as "rights," the much-traveled ground to be trodden by prophecy is replete with testimonials to past confusions. Some order will be introduced into its task if prophecy conforms to some of the lawlike tendencies (e.g., for power to gravitate as it fills a vacuum, for rivals to converge and third powers to impact differentially on two-power conflicts); if it is consistent with other laws (such as those positing a constant sum of conflict and energy in the system); and if it merely aims to delay or moderate the impact of still others (e.g., those decreeing the unavoidable decline of once-dominant powers). Respect for such laws is a path to orderliness. However, the path to practical utility is for prophecy to exploit the latitudes that are present in the environment, if for no other reason than because the laws are only tendencies and the laxity peculiar to each is augmented by contact with ambiguities inherent in all others.

An element of prophecy is especially needed in a grand strategy that aims at restoring a state system caught in the throes of a potentially receding revolution in the center of the system and a revolution possibly incipient at its peripheries. Yet the successful implementation of a grand strategy consciously keyed to system restoration would in itself constitute a revolution in statecraft. Statecraft is an activity more commonly consigned to less grandiose enterprises, and system restoration is commonly the unintended result of step-by-step reactions to immediate challenges. It does not help that social dynamics focused on welfare issues within states feeds into drives for external security or superiority and distorts the gravitational revolutions that states qua territorial entities would enact in a field of forces subject only to the laws of their motivation and motion. But, even if left to themselves, and isolated from doctrine and prophecy, the drives and the laws would be most of the time reflected in less-than-grand strategy, shading off into tactics.

In the relations between the United States and the Soviet Union, drives shaped by the triangular configuration point to a competition that structurally conditioned inhibitions to accommodation cannot but aggravate. Accommodation between a predominant sea power and an aspiring land power is all the more difficult the more the two are, first, asymmetrically situated in terms of geography and resources and, second, caught up in an intense phase of the ongoing process through which a seemingly constant sum of conflict in the system is being distributed, and that of political energy subdivided, among unequally rising or declining and assertive or defensive powers. Yet attempts at accommodation will be prompted again and again by the desire of the principals to escape either escalating conflict or deepening captivity to third parties. A total loss of control over either the third party or the conflict's momentum is apt to ensue from the main rivals blindly yielding to the laws of motivation and motion that promote competition between them. One such "law" enjoins the Soviet Union to yield to the attractions of overseas outlets in recoil from territorially contiguous China; another prompts the United States to respond to the attractions of an alliance with the same China in recoil from the damage done or threatened to its own interests and activities in the peripheries by Russia's centrifugal escape overland or overseas.

Situationally prompted tendencies of this kind make it necessary to take a more than casual look into a segment of reality larger than is readily perceived; they make it necessary to escape the tyranny of a manifest (i.e., bipolar) structure through timely awareness of the dangers hidden in the largely still latent (triangular) configuration; and they make it necessary to adopt and implement to this end a grand strategy dedicated to anticipating and precluding what policymakers applying "mere" strategy would first precipitate into being, later try to cope with, and then be coerced too late into trying to undo. Such would be a situation wherein the United States becomes wholly dependent on a China increasingly conventional as a power and traditional as a culture, and the Soviet Union dependent on a Third World increasingly radical or rebellious; or wherein both principals are in different ways immediately and tangibly threatened by one or the other—or both—"third" parties.

IV

THE PRESENT AS HYPOTHESIS.

Assmptions and Beliefs

Historical analogies and projections from history articulated within a longer or shorter perspective will not produce propositions about foreign policy that meet the predictive criteria of rigorous scientific theory. Nor will such an objective, if it is a feasible one, be achieved by explicating the sets of competing assumptions behind alternative strategies. However, in exploring all these avenues—analogy and projection; assumptions and perspectives—even if it is not possible to be "scientific," the potential does exist for an analysis that is more than sagacious in the sense of displaying political sense and judgment, and is also scholarly in the sense of laying a basis for a disciplined discussion of controvertible propositions.

When the object is to isolate elements of a doctrine with a view to proposing a strategy, the different planes of reality reappear in different levels of analysis. The approach on one level is to break down historical antecedents into especially significant structures and sequences of a rather general kind; this has been done in the preceding chapter. The complementary approach, on a different level, is to narrow down generalized premises to specific assumptions actually or logically tied to alternative strategies. Exactly which structures and sequences are best suited to inspire doctrine and inform strategy depends on their capacity to permit projections into the future, with an eye on the possibility of amending the historical consequences of past policies; the validity of alternative assumptions can be tested by reference to specific past events as much as with help from an eclectically formed sense of what is plausible.

Assumptions about policies: internal and spatial dimensions

The same reasons that place the U.S.-Soviet relationship at the center of world politics are reasons for viewing the policies of the two major powers in the broadest possible setting of both politics and history. As part of such an effort, the intellectual subsoil of the principal strategic options—rigid containment and its controlled opposite (to be called here "decompression")—will be broken up into assumptions that more or less consciously underlie advocacies of either.

Soviet foreign policy as "adventurous"? One of the central concepts in current western perceptions of Soviet foreign policy is that of adventurousness. From this a pressing question becomes evident: Under what definition of the term is Soviet foreign policy "adventurous" and, as such, both unpredictable in specific detail and direction and unmanageable by means other than massive blockage or repression by counterforce?

A policy can be judged adventurous from two viewpoints: that of underlying motive and that of ultimate effect. Whereas the ultimate effect is chiefly international, it is the domestic base of policy that is essential for the first category. A foreign policy is radically adventurous if it is intended to distract attention from, or make up for, internal inefficiencies even more than external weaknesses. These internal inefficiencies are usually those of an unstable and poorly institutionalized regime that has become almost totally dependent for survival or legitimacy on foreign-policy success that is both spectacular and "cheap." There will then tend to be no connection, or only the slimmest, between the contemplated object of foreign policy and the available means, as well as between the specific foreign-policy action and a sustainable long-term program or strategy. The object itself is more spectacular than substantial, and is to be attained owing to surprise, external underreaction, or, generally, some kind of default or special circumstance. From this perspective, an adventurous foreign policy is essentially reactive at home and opportunistic abroad.

Two separate antecedents to the supposedly adventurous Soviet thrusts into the Western Hemisphere offer illustrations. One of them, Napoleon III's attempt to penetrate Mexico, was unquestionably adventurous. The installation of a dependent Habsburg archduke while America's involvement in the Civil War immunized the intrusion against the interdicts of the Monroe

Doctrine was neither sustainable nor was it related to a coherent global strategy. It was designed, instead, to refurbish the regime's domestic image as well as, perhaps, camouflage its inability to substantially revise to France's advantage the consequences of Napoleon I's defeat in Europe.

A contrast is offered by an earlier French bid to secure an indirect stake in Spain's American empire by way of installing a junior member of the Bourbon dynasty as heir to the Habsburgs. This policy was not adventurous. It was an integral part of France's struggle with England over a fair share in overseas dominion. Securing such a share was a condition of making France competitive in the new economic forms of national and world power, and of matching England's economic and naval proficiency while complementing France's own land-military role and status. Louis XIV's policy choice was, under the circumstances, a rational one among the available options, and its object was in principle commensurate with French means. The policy addressed the long-term conditions of internal stability in the age of incipient world politics and developing world economics. But it was in no way prompted by an immediate need to shore up the regime or compensate for its failures—a need that only followed upon the effort's only partial and costly success.

In such a perspective, does Soviet foreign policy (likewise enacted in part by surrogates or auxiliaries world-wide) compare more with that of Napoleon the Little or that of the Sun King? If the criterion is accepted and the "facts" are construed in a certain manner, the answer can (and will) be in favor of similarity with the latter.

Soviet foreign policy can also be compared with the more recent example of Imperial Germany. Without being wholly so, the latter's *Weltpolitik* was relatively more adventurous, not only in the surface appearances of its implementation, but also insofar as it had one of its sources in internal social dynamics as it attempted to solve the problem of solidifying the increasingly archaic imperial regime. The object would be achieved if world policy and the related naval build-up, next to reconciling the conflict of interests between the agrarian gentry and the more modern industrial-commercial middle class, would also appease the working class through a combination of spectacular display abroad and material dividends from abroad.

Another criterion, comparatively less significant, is international effect. A policy is meaningfully adventurous when it is an independent source of disturbance, unfit to offset or constrain parallel sources of disorder. Moreover, the risks that the assertive power incurs must be far in excess of its supportive resource base. The resulting disparity is then likely to encourage external restraints, and it may elicit punitive responses, which will tend to further aggravate instability—probably beyond the degree implicit in or justified by the frivolous policy's likely or possible impact on the balance of power.

The use of military means for policy implementation is not a sufficient criterion of adventurousness when taken alone. Affirming that would replace a legitimate criterion, that of extreme disparity between available resource and incurred risk, with an attempt to elevate unavoidable disparities in resource between differently endowed and situated powers into a barrier to change. All the continental powers in question—old-regime and second-Empire France as well as Imperial Germany and Soviet Russia—depended on their military power to stay in the running for global sweepstakes against the economically stronger or better-entrenched maritime states. There is, of course, a very real difference between Napoleon III's attempt to infiltrate Latin America through an Austrian archduke backed by French soldiery and the efforts of William II's Germany to do likewise through foreign trade and commercial consuls. But Germany, too, despite her industrial performance and proficiency in export trade, remained weak relative to Britain and France in the financial markets even after she became a net capital exporter. She caused offense by combining the build-up of military power with the export of military-aid missions, such as that to Turkey in the Middle East.

Consequently, before Soviet foreign policy can be objectively identified as adventurous, it is necessary to assume certain things. As to the second criterion, the international system must be visualized as one that, if free of Soviet power and policy, would be inherently stable or, at least, readily and easily manageable. It must not, that is, be possible to judge Soviet expansive policy as a normal one for a state of its kind at its stage of development; and it must not be possible to view that expansiveness as one that, if kept within limits by a combination of restraint and a reasonable resource-risk ratio, can have positive effects on both the world-wide configuration of threats to order and on the internal structure of Soviet power.

As to the first (domestic) criterion, in order to consider Soviet foreign policy adventurous, the Soviet political system must be viewed as radically unstable and unmanageable—and not merely unpopular and sectorially inefficient. It must also be viewed as wholly or primarily dependent on conspicious foreign-policy coups for survival and legitimacy—and not merely as a system of rule wherein the limitations of popular support can be supplemented, and shortcomings in internal performance compensated for, by a foreign policy sufficiently successful to satisfy the patriotic values and nationalistic desiderata of the people. Any political regime facing a politicized populace must have the ability to generate satisfactions of this kind. To admit this particular connection between domestic inducements and foreign policy weakens the case for foreign policy as an outside projection of a particular (including Soviet) ideology. But it does not confirm the interpretation of such a foreign policy as being principally a response to internal pressures and compulsions. One reason is that, in the Soviet case, any internal rewards for the regime's success abroad are offset by widespread popular reluctance to sustain the material costs of an ambitious foreign policy most of the time. Another, that the regime is politically much too strong and stable to be guided abroad by pressures from within, much as it might prize increases in popularity gained abroad at reasonable cost and risk.

Thus it is possible to conclude on the basis of both criteria that Brezhnev's Russia compares favorably with Wilhelminian Germany on the issue of adventurousness (and still more favorably with late-Bonapartist France and some other regimes, such as that of fading Austria-Hungary). While Soviet policy is unquestionably assertive, it is not technically adventurous. Were a different conclusion embraced, it would be necessary to overcome a formal or logical objection: Is it consistent to treat Soviet foreign policy as being at once adventurous and as implementing an unchanging long-range design?

In principle, the two features—adventurousness and design—could be reconciled in a view of Soviet Russia as a revolutionary power, with transitional disorders as the object of a medium-term design. In practice, a genuinely adventurous policy (however defined) is unlikely to relate effectively means to ends and promote any design—including that of imposing a provisional instability on the system that would be more than a transition to widely concerted countervailing response. Nor is this all. A genuinely revolutionary power is likely to be adventurous under our definition. While formally distinct, the internal and the external aspects of a revolutionary identity cannot be wholly separated in fact: an internal-revolutionary condition will tend to satisfy the domestic criterion of foreign-policy adventurousness; the French revolution in its later stages, as well as the Communist revolutions in Russia and China in their early ones, support that contention. Hence, pronouncing against Soviet adventurousness in foreign policy implies an argument against the continuing character of Soviet Russia as an internationally "revolutionary" power.

No irrefutable basis for a correct judgment on these issues can be laid by either empirical analysis or hypothetical reasoning. Yet if a policy based on an incorrect single assumption proves disastrous, it is impossible to repeat the experiment under a different assumption. When replication is impossible, the second best approach is to explicate the widest possible range of assumptions when fashioning a response to Soviet "world policy" in the hope that one set of such assumptions may emerge as more coherent or convincing than any other.

The Soviet Union as a rising or declining expansionist power. No assumptions are more critical for U.S. or western foreign policy than these: As a power expanding outward either actually or in intention, is Soviet Russia an inherently ascending power? Or is she a stagnant or even declining power, either absolutely or relative to western or farther-eastern powers? Is, therefore, her expansionism an awkward but necessary part of transition to an essentially conservative foreign-policy phase keyed to a balance of power, or is it of the compulsive variety compensating for internal slippage? These questions pose in a different way the issue of adventurousness versus assertiveness. And the way in which the questions are answered determines assessments of the long-term significance and permanence of Russia's ostensible expansion: how effective increases in Soviet control and influence are apt to be over time, and how lastingly the Soviets will be either able or inclined to interfere in depth with vital western interests.

Whether the Soviets are inherently rising or declining depends chiefly on the internal performance of the regime. What is its industrial-technological or agricultural efficiency? And how great is its capacity to maintain the cohesion of a growing and diversifying elite while mobilizing a potentially flagging mass support? By the time we know, it may be too late. Moreover, the significance of the associated Soviet expansiveness abroad for the foreign policy of other powers depends on additional assumptions about the *international* system. Is it expanding, static, or even contracting; is it flexible or rigid, and in what terms? It will be easier to justify the strategy that aims at assimilating an expansive great power into the international system without war if the system itself can be assumed to be expanding or expansion-capable; if, that is, the expansionist thrust mobilizes so far dormant powers or helps crystallize the so-far inchoate forces in ways susceptible of reequilibrating the enlarged system, as well as helping realign powers that have been active throughout. In addition to being rich in elements of counterpoise (to the "expansionist"), a flexible system will be also endowed with elements of substitution (for the expansionist's "victims"), as well as with ample geographic or functional outlets for expansive energy.

Without being squarely faced, the issue arose in the 1930s when the debated question was whether to appease Nazi Germany or "stop" Hitler. The proappeasement option, while selected by default or through timidity, was neither publicly nor, one suspects, intramurally rationalized in terms of a world system capable of expansion and reequilibration. Logically if not otherwise, the antiappeasement position hinged on the assumption of a static all-European international system (minus Soviet Russia?), incapable as such of absorbing German expansion in east-central Europe.

More recently, the tendency has been to postulate an international system that is expanding in terms of new actors and emergent forces, especially at its peripheries and in its most intensely embattled sectors. That assumption has directed attention to the wide range of possible targets for Soviet expansion, but it has not been positively related to strategy options toward that expansion. Nor has another implication been weighed. Whereas the interwar antiappeasers implicitly held the then system to be static—that is, including neither Soviet Russia nor, *a fortiori,* the United States in a way permitting (for different reasons) the expectation of them both gradually if separately responding to the expansionist tendencies of Nazi Germany—the system did encompass the two as significant reserve powers. Within different time spans, a German enlargement that continued and extended beyond east-central Europe was likely to set off system-wide pressures sufficient to mobilize not only Soviet Russia but eventually also the United States into countervailing involvement in conditions of formal peace. If this is a tenable hypothesis, and both Russia and America were activable reserve powers, the antiappeasement option was finally adopted in 1939 on an only partially, or questionably, correct assumption about the international system as structurally less expansible than it actually was.

It is anybody's guess whether the present international system will dispose for the next half-century or so of reserve powers that are comparable with interwar America and Russia (be they China, Japan, Western Europe or, say, Brazil or India)—powers, that is, that are readily mobilizable in terms of either morale or matériel from a politically neutral or neutralized posture. The uncertainty makes assumptions about this facet of the problem all the more important.

At least two conclusions for policy can be drawn from what precedes. One is that, if Soviet Russia is assumed to be a materially rising as well as a policy-wise expansionist power, the larger system's capacity to expand in terms of either countervailing forces or spatial and functional outlets permits some Soviet expansion. Another is that, insofar as these forces are fragile or underdeveloped, and outlets for Soviet expansion are located in areas of the system that are not readily reequilibration-prone, there are definite limits on the degree of readily permissible expansion. Thus there are equally definite limits on the margin available to a responsible policy partaking of appeasement—and amounting, as it will be more amply explained, to the obverse of rigid containment: a strategy of decompressing the both external and internal environments of Soviet foreign-policy making. Yet again, even if finite, a limited margin can be assumed to exist, and there are corresponding limits on the policy of inflexible denial of all Soviet geopolitical expansion. These limits result from the uncertainty about whether there is significant major reserve power with a willing disposition that can be readily mobilized and whose material power base is not simply illusory. Were, therefore, the Soviet Union to view inflexible denial as provocative, this would tend to advance the Soviets' necessity for choice—between abandoning external objectives regarded as legitimate and prosecuting them more forcefully—to a point in time preceding the materialization of any such reserve power.

It is plausible to assume that Soviet Russia rises or ascends in her internal capacity to expand, and the international system increases its capacity to absorb Soviet expansion, in a similar and similarly precarious fashion—although somewhat unevenly in degree and time. This assumption may be held to support a western policy tolerant of moderate and controlled Soviet expansion. So might the assumption of Soviet stagnation or even relative decline. Under this assumption, the expanding or contracting nature of the international system over time is of less importance than is the question of what is best for its stability in the shorter run. The strategic choice between rigid containment and decompression is then keyed to the related question whether to seek to accelerate the rival's stagnation or decline and its external ramifications, or adopt a course that would ease both; whether to increase or decrease the likelihood of a power vacuum or of Soviet overreaction. In regard to the latter, it is possible to either advance or defer the possibly irreversible choice faced by the Soviet leadership: whether to respond, perhaps as part of a struggle over succession, to stagnation or decline by resorting to foreign-policy adventurism (as defined previously) or by adopting the stance of renunciation; whether to stake the future on a gamble or definitively abdicate from great- or world-power ambitions.

Deferring the choice might make the need for it disappear. Should the delay cause Soviet leaders instead to opt for the path of adventurousness, any intervening advancement of the internal decay would lessen the impact of this adventurousness even further. In either case, conceding a measure of foreign-policy success to a faltering Soviet regime is meant to compensate for internal inadequacies rather than to moderate Soviet conduct by facilitating the outward projection of internal efficiencies. It may come easier to concede external success to a faltering regime if doing so fits another assumption, one that bears on the predictable effect of internal stagnation on foreign policy over the short or middle run. The Soviet political system being what it is, it is possible to assume that even stagnation or decline, when measured by criteria such as economic growth rates or agricultural productivity, will be compatible for some time with a persistent middle-level assertiveness.

A related question is whether, in such circumstances, the Soviet leadership will be receptive to a barter between access to outside resources and self-restraint abroad. A positive answer to this question is possible only so long as receptivity is not confused with disposition to "sell out" on the score of political goals and to be "bought off" in the coin of material grants.

One approach is to offer the Soviets economic and technological substitutions for foreign-policy ambitions: that approach was in evidence in the Nixon-Kissinger era. Another approach, one that has become more tempting in that era's aftermath, is to deny the Soviets economic and technological favors in the hope that internal disabilities will impede their foreign-policy enterprise. The first approach could work only if the Soviets already were so (conventionally) adventurous as to try to dupe the West by sitting pretty until sufficiently strong, while not yet softened, for striking out; the second risks making them adventurous (under our definition). Both approaches differ from conceding foreign-policy successes of a kind that augment the need for internal efficacy. If the efficacy necessary for action abroad cannot be fully secured either at home or coercively from abroad, it can be assumed that a continuing prospect of some foreign-policy success, and an access to resources from abroad impliedly contingent on self-restraint, will jointly moderate the intensity of foreign-policy aspirations.

It will matter for the quality of self-restraint and external restraint whether needed resources originate within or also without. As critical as the resource-restraint relationship is one between resource and risk. Soviet resources available for foreign-policy purposes over the short-to-middle term are unquestionably finite. Taking commensurate risks will have to make up for the different degrees of resource limitation if foreign policy is to remain active and have a chance to be effective. The question then is what kind of risks the leadership will be prepared or forced to take in order to maintain in balance another possible trade-off: between progress toward domestic prosperity western-style and advances toward parity with the West in the world at large. Some such trade-off seems necessary if the regime is to maintain the irreducible measure of popularity, popular mandate, or mass apathy necessary to avoid relapse into Stalin-like coercion.

The equations involving available resources, necessary risk, and acceptable restraint on the one hand and domestic prosperity, intersuperpower parity, and regime popularity on the other hand are complex. But they do have a definite relation to external as well as internal stability and peace. This is readily apparent on the energy issue, as it relates to the alternatives of Soviet access to increased supplies through domestic exploration (with or without western technological assistance) and access to Mid-Eastern oil supplies with western toleration or against western opposition. For the Soviets, different ranges of risk-taking will be judged necessary under different conditions of resource availability and western constraint. They will depend more generally on the state of Russian development along the not necessarily parallel lines of mass consumerism and nationalism; that is to say, they will depend on whether and how the popular expectations of a steady if slow improvement in the standard of living inside Soviet Russia can be traded off in popular perceptions against a steady if slow enlargement of Russian role and influence abroad.

It is an altogether plausible assumption that the Soviet political system is unpopular and is internally perceived as inefficient. However, it is also essentially stable and capable of adopting rational foreign-policy perspectives of at least a medium range. Under such an assumption, even a relatively mediocre internal performance ought to make it possible for the regime to steer clear of both the external risks of adventurism and the domestic penalties of renunciation in foreign policy. If it does, the internal costs of a moderately expansive foreign policy with only indirect or prospective material benefits ought to be acceptable inside Russia. So might be to others its international costs, also with only indirect or prospective political benefits.

External acceptance will be contingent on the plausibility of the assumption that moderate expansiveness will satisfy not only the present but also any likely future Soviet leadership; that it will be sufficient as well as necessary. Any Soviet regime of the immediate future, whether more inward- or outward-oriented in its efforts and ambitions than the present, will be unable to base its legitimacy on meeting only internal demands for continually improving the people's standard of living (or, at least, maintaining it if the pessimistic forecasts about future performance levels prove correct). Nor will any regime be able to ignore the reciprocal influence between its foreign-policy orientation and the domestic interethnic balance or dynamic, much as it may continue to be committed to the Soviet-statist formula or look to a gradual crystallization of an ethnically neutral Eurasian identity. Considerations such as these suggest that the regime optimum will be to safeguard the bases for both intangible prestige and concrete performance by action abroad that is consistent with "reasonable" relations with the West.

Only on such a basis can internal, economic or ethnic, problems be approached steadily from a position of regime strength. Only regime strength will minimize pressures for precipitate concessions to demands for material betterment by all groups, or demands for redistribution of political power by so far disadvantaged ethnic groups. All such pressures, as well as the pressure for relapse into countervailing internal terror, would be harder to withstand if the regime's external behavior either tightened U.S.-Chinese confinement or created the need to appease China as a means of loosening the vise. The problems with which the non-Russian or non-Slavic ethnic minorities face the Soviet regime have points in common with those of the West facing demands from the Third World. To the extent that this similarity sinks in, the "southern" or "eastern" dilemmas of the predominantly Russian Soviet leadership will set a rational limit on its exploiting the West's world-wide problems of a similar kind. There are ideological or immediately tactical inducements to do otherwise. However, they will all pale before the high probability that to intensify the conflict with either the West or China is unlikely to inspire all of the divergent ethnic elements evenly and simultaneously with a heightened sense of Soviet-type patriotism convertible into material self-denial and heightened political loyalty or only conformity.

In the circumstances, any Soviet leadership that is dependent on foreign-policy success, but is constrained in regard to its scope and the methods of pursuing it, will have to tread a delicate line between over- and under-assertiveness abroad. It cannot reconcile otherwise the modernist needs for technological and related progress (least of all with western assistance) with the traditional urges of ethnically differentiated groups for self-expression (in the face of western or eastern cultural attractions). However, one condition must be met if any leadership is to be able to embark upon a gradualist evolutionary path with an ideologically inadmissible, but practically unavoidable, terminus for adaptive conventional power politics. The western strategic response must be likewise nuanced; it must be minimally permissive or even supportive. It will not be such so long as western policymakers keep proposing a simple barter between Soviet restraint (defined as quiescence) and western resource infusion. Nor will it be such so long as they offer undefined substitutes for forceful, including military, Soviet self-assertion as a way to enlarging the Soviet role in world affairs. Such offers ignore the ample evidence that it is impossible for a revisionist power to separate forcible approaches to change from "peaceful change" in cooperation with a concession-prone status quo power. Thus, most recently, western offers of a diplomatic accommodation of Soviet security needs in Afghanistan only followed the Soviet invasion, whereas the fragility of forceful Soviet leverages in the Middle East made it both possible and irresistible for U.S. diplomacy to keep the Soviets out of that area's peacemaking.

One point is worth noting before proceeding further. It is a rather safe hypothesis, supported by experiences all the way from Ethiopia in the 1930s to South Africa more recently, that economic or technological reprisals or sanctions "short of war" are not an effective punitive reaction to undesired conduct. But they are least ineffective if, designed to do no more than increase receptivity to an eventual inducement, they are aimed at constraining the overall power potential of the (preferably small) target state (e.g., Rhodesia) over a prolonged period of time. In that form they are superior to selective and transient ad hoc measures, be it against military violence (e.g., Italy's in Abyssinia) or political violence (denial of "human rights," e.g., in Latin America)—and this with only rare and special exceptions (e.g., the U.S. refusal to relieve the run on the British pound in the 1956 Suez crisis).

Much the same is true of external inducements. Most promising is a long-term strategy calculated to affect the connection between the internal evolution of a political system and foreign-policy dispositions on the level of changing, and up to a point influenceable, relationships between the dominant political class and other key groups, including the public at large. Least promising—and least capable of being assessed as to their effect, as well as most susceptible of being manipulated from abroad—are haphazard acts of concession or constraint intended to tip the balance of insufficiently known factions, "radical" and "moderate," in a particular foreign-policy debate within the target country. U.S. efforts to outguess internal Soviet policy-making dynamics with the view to aiding the moderate viewpoint were most prominent in the waning cold-war era, during the Khrushchev stewardship, before giving way to an experiment with long-term structural inducements—if only ones confined to economic means and to nuclear-strategic or nominal-status issues. In the face of disappointments, the most recent administrations have vacillated between ad hoc punitive reactions to Soviet foreign "adventures" and sanctions targeted at imposing long-term constraints upon the growth of components of Soviet national power that could be allocated to such adventures. Neither tactic has produced visible results.

Soviet global outreach and inner nature. Within the broad setting of assumptions about Soviet Russia and the international system, the makers of U.S. foreign policy will confront a range of other uncertainties. Should American or western responses to Soviet expansiveness be essentially containing or constraining, and if so, should this constraint progress through frontal confrontation? Or else should one relax frontal opposition throughout in favor of flanking rebuffs performed at points of Soviet overextension and, thus, overexposure? A related question will arise about the principal object of U.S. foreign policy. Is it a purely preventive one, or is it to promote, beyond mere mellowing, the maturation of the Soviet sociopolitical system toward compatibility with the western system? Is the purpose only negative or also positive?

Much will depend on what is the principal kind of Soviet expansion—according to its direction and radius, rationale and requisites—and on the anticipated results of fostering one or another form of Soviet self-assertion. Soviet efforts to extend influence overseas across long distances differ from overland expansion into areas directly contiguous with the Soviet Union. They are apt to confront the Soviet system with qualitatively different requirements of efficacy, inasmuch as the requisites of long-distance outreach will be less directly or exclusively military and will be also and increasingly politico-economic. They will be, consequently, more conductive to an overall rationalization of the Soviet system.

However, because all continental powers challenging the economically dominant maritime power depend initially on a military edge (e.g., France on the Continent to offset British advantage at seas and overseas), a caveat is in order. It is impractical, and suggests the application of a double standard, to rule out military means for seeking advantage on formal-procedural grounds while averring commitment to international equity, which might or should include an equal chance for the "other" great power. The more such an attitude is impractical or hypocritical, the more it is necessary to condone if not encourage the continental state diversifying the means available to it outside the military sphere. On the assumption that external and internal efficacy are interdependent, this will involve adopting a tolerant view of what constitutes a "fair" distribution of strategic access overseas also from the land power's perspective. In the present case, that issue is anterior to the question as to what constitutes "fair" trade—a question raised simultaneously with the first-mentioned one in the case of differently imperial Britain and Germany.

In a still fluid and inchoate international system, the criterion of means cannot be the only controlling one. It must perforce yield a large part of its claim to the standard of use—and, consequently, effect. The actual or likely use of a geopolitical or other "gain" or "asset" to weigh in formulating response to the power or policy responsible for acquiring it can be external or internal. In the first case, the gain can be employed in a way more or less threatening to the vital interests of other parties; in the second, either induce repression of truly essential needs, rights, and interests of the citizenry, or improve the conditions for these being met or satisfied. The pursuit of a relationship between a predominantly continental and a chiefly maritime power that would or could be perceived by both as equitable may only with difficulty mesh with the continental-autocratic state gradually increasing social—interclass or ruler-ruled—justice or well-being within its bounds or orbit, even as the achieved state of the maritime-constitutional republic's essential values remains intact. The difficulty, and the related challenge, are not least in contemporary conditions. But, however difficult it may be to find the exact point at which such a dual, internal and external, state of equity and equilibrium can be achieved, it might just as well be the operative assumption of responsible statecraft that there is one to be found if striven for.

It is part of the problematic nature of the effort that the question of "whither" expansion is directed will overlap with the question of "why" it is attempted. A land power's elite may feel it necessary to expand in order to make up for a pressing deficiency in essential assets, or it may choose to expand in order to inflict a crippling deficiency or abridge the surplus (in the same or different resource) of another party. The difference between the two "whys" is especially telling for the risks the expansionist is prepared to run: they will be much greater in the instance of felt necessity than in that of fancied opportunity. By the same token, it matters whether the rationale behind expansion is the desire to achieve a major or qualitative new strategic advantage (i.e., the expansion is wholly or largely "offensive"), or merely to offset a threatened disadvantage (i.e., the expansion is largely "defensive"). A move does not necessarily cease being primarily defensive if it also marginally improves the expanding power's preexisting situation or if restoring a compromised prior position also pre-positions the expansionist for further advance, should the adversary's reaction recommend or impose it.

Thus, regardless of the means of achieving it, the newly—even if not necessarily lastingly—strengthened Soviet position in Afghanistan looks different depending on how it is perceived. It can be seen as part of an unprovoked thrust toward the Persian Gulf, undertaken with the intention of disrupting western access at the first available opportunity locally or at the first sign of risk-reducing superiority globally. Or it may be viewed as a last-resort move to check the unfolding consequences of prior western efforts, both direct and by local or regional surrogates, to change to Russia's disadvantage the preexisting domestic and foreign-policy orientation in

Afghanistan.* Offensive under the first perception (provided the thrust is "unprovoked"), the Soviet move is, under the second interpretation, an offensively enacted defensive measure—as well as, perhaps, part of a defensively motivated *diplomatic* offensive, on a par with Soviet moves to counterencircle either the West alone or the U.S.-Chinese "alliance" in the Middle East or southeast Asia. As such, the Afghan invasion would be one of the measures signaling the Soviet intention to be treated, and to insist on being treated, with new caution and heightened consideration—that is, as to the latter, be included as a codetermining party in critical dispositions for the region and resource distribution within it.

Most of the important acts, especially those of the great powers, will mix offensive and defensive intents. It is thus the internal ratio between the two that matters for evaluation and response. Yet the way in which and the bias with which the uncertainty in assessments is arbitrated will tend to substantiate, in the guise of specific policy-relevant outcomes, the general premise about the adversary's policy intentions. Hence, the more inadequate are ad hoc assessments based on debatable premises, the more will even a self-consciously pragmatic policy have to mobilize into its service perspectives from history or theory.

An estimate of "why" the rival expands will weigh on "what" effect on him can be sought and achieved. In some respects, the long run is but a sum of the short runs; in others, it is qualitatively different. It will be different in regard to the kind of impact to be anticipated from guardedly permissive and from actually, or in intention, preventive responses to another party's expansion. A short-term impact or effect of any U.S. response on current Soviet foreign-policy (its becoming more accommodating or aggressive) is likely to vary from its middle-term impact on the composition and general orientation of the Soviet ruling elite and immediately subordinate elites (e.g., the issue of succession to Brezhnev). Both differ from the longest-term impact on the evolution of the Soviet political and social systems toward emphasis on warfare or welfare, toward differentiation of elites by function or toward ever more centralized organization.

It is unavoidably difficult to responsibly evaluate or reliably orchestrate the dialectical relationship of the several layers of effects and events in the different time spans. Imposing restraint by an effective denial policy in the short run may well produce the desired immediate result of dampening Soviet initiatives, but it may also conduce to a reactive later hardening of the incumbent or successor elite and lay the basis for a greater rigidity in the total system over a yet longer period of time. Conversely, an accommodating or

*On the Afghan issue, see Selig Harrison, "Dateline Afghanistan: Exit through Finland?" *Foreign Policy* 41 (Winter 1980/81): 153–87. On the wider implications, consult my "Russia and the West: The Next to Last Phase," *SAIS Review* 1, no. 2 (Summer 1981): 141–53.

merely discriminating response that seemingly rewards aggression may briefly encourage either expansionist tendencies or totalitarian residues, while it reduces the pressures behind either or both in the longer run.

The Soviet system is one that negotiates an awkward exit from totalitarianism. Any lessening of international tensions in such a system will highlight the often perverse relationship between its short- and longer-term effects; it will foster within the autocratic apparatus a defensive reflex in favor of tightening up internal ideological orthodoxy without by any means ruling out a relaxing effect of détente on both doctrine and practice over time. Because no reliable empirical judgment can be made within a narrow frame of reference in this as in many another operationally important matter, assumptions have to be made about the essential character of the Soviet polity. Making assumptions on this subject need not raise the issue whether or to what extent the Soviet system is, or is likely to remain, Marxist-Leninist or is likely to become "socialist" or "communist."

There are at least three possible images or models of Soviet polity, each with some empirical and analytical validity. They must be evaluated as a prerequisite to rational policy decisions. Is Soviet Russia an Asiatic despotism on the model of, say, the Ottoman Empire? Such a system will depend on continuing territorial expansion, because it requires a continuing supply of material and human resources from the outside if it is to remain at peak efficiency. And, depending on expansion, the apparatus will also promote it, inasmuch as the bureaucratic-military personnel is highly competitive because individually insecure, and the nonhereditary leadership is daring because individually dependent on striking achievements. Both the makers and the executors of policy will be devious, because they are equally subject to the capricious whims of a remote tyrant and the rigid canons of a pervasive belief system.

Russia in the Stalin period did not display all of these external symptoms or effects, but was far from free of such traits internally. They have been weakening lately within the Soviet system, if only because the trend has been toward the collective principle at the summit and, equally important, toward the hereditary principle at the wider elite level. Whereas individualized co-optation into a ruling group is at its most efficient when it is contingent on high competence and only ritualistic conformism, a shift to inherited preferment (not wholly unknown to the late Ottoman Empire) marks a postheroic age. It may signal irreversible decay. Even when it does not, the drift will be toward a bastard mix of "conservatism" and "liberalism." As fear of the consequences of rigidity battles fear of change, a growing caution abroad allies with concern over staying power at home.

The less she is an Asiatic despotism, the more is Soviet Russia the typical premier continental-European land power, with pronounced easternness as the qualifier. In such a state, autocratic government fosters, while controlling, integral nationalism at the mass base and is supported by it. In regard to the outside, the mutually reinforcing internal tendencies are held up by a delicate balance between opposing instincts. One inclination is to feel alienated from the dominant western-maritime culture and power; its opposite is the readiness if not eagerness to move closer to the West if it can be done on an equal basis. However, a coequal role is construed as something more than a status-satisfying association in symbolic gestures; it will be sought as a matter of one's admitted and enforceable historical right, rather than of another's momentary convenience and revocable concession.

In the chosen form, equality will be pursued almost interchangeably by cooperation and concert or by conflict and conquest. Much will depend on whether the other side offers the prospect of a positive response or persists in a negative one. However, the aspiring land power will have to moderate its expansion if it is to promote one kind of response and guard against the other kind. Being necessary, a but moderate expansion will be also sufficient to substantiate the claim to an equal role in the first, exploratory, phase. In that phase, too, the material and social conditions in the continental state traceable to either a late-developing economy, or a severe early (as well as prolonged) exposure to politico-military disruptions, will set limits to the degree and rate of either feasible or sustainable regime liberalization, including one linked to foreign-policy success. This will be the case not least if the continental regime is exposed to pressures from within or without to accelerate change before it has been immunized against both "reactionary" and "revolutionary" pressures.

The third and final possibility is to identify Russia's essential character with the changes in internal socioeconomic conditions and political and administrative institutions that were initiated under the last tsar and have been eventually pursued by the Soviets in new ways. The combined process can then be seen as moving the country and its internal regime into the category of an industrial society and order, which, if not wholly western, is eminently capable of being westernized; wherein an outward and especially an overseas projection of power is most likely to be soon followed by greater social mobility and functional equality. From the empire-founding warfare stage, such a society will pass fairly quickly to a welfare commitment that is at first tied to empire and later tends to dissolve it.

Not just any assumption will do if a strategy is to aim realistically at lowering pressures on Soviet Russia so as to mitigate oppression within her and by her, and at appeasing the East-West conflict. The Soviet system must instead be assumed to be located somewhere between the second and the third image. Only residual and marginal elements of the first, oriental-despotic model may be posited, without ruling out their being reactivated or magnified in certain conditions. By contrast, for a policy of indefinitely continuing rigid containment to be fully consistent with its premises and be defensible in normative terms, it is necessary to presuppose the first image as the dominant one and in essence unalterable. The policy must, correspondingly, have for its ultimate aim the acceleration of the decay of an expansion-dependent conquering empire and the collapse of its core regime. As the precedent of failure in, and in regard to, the Ottoman Empire suggests, neither restraints nor exemplars from the outside will then induce in-depth reform of either the empire or its executive power; economic and technological compensations for political reform will help no more than will their coercive denials.

Believing otherwise is to be captive to essentially western, liberal assumptions about the relationship of state and society. It is, furthermore, to hold that such assumptions could be not only relevant but also ultimately controlling for the Soviet state as an east-European land power—quite apart from their relevance for a Communist system. Not all positions are open to any possible Soviet candidate group for leadership in the tension between consumerism and nationalism. No such group could effectively bid for office and authority on the platform of an unequal integration into the international system on western terms; on terms, that is, of arresting Russia's progress on her life path to great and world power in exchange for outside help in raising the living standards of individual Russians.

A more significant choice is likelier to surface in any competition over internal Soviet authority: between one party arguing for a steady pursuit of limited external gains, and another pleading for a stepped-up rate of expansion. Among the would-be accelerators, an individual or group might invoke the possibility to exploit western debility, another individual or group assert the necessity to break through an implacable western determination to deny Russia her destiny, while ability served. The argument from necessity is likely to be more convincing and compelling than the argument from opportunity in foreseeable circumstances.

One-power expansion and interregional and intercultural equilibria. Whether assumptions are about features that only condition U.S.-Soviet (or East-West) relations or about ones that touch upon operationally significant factors, new issues appear constantly while old ones reappear. Thus an assumption widely embraced as early as the mid-1950s has come under fire. According to that assumption, the conflict is not one between ideologies, between Communism and either liberalism or capitalism, but between states; at issue is not "world revolution" but world power distribution—or, in more contemporary language, management of world order. When this view is shaken, détente sinks to the bottom of serious agenda, and divergences in assumptions as to what it can reasonably mean between two great powers lose their urgency.

But the quandary does not go away. Can détente be separated from a reapportionment of geostrategic positions of influence, coincidentally with recasting the nuclear-strategic balance in the direction of parity? It does not help that "parity" itself is a controversial subject as to both the criteria for determining its existence and its current state in the realm of military capabilities.

Other questions can be raised. What, quite apart from philosophical questions regarding historic justice or internation equity, is the generally applicable empirical theory of international relations under which the United States could plausibly insist on a code of conduct that, congenial to it, would be binding on the Soviets as well? A code, that is, under which U.S. policymakers could expect or stipulate that Soviet Russia display passivity or offer cooperation in perpetuating a geostrategic status quo still unfavorable to her (or, by renouncing military means, countenance its changes to her disadvantage only), so that she qualify as a worthy partner in observing détente as a "two-way street"? Moreover, under what particular theory of intersuperpower or interempire relations could one legitimately interpret the two-way-street condition in a manner that shuts off one of the directions? Could it be one that asserts or implies, for instance, that whereas détente is expected to stimulate sociopolitical transformations inside a Soviet-controlled region, such as eastern Europe, it also abrogates the previously conceded Soviet entitlement to control and manage the rate and scope of the transformation? That is to say, that the additional impetus to social change does not instead provisionally enhance the regime's title to inhibit radical change as a compensation? It is safe to assert that no such proposition would command intellectual or any other authority if formulated in general terms stripped of partisan bias and unreal if laudable desiderata. It is equally safe to believe that the proponents of such a theory or theories would not wish them to be invariably applied to themselves even in realistically defined contemporary, as compared with "classical," conditions.

Closely related to assumptions pertaining to détente are those about an ideal world equilibrium. Such assumptions can be formulated on several levels. They are highly controversial in regard to military-strategic capabilities. Is there or is there not, at any one time, parity or "equal security" between the two superpowers or alliances, be it in terms of so-called static measures (referring to different categories of capabilities) or under more dynamic criteria (postulating various war-fighting scenarios regionally and globally)? Underlying the strategic balance is the distribution of organic power and territorially focused political influence among the differently situated powers. Were assumptions and criteria regarding the latter condition ever explicitly formulated, they would be even more controversial. Assuming the thus-far evolved structure of the international system to be essentially bipolar, or incipiently tripolar, or marginally multipolar, what does in either case constitute equilibrium between Soviet Russia as a continental heartland power and the United States as a continent-wide offshore insular power? And, then, under what present and prospective technological conditions for organizing resources internally and projecting them externally? Is there more of an equilibrium if Soviet Russia remains as is—an essentially regional power? Or is the system a more stable one if Russia moderately expands overseas in order that she may effectively participate in promoting or maintaining "world order" by right and obligation rather than by occasional invitation? Or must she first disintegrate into her constituent parts, be these ethnic groups or geoeconomic sections?

Even attempting to answer these all-important questions involves weighing and weighting a multitude of factors. What is the resource endowment and the wider capability of each of the powers to use both tangible and intangible resources for generating, purposefully applying, and persistently projecting power and influence abroad? Among the more tangible assets are the different lines and means of communication (interior or exterior; overland, maritime, and aerial) for access to areas and resources peripheral to either power's and its key allies' homelands, continuous or remote. Less tangible is the capacity to engender economic, cultural, or ideological attraction, or else provoke similarly or otherwise inspired revulsion.

Defining the issue in such broad terms may be impractical and incapable of producing consensus. It then becomes useful to subdivide the issue into its subsidiary aspects. Each is rooted in some assumptions and may lead to others.

The first aspect concerns the relation between regional and global power distributions (or "balances"). What is the relationship between regional (or subsystemic) and global (or system-wide) configurations of actual or potential forces and policy foci? Operationally, the system-wide balance will be adjusted most of the time only unwittingly, as major states define and defend their specific interests in relation to a critical region or regions. The rare exception is when a hegemonial threat to the overall equilibrium is widely perceived and instigates a uniform reaction. Thus, in the sixteenth century, the all-European balance of power was incidentally regulated by the major powers attending to the distribution of power and to access in Italy on land (chiefly France and Spain) and in the Mediterranean at sea (chiefly Spain and the Ottoman Empire). By the eighteenth century, the intra-Germanic regional balance has moved up to the status of a prime regulator, alongside with the North Atlantic cum American balance, with France and England as either allies of the local parties or as principals. And the various phases and manifestations of the Eastern Question played the role well into and beyond the nineteenth century. After World War II, first Europe and then, in succession, southeast Asia, the Middle East, and southwest Asia were the shifting targets of Soviet initiatives, seats of consequent crises, and thus, critical regulatory regional theaters. Outcomes therein have had both intended and unintended implications for power distribution world-wide.

It has continued to be impossible intellectually to assess and monitor, and nearly impossible to manage, the global distribution of power on its own, independently of local situations and outcomes. At the same time, global equilibrium has acquired a greater than ever conceptual priority over regional equilibria both objectively (from the viewpoint of world order) and subjectively (from that of the world powers). Unfortunately, to state the paradox is not to resolve the issue of the relative merit of "regionalist" and "globalist" approaches to particular issues. It merely suggests that, while legitimately concerned in the last resort with their relationship and standing system-wide, the major powers will not be effective regionally (and thus, in the last analysis, globally) if they apply the globalist priority simplistically. This might mean, for the United States, applying the "China card" against Soviet Russia in southeast Asia in ways that align U.S. policies integrally with the Chinese position; one effect among others has been to alienate the Vietnamese (on the Cambodian issue) and align them ever closer with the Soviets. Or it might mean conceptually polarizing the middle-Eastern or the southwest-Asian areas of many-sided conflicts and tensions by framing the issue in terms of Soviet "expansionism" or support for "international terrorism." The operational result is to distort American initiatives and responses in regard to strictly local sources of stability or instability, and to paralyze the possibility of a joint U.S.-Soviet efficacy in regard to local conflicts and challenges—be these political or military and, when military, conventional, subconventional, or thermonuclear.

Supposing, furthermore, that it is necessary to imaginatively interrelate regional and global equilibria when either assessing or seeking to influence evolution in the larger arena, a related question will elicit additional assumptions. What is the better or easier way for the two arenas to be linked in practice? Is it by attempts to divide the world and the several regions vertically into static spheres of control, hermetically sealed-off and separate? Or is it by efforts to divide both arenas horizontally and dynamically? In the latter case, influence and leverage by both superpowers must interpenetrate within the several regions before the two rivals can effectively co-manage regional or world order. An area can be either assigned, not yet assigned, or no longer assigned to either superpower as its sphere of influence. Reflecting this variety, superpower access will be apportioned both unequally and flexibly: unequally, to reflect the degree of intensity of the stake each power has in different areas or countries; flexibly, in that either power's presence or influence is the object of a mobile diplomacy of penetration and counter-penetration, encirclement and counterencirclement. Thus, the competition is kept in bounds by mutual regard for the truly vital interests of each. But it is kept mobile by the resistance of both the major states and the lesser local parties to a permanent or unqualified, monopolistic entrenchment of either superpower in an area.

Sharing access in a fashion differentiated as to its scope and intensity is a condition for the equilibrium being a dynamic one, especially if the critical powers are asymmetrically situated and equipped heartland and offshore-insular powers. An offshore insular power must keep open its access to continental rimlands. If it does not, it must be prepared to rely on conflicts among the major continental states for the balance of power and, thus, its own security—for preventing an eventually irresistible land-based power from being concentrated in one state. On its part, the heartland power will seek overseas outlets from continental confinement. It may be allowed or even encouraged to do so as an alternative to consolidating its land-based capabilities in secrecy. While it enhances power and influence abroad, the heartland power will also disperse both. This trend will be preferable to its simulating restraint and remaining inaccessible to constraint in the period before its breakout in mass releases pent-up frustrations—while the outside powers (including the insular one) have been lulled into complacent dependence for security on the heartland state's inner erosion or disintegration intervening before it has become capable of acting decisively on the wider, global stage.

Appealing to the heartland state's self-restraint is no more realistic than is voluntary self-limitation on the part of the offshore-insular power. Self-limitation as fact or precept will be rationalized by a doctrine that stresses a narrow construction of vital interests. A strict delimitation of mutually exclusive spheres of interest will be favored within a balance of power that was made favorable and is kept secure by an assured control over major industrial and other material resources within reach of safe maritime approaches. The attractions of self-limitation for the insular power have an aspect in common with appeals to the land power's self-restraint. They reflect a strategy that ultimately depends for a felicitous outcome on both unpredictable and largely uncontrolled, as well as uncontrollable, developments of a special kind: the fractioning of continental power. If it is the foremost maritime power that forswears access to continental rimlands, the continental power to be fractioned is between or among competing land powers, which neutralize one another as a result; land-based power is fractioned within the premier continental state if internal dislocation precedes its abandonment of self-restraint. The self-limitation doctrine lay, in America's imperial phase, behind strictures against U.S. involvement on the "mainland" (actually rimland) of Asia. Then or now, it entails preference for an offshore-insular containment strategy outside an exclusive interest-sphere in western Europe, Japan, and the western hemisphere. The self-restraint theory continues to preside over efforts to keep Soviet power within regional confines. Its corollary has been the hope that the inner-Asian ethnic and the economic lines of latent fissures in the Soviet system will complement in due course outer-Asian (Chinese or Sino-Japanese) power and pressure, and both serve as the West's safeguard against the internally exacerbating or globally destabilizing consequences of the compression strategy.

It is a tenable operative assumption that it is easier to divide strategic space—or, more precisely, access to it—than physical space. So is influence supporting a role more readily divisible than is exclusive control amounting to rule. Moreover, the fact that influence is more easily or readily divisible than actual hegemony may also mean that the division is more peaceful, and greater mobility may entail greater or safer stability over the long run than does fixity. It may be further held that the West is still favored as much in the allocation of space by way of superpower control as it is in the present distribution of access. This assessment would seem correct in terms of access by either superpower as well as in terms of either power's capacity and commitment to bar rival access. And it would seem to cover Soviet control in eastern Europe, Soviet attitudes to western access thereto, and western attitudes to Soviet access in all of the other regions. This assessment is not negated by differences in the modes and the instruments of reciprocal counterpenetration, these being slanted on the western side toward economics in eastern Europe and on the Soviet side toward politico-military instruments elsewhere. Nor would the judgment be overthrown if additional criteria were taken into account, such as that of the "legitimacy" of an entrenchment and the resultant leverage in terms of an area's proximity to the more influential superpower or the latter's vulnerability.

A final assumption is that the intrusion of third powers or parties will bar or displace the superpowers equally. Under this and the preceding hypotheses, there would seem to be a safe margin for continuing moderate Soviet expansion, one that could satisfy Russia's needs and might be helpful in a world-order perspective. Hence, wholly denying Soviet claims to additional access would do little more than disguise the assertion of the right to continuing favorable imbalance by the West. The right might be viewed as innate or prescriptively acquired and be anchored in the desideratum of unabridged regional security or unlimited resource abundance. In either case, validating such a pretension would call for commensurate efforts distinct from camouflaging rhetoric.

The West could not experiment with the more dynamic approach to regional and world equilibrium so long as its policies remained hostage to worst-case scenarios regarding Soviet intentions vis-à-vis third-world regions or resources. That hindrance as centered in the Middle East and oil alone could irreparably derail a longer-term approach to a more enduring problem: Russia's historic encounter with Europe and the current one with the West. In either formulation the larger problem is likely to retain if not increase its importance when the technological parameters of the energy issue have been changed. The present is not the first era of interstate politics focused on one resource or commodity; it is likely to be equally transient and not necessarily the last.

The scenario of the Soviets casually blocking western access to oil is implausible in the light of precedents. One precedent is Napoleon's attempt to bring England to her knees by the so-called continental blockade; another, Imperial Germany's bid to achieve the same result by unrestricted submarine warfare. Both of the continental powers employed the "ultimate" economic weapon against the sea power only in the very last resort. Other means had failed by then to move toward geopolitical parity before the climactic military conflict, or to either circumvent or eliminate the leading maritime belligerent by other means during that conflict. That is to say, employing the economic weapon was not the preferred method to provoke a military enactment of the competition; nor, at an early stage of the military phase, to bring it to a speedy favorable conclusion. Are there valid grounds for assuming that the Soviet leadership would act differently and gamble more recklessly so long as it did not exhaust other recourses or remedies? A bid for economic coercion that, if in earnest, will provoke a nuclear response is an unattractive substitute for nuclear preemption.

When propounding either an extreme or a moderate version of the oil cutoff scenario, it is necessary to ask one question: In exchange for what advantage, or in retaliation for what inflicted distress, would it "pay" the disruptor to fundamentally change the diplomatic—not to speak of the military—environment inside Europe or globally, by separating the West from an absolutely vital resource? This is true whether the hypothetical disruptor is the oil cartel again or the Soviets for the first time. As in the case of the oil cartel, their first interference was likely to be the last one with a reasonable prospect for total or relative impunity. If the consequences of a more thorough and lasting disruption are properly assessed, the incentive to attempt it is hard to imagine, so long as the will to implement the consequences is presumed.

Overshadowing the day's critical resource issue is the reemerging historic issue: Which of the two possible lines of East-West divisions should have priority in formulating strategies? The one currently stressed within Europe or the briefly repressed but reviving one between Europe and her offshoots (America and Russia) on one side, and the extra-European larger "East" on the other? The third party critical for the U.S.-Soviet divide running through Europe has been western Europe generally and West Germany specifically; the Third World in general and China in particular occupy the third-party position relative to the divide running figuratively outside Europe. In either case, the third parties and their controlling priorities give rise to critical assumptions; so do the concerns that primarily propel them into choice and action.

In the narrower East-West setting, at issue is the effect of alternative U.S. policies on western Europe. These might make Russia into a power that is increasingly European or else, whether or not she is moving or is being displaced diplomatically or otherwise eastward toward Asia, make her resort to overt aggression westward in Europe. Were the latter trend to become likelier, would west European statecraft opt in a crunch for an all-European solution with Russia or for an Atlantic-wide refuge and U.S.-made remedies? In the wider East-West setting, what would be third-world responses to comparable stresses? They might be pragmatic and rational or be motivated by racial or otherwise "irrational" biases when influencing politico-diplomatic alignments and options; be governed by consumerist criteria or be culturally biased when alternative socioeconomic pathways were at issue.

In this same context, what about interdependence, co-optation, and convergence? The prevailing assumption about economic interdependence or complementarity between industrial western and industrializing third-world (including OPEC) countries has been that it will foster more than superficial politico-cultural unison and more than token or opportunist politico-diplomatic or military alignments (be it generally or between western Europe and, say, the Arab OPEC members in particular). Diametrically opposed has been the dominating assumption, not least in the United States, concerning economic interdependence between western and eastern Europe. It is not assumed that a sense of politico-cultural community and politico-military interdependence for survival was an either extant or legitimate prior basis for seeking its advantages and incurring its risks (e.g., the widely heralded risks of west European dependence of Soviet gas, and Soviet dependence on west European technology). Nor has it been fashionable to assume that economic links would be sought not only or even chiefly on the grounds of their economic or security-enhancing expediency, but also as a way of imparting substance to a political principle or even ideal of a pan-European character.

Making the prevailing assumption about the Third World overrates a prospect and underrates its prerequisite. It tends to overrate the chances for lastingly co-opting third-world elites, let alone masses, into the West-centered liberal-capitalist world system on the strength of either the elites' rational economic calculations or the West's economic competences; it risks underrating other, cultural or racial, psychopolitical factors. Moreover, the optimistic estimate also underrates the military-political requisites for managing such a co-optation process in conditions aggravated by acute conflict with Soviet Russia. Conversely, widespread assumptions about the latter have incidentally lowered its posited potential for converging with the West, let alone becoming part of an enlarged Occident. One way of making the pessimistic estimate more convincing has been to settle on very short time spans as sufficient to provide conclusive evidence either way; another, to ignore the degree of assimilation already realized; and yet another, to overstate the ideal norm of total convergence as if amounting to identity. Just as convergence is confounded with conversion, so process is confounded with phenomenon—to wit, the narrowing of differentials in regard to patterns of action directly relevant for international behavior with either system's innermost essence.

When the East-West framework of reference is expanded into a global one, the makeup of an ideal equilibrium will likewise be expanded. The focus will shift from one between the United States (and allies) and Soviet Russia (and clients) as territorial states to one among major cultures or civilizations. An intercultural equilibrium emerges as one that might become increasingly significant in the aftermath of half a millennium of ascendancy by Europe or Europe-derived powers. Far from diminishing it, this emergence actually adds new significance to assumptions about whether the intra-European East-West cleavage can be influenced toward Russia's assimilation, rather than alienation; it underscores prescriptions on how to manage the split.

It is also in a long-term perspective on both of the East-West arenas that assumptions about the United States become critical. What is its material and moral staying power as a nation in a world no longer fortuitously arranged to its advantage? These assumptions match those about Russia being a rising or a stagnant cum declining society and polity. The related question is whether the American nation is or is not capable of dealing simultaneously with different kinds of perceived or actual threats emanating from the two Easts while ranking them in a realistic hierarchy: and whether it can do this for an indefinite period of time.

The so far dominant assumption has been that the several threats could be managed concurrently, while degrees of attention could shift as local disruptions alternated with brief détentes over both time and space. The assumption has militated against a serious attempt to transcend an ingrained *modus operandi.* Any release from habitual pragmatism other than a flight into its reverse—inherited providentialism—required attempts to view events and policy in long-term sequences. This type of perspective requires policymakers to accept that different issues and relationships are apt to mature simultaneously but become ripe for composition in depth at different future points in time; and that not the least challenge to statecraft is to anticipate the nearest point in time when reciprocally reinforcing separate outcomes could be made to coalesce in an acceptable overall outcome.

Assumptions about strategy-related time spans: the temporal dimension

Proposing historical parallels suggests belief in a decent measure of continuity in the pattern of concerns and actions within the same or comparable space. And, because the parallels are historical, they will highlight the importance of time and time-related perspectives in adjusting conflict and promoting accommodation. The time factor gives rise to two main concerns of a truly "grand" strategy: one, how to integrate antecedents into present choices; two, how to synchronize outcomes of policies. The first, as amply illustrated earlier, involves gaining perspective on a stream of already transpired evolution; the second, guiding foresight along segments of a hypothetical future.

Different assumptions are possible on the latter score. One assumption holds that strategy-related time is mechanically divisible. It is, consequently, possible to serialize outcomes, to make one follow another in orderly sequence. This might mean practically that one can eliminate Soviet Russia as the main present threat now, and only later deal with China or whoever is the next threat.

The second assumption is that strategy-related time spans are integrally simultaneous. It is, consequently, possible to aggregate both provisional and terminal outcomes—make all issues unfold at all times toward resolution in a more or less harmonious interaction of policy strands. This might mean that on a practical level one can manage and solve the different problems raised by Soviet Russia, China, the Third World, and so forth, at one and the same time.

The third assumption is intermediate between the two with an added emphasis on the organic-evolutionary dimension. It holds that unevenly long and active strategy-relevant time spans overlap, but are also staggered to match the uneven maturation of the conditions necessary for dealing with the several issues or problems effectively. It is, consequently, in principle possible to synchronize outcomes, but only over a very long term. This should mean in practice that if shapers of policy have correctly assigned priorities and have rightly assessed and managed the interconnections among the currently perceivable factors and forces at all times, policy can bring about an at least temporary equilibrium situation among them at some time in the future.

It is obvious that the last assumption as stated gives rise to conceptual and practical demands on statecraft that it cannot meet fully. It is not possible to perfectly synchronize outcomes fostered over unevenly long terms, least of all into the ideal equilibrium-state initially contemplated. Presently manifest "forces and factors" will not be perfectly calibrated and interrelated to begin with, while new ones will emerge and intervene before the envisaged (and in the best of cases only provisional) equilibrium point has been reached. Nevertheless, this assumption is superior to the other two assumptions as a fundamental conceptual premise of, and a normative commitment behind, a "grand" strategy. It can, as such, give rise to practical prescriptions so long as these are constantly reevaluated and revised in function of changing realities. Its superiority is solidly anchored in the manifest inadequacy of the other two assumptions and their related practices.

It ought to be self-evident that trying to deal with all problems indiscriminately at the same time—in keeping with the second-named assumption—amounts to but a reactive statecraft. Such an approach will at best only blindly aggregate random outcomes into occasional deadlocks or stalemates, which are situations easily mistaken for equilibrium or stability. It will be long on tactics and extremely short on even low-level strategy let alone "grand" strategy, which must coordinate the temporal along with the more material dimensions.

It is less self-evident that it has become ever less possible to abide by the first-named assumption of mechanical divisibility: to segregate threats or challenges and deal with them effectively one at a time. But it remains tempting to do exactly that. Thus, why not first thwart the Soviet aggressor and then use Russia as a codefender against the next threat or aggressor? In that same manner and in succession, a defeated or thwarted Spain served against France, France against Germany, and West Germany most recently against Soviet Russia. However, even at the best of times, the approach has never been free of costs and crises during the transition from one would-be hegemon to the next. Failures abounded of attempts to correctly assess when and how checking efforts should shift from an already declining or past threat to the similarly rising future one. Thus, England's policymakers were uncertain whether to contain primarily the straggling Spanish empire or a temporarily paralyzed but eminently revival-capable French imperialism in the sixteenth century; but their fixation on the threat from France continued and helped promote or ignore the intermittent rise of tsarist Russia and, with increasingly grave consequences, Prussia-Germany. Britain alternately under- and overcontained Germany from the late-nineteenth century on. Even before passing on the torch to the United States, British statecraft thus indirectly helped the eventual emergence of Soviet Russia to the status of the presumed main threat.

It has not rendered America's task easier that recruiting the defeated would-be hegemon into service as a counterweight to the next one has become newly difficult. In modern times, the thwarted expansionist is not only a power state but also, underneath that carapace, an industrial mass society. Such a society's defeat in the climactic effort at mastering other powers and, in the process, also its own destiny will subjugate the defensive instinct to the desire for repose. Defeat breaks the all-important collective morale, and it alters the values that are needed to sustain either a massive war effort or a prolonged conflict. This will bar any but a half-hearted or token support for the next counter-hegemonial coalition. France's commitment against Germany was gradually weaker as the French state decayed and the society matured in the twentieth century; rump Germany's engagement against Soviet Russia has been less than was France's in the first phase of defense against Germany before and during World War I. This may portend something for the capability of a defeated or truncated Great Russian nation to take part in resistance against any later assault on a further fragmented and unbalanced international system.

For practical purposes, another change in balance-of-power politics might make up for the lessened readiness of the previously defeated party to perform as part of a counterpoise. Despite retrogressions, the drives for hegemony themselves may have become weaker and less efficacious as part of the gradual erosion of completed transformations (or, inside Europe, near-transformations—e.g., of an equilibrium system into an empire system) into mere temptations and unconsummated tendencies keyed to the integral end results. However, so long as international relations are conducted as if either temptation or tendency could result in a catastrophic transformation, related conflicts can eventuate in warlike catastrophes that alter profoundly the distribution of power even if they do not change the fundamental character of the international system. And so long as the presumption of continuity and its consequences prevail, any change in the disposition to countervail is more significant than is any change in the capacity to coerce. It is especially significant for the issue at hand: how long and how astringently to go on containing Soviet Russia (with China's assistance) on the supposition that being frustrated or defeated will reform both the state and the people and make them ready for a part in common defense in the next, separate and separable, time slot (against China, if necessary).

Like everything else, the pretension to preserve intact a nation's capacity for defense after first breaking its will in contention can also be diluted. The watered-down assumption is that sweeping denials and occasional sanctions can be employed to wear down a major nation-state while holding aloft the reward of intimate collaboration when the rival has ceased to "misbehave." The possibility that the approach to détente could be thus amended was a premise behind the theory of U.S.-Soviet relations as a compound of competition and collaboration. Staggering the stick-and-carrot approach over two discrete time periods may work in some cases. But a power such as Soviet Russia will more probably have to be conceded a substantial role in managing the international system while it asserts itself from a position of still undiminished ambition and still rising strength—not the least if the objective is to synchronize multiple outcomes in the very long term. It will be up to the defending side to display strength and determination equal to the challenger's; and it will be necessary to entrust the future to gradual shifts in the assertive party's motivation. These will reflect changes in the environing configurations of power and threat, and could themselves be reflected in both the mode and the purpose of one's accommodation with such a party.*

*The assumption of divisibility of the balancing process over successive time spans is very much part of a "geopolitical" approach (from "equilibrium") to the triangular relationship, put forward in the name of distinctive strategic sophistication. (Thus Henry Kissinger's, in *White House Years* [Boston: Little, Brown, 1979], pp. 1090–91.) The underlying conception of preferred global equilibrium is that of Soviet Russia remaining a regional power. Actually the Soviets are at one and the same time an "inherent threat" to the global balance of power and (somewhat contradictorily) their position relative to major power centers is "uncomfortable"—to wit, inferior—despite their "seeming" power. Their "constant probing" (solely responsible for the adverse alignment?) is keyed to testing "every equilibrium" (supposedly identical also with prior western predominance if not monopoly, thus in West Africa?); but if they show interest in superpower cooperation regionally, thus in the Middle East, their diplomatic probe becomes a transparent bid for an unthinkable U.S.-Soviet "condominium"—or, relative to the Chinese, U.S.-Soviet collusion. Conversely, it becomes an additional proof of adventurism or hegemonism for the Soviets to ignore an occasional U.S. offer to be saved from the embarrassment of local American weakness by "acting jointly" in what is then laudable association. While "den[ying] the Soviets all opportunities for expansion," the door is thus presumably kept "open for genuine cooperation" (ibid., p. 1204; and pp. 1142, 1143, 1151, and 875, respectively, for preceding quotes).

The approach is best illustrated in the book's chapter on the Indo-Pakistani conflict over East Pakistan in late 1971. Having just been exposed to a dramatic U.S.-Chinese rapprochement, the Soviets are expected to gratuitously jeopardize their diplomatic riposte and regional counterpoise in the form of the friendship treaty with India by joining the United States in pressuring the latter into restraint. When India finally does abstain from implementing her supposed design—to disintegrate Pakistan also in the west—the merit is ascribed wholly to U.S. naval pressure: the Soviet role in restraining India in the last stages cannot be due to an independent concern for regional equilibrium (shades of Tashkent?), if only as the precondition of India's continued interest in the Soviet connection and a barrier to an uncomfortable contiguity between Soviet and Indian spheres of interest in southwest Asia.

Part Three

STRATEGIC ALTERNATIVE AND ALTERNATIVE SCENARIOS

Mr. President, should we not be concerned with eliminating the obstacles which prevent our people—those you and I represent—from achieving their most cherished goals?—Ronald Reagan (letter to Leonid Brezhnev, cited in address to the National Press Club in Washington, 18 November 1981)

The end of our empire, if end it should, does not frighten us: a rival empire like Lacedaemon, even if Lacedaemon was our real antagonist, is not so terrible to the vanquished as subjects who by themselves attack and overpower their rulers.—Thucydides, *History of the Peloponnesian War* (Athenians to the Melians)

V

TOWARD DECOMPRESSION.

External and World-wide

Configurations of power, sequences of events, and processes of socializing new or resurgent powers into the system recur. The recurrence will be qualified by a blend of similarities and differences on the part of key actors and conditions, while a properly adjusted strategy can steer future developments away from past outcomes seen in retrospect as undesirable. The framework of strategy blends "necessity," in the form of the full range of historically manifest constraints, with "freedom," in the form of alternative options; the degree of freedom is circumscribed by the need to pay regard to fundamental tendencies operative in national behavior and international politics.

One such tendency is that two competing powers will not relax their competition unless a third-party danger to both is superior to the threat each poses for the other. From the viewpoint of theory, the threat must be invented—that is, magnified—if it is not clearly present; for purposes of effective statecraft, it must be acknowledged and highlighted while it is still latent. If theory alerts statecraft to the need for surfacing trends or threats, alert statecraft vindicates theory when it deals effectively with the underlying facts.

Another tendency concerns the party making the more obvious initial concessions for the purpose of relaxing a two-power conflict. It will find it unattractive to do so unless the two key levels—the international and the domestic—can be related in such a way that concessions to the more forward party will be somehow compensated for. They can be so compensated by countervailing changes in either the external environment (if the concessions activate new resistance) or, more importantly, in the more forward party's domestic structure. Thus, successes in foreign policy may trigger inside the expansionist an evolution toward greater affinity with the internal order of the defending side. Again, the possibility of such internal changes occurring must be theoretically posited to make the strategy of concessions and appeasement formally realistic; the strategy itself must in turn be keyed to making such developments more likely than they would be otherwise.

The interactive factors—threat or compensation by third party; outside constraints and internal relaxation—are basic to combining the negative and the positive aspects of a grand strategy in a theoretically coherent way. For a strategy to be grand, it must be for something (e.g., appeasement, "liberalization") because, if it is to work, it must necessarily be also against something (e.g., anarchy) or someone (a third party). However, the strategy need not be negative in the sense of allowing for lessened constraint on the rival party only if it is impossible to do more and better, or because the particular stake or space are not worth defending. Instead, even feasible checks will be avoided when avoiding obstruction will promote a positive trend in the rival's foreign-policy orientation or domestic political system. Yet again, if accepting risks on behalf of long-term positive goals may qualify the prime preoccupation of responsibile statecraft with maintaining a margin of safety, it cannot nullify this obligation. Only when the survival of essential values is assured can attention shift to rationales for concessions that would look past favorable or stable balance of power to more dynamic or dual (intra- as well as interstate) equilibrium, one sufficiently widely perceived as equitable to replace standoff with in-depth appeasement.

American relations with the Soviet Union in the era following World War II were dominated by containment. The doctrine was originally formulated as a set of assumptions and concepts remote from the routine contingencies of statecraft. But, as doctrine was translated into operative strategy, the issue of military capabilities and responses moved to the fore. Among the early questions faced by the framers of containment was how the United States ought to implement the strategy in Europe, and whether the strategy could at all be applied outside Europe. Of a somewhat more speculative nature were questions about Soviet internal power structure and foreign-policy behavior. Were they self-regulating or also responsive to what other powers, meaning chiefly the United States, did or failed to do? Responsiveness to external stimuli was bound to replace unresponsiveness as the dominant hypothesis when a crude version of Marxist "historical determinism" lost luster as the main presumptive determinant of Soviet behavior.

Two conclusions can be drawn from this revision. One, of principle, is that conceding latitudes to the Soviets can influence their behavior no less than can inhibitions imposed upon them. Another, for practice, is that the latitudes might be usefully extended from conceding nuclear-strategic parity to envisioning movement toward parity in geopolitical access or assets.

Varieties of factors conditioning strategy: structure and process

If a grand strategy is to take into account events and trends from history and be usefully informed by them, it must have a temporal as well as an operational dimension. To be considered in the temporal dimension of grand strategy are the time spans within which structures took shape and sequences unfolded in the past and might comparably do so again in the future. To be taken into account in the operational dimension is the extent to which diplomatic or any other activity can influence events. The supreme challenge for a grand strategy is thus how to achieve desired results at various points in time with regard to parties that are unevenly open to influence and are of unequal priority and importance; and how to do this so that one element in the total strategy more frequently promotes other elements than it fatally impedes them. At the same time, all results should "ultimately" converge in a preferred configuration of world power and order.

No grand strategy can exist unless conscious judgments and efforts unite structural with synchronic components. To insist on this is not to deny that such judgments and efforts will be highly problematic. Implementing them will be subject to constraints ranging all the way from the play of accidents and other random factors to the operation of the "laws" (i.e., recurrent tendencies) of both power and psychological nature in interstate relations.

Different ranges of the East-West dynamic. An intercultural dynamic of a kind that currently affects relations between the West and the Third World tends to unfold over the longest time span. That dynamic will be less responsive to conventional diplomacy than to dramatic demonstrations of power and will, so long as alienation on one (the Third World) side and drift to self-abdication on the other (the western) side call for a new balance to be forged between the appeals of anarchy and the imperatives of elementary order. Only if, and insofar as, the new balance has taken shape, will it be safe for what is now the periphery to move functionally closer to the center of a multicultural international system and for power to migrate in the opposite direction. Anything else would disrupt vital relationships, including those denoted as South-North in chiefly economic terms and denotable again as East-West in traditional politico-cultural terms. One way or another, the complex external manifestations of the southern (or eastern) resurgence have been seeping insidiously into the innards of western societies. They are more threatening in the long run than is anything else if the objective is to surrender the residual supremacy of the West only gradually, and then in favor of a genuinely global and stable international system.

Compared to the "awakening (non-European) East," the Russian factor can be managed both more readily and over a shorter period of time. It has a more specific ideological component and its cultural component is less inherently antagonistic than are the several sets of beliefs, prejudices, and pretensions that impinge on western relations with much of the postcolonial world. It ought, therefore, to be easier for the official Soviet belief system to erode, for the cultural animosities between Russia and the West to subside, and for Soviet Russia to be integrated into a stable role in the world system.

In the middle range between third-world countries at their least manageable and Soviet Russia at her most assimilable are the large and ancient countries like China and India. Their long-term power potential is less transient than is, say, OPEC's and their cultural self-confidence reaches deeper than does, say, the Africans' into the making of policy most of the time. To influence their orientation, demonstrations of power and will, critical in relations with much of the Third World, are only supplemental to diplomacy. And both diplomacy and more tangible demonstrations of power will work in their case best when they operate circuitously. Just as the demonstrations will impress the two Asian powers most beneficially and least offensively if they are targeted at lesser powers, so the effect of diplomacy will often be greatest if mediated through western grand strategy toward Soviet Russia and its outcomes in areas of concern to either China or India. What matters most is to avoid provoking one or the other into responses that would seriously jeopardize the highest-priority strategy or would fundamentally revise the framework of the long-term approach toward the Third World.

The two foci of grand strategy. The West's and, specifically, America's highest-priority strategy for relations with Soviet Russia has two foci. One is superficially more compelling but is potentially more malleable over a shorter time span than is the other. It consists of the two-power U.S.-Soviet conflict in its concrete geopolitical settings, whereas the other object of concern is the three-power configuration and broadly systemic conflict also involving China. The bilateral conflict partially revives the pattern of the nineteenth-century Anglo-Russian competition in southeastern Europe and in Asia, when the features of a land-sea power schism were not yet fully developed. The tripartite pattern reactivates a recurring model that was most perfectly exemplified in the Anglo-German-Russian triangle before World War I. While in the current world situation the full implications of the triangular configuration are still only latent, the two-power structure is more fully manifest by comparison. The shadowy coexistence of the two- and three-power foci leads to a conflict of perceptions and priorities that has to be mastered if the primacy of structure in conditioning policy is not to degenerate into the tyranny over policy of the structure's most conspicuous aspect. But, although the two strategic perspectives could easily diverge in one respect, they also converge in the key role of a third party. That party can be the same (if it is China in both structural settings) or different (if it is the Third World in the two-power setting), but to identify it correctly in different circumstances, for different purposes, and at different points in time, is *the* most critical task for strategy.

In the full-scale triangular setting, the strictly continental power in the rear of the navally ambitious land power, the would-be amphibian, has been historically critical. Its rate of material growth or its political closeness to the preeminent insular-maritime power will not be always easy to calculate, an uncertainty apt to set an elastic time limit within which the would-be amphibian will feel he can or must break out for more breathing room overseas. In an early and imperfect triangle, the rivalries and ambitions of the principal German states pressed on France's rear, and the raw power of Russia later threatened Germany when, unified, she superseded France as Britain's challenger outside Europe. China looms even larger for Soviet Russia as the latter challenges the United States. The Asian power has outgrown the status of a mere seat of disturbance and an object of competition in the U.S.-Soviet bilateral conflict on a par with the Third World and as part of it. But, as a continental-rear power in the triangle, China is still not much more than an important background factor.

Facts and perceptions differ when conflict on land and sea is, or is viewed as, confined to two major powers. Of immediate interest is then whatever might become a greater threat to each than they are to one another; the focus is on the likelihood that a third actor or group of actors will eventually soften the bilateral conflict and then defuse it, not on the known third major power's propensity to intensify the central conflict by growing in power and in threat to one of the parties to it only. The third party can defuse the two-power conflict if, but only if, the two main contestants do not ignore it for too long or assess it too differently. If the two-power conflict is not attenuated, it will tend to deteriorate to the advantage of the third party. Competing over the latter will impede timely adaptative responses within the great-power triangle when the third party in the two-power contest and the third major power in the triangular one are not one and the same. This will matter because, though the tripartite bigger-power conflict may have a long time dimension, it does not have an indefinite one. Where the potential for such a conflict exists, keeping it within the bounds of manageability is more important than anything else; that desideratum will militate not only in favor of concern about the third-party factor but also against extremes in the relations between any two of the three major powers, be it zero-sum competition or full-fledged collusion.

It will take some change of perceptions before the two superpowers can see eye to eye on the issue of a common threat. And it will take some time before China presses effectively enough from the rear on Soviet Russia as the latter faces the United States. This gives Soviet Russia a longer respite than the makers of German policy thought they could count on against tsarist Russia. It also wins enough latitude for the United States to shift gears from drawing on the Sino-Soviet conflict for tactical advantage in triangular diplomacy, to defusing a systemic crisis implicit in the triangular structure by a grander strategy. But the grace period for both powers could be easily wasted. It would be wasted by the United States if a single-minded preoccupation with the global Soviet outreach continued to impede agreement on who or what is the common threat. Although this threat may not yet be as concrete as Imperial Germany's finally became for England and Russia, it is sufficiently determinate to scale down the U.S.-Soviet conflict to a reasonable level of intensity.

China's ultimate strength, status, role, and ambition are in abeyance, as is her internally and internationally revolutionary character. But neither of the relatively conservative superpowers is alone able to lastingly manage culture-induced alienation and to control outbreaks of anarchy in the Third World. On that hypothesis, it is the global periphery that is likeliest to produce early candidates for the status of a shared threat. Perceiving a threat as common would recommend reviewing the sources of superpower conflict on both sides; keeping China from becoming part of the common threat for as long as possible would set limits on the pace and extent of superpower accommodation. Initiating the latter is the both logically and operationally prior task of strategy; intimating why and how this should be done is the main purpose of this study.

Two strands in a complete strategy. Just as there are two foci for a grand strategy toward Soviet Russia, so too are there two interdependent strands within a promising strategy, with unequally negative and positive aspects. One strand, that of extended deterrence, would extrapolate capability requirements and limitations commonplace to the mutual-deterrence doctrine from the nuclear-strategic into the geopolitical arena. The other strand, that of decompression, would substitute for systematic containment a more discriminating effort to lower strains within the two linked environments of global power distribution (or access allocation) and internal Soviet authority structure. Within a strategic concept freed thus for expedient choices between condoning and constraining Soviet expansiveness, two-level (strategic and geopolitical) deterrence capabilities for both superpowers and two-sided (internal-Soviet and systemic) decompression would tend to entail and promote, as a subordinate means-end strand, the diversion of Soviet power to lower-pressure areas and lower-risk activities than it is or might be drawn to while either overconcentrated or overcontained.

When two powers accept to share the capacity for deterring one another's interdicts on access within or across regional boundaries, it is usually due at least in part to a shared concern about a third party. Such a concern is essentially negative. So too are the intentions immediately underlying the extended mutual-deterrence capacity itself. Only the indirect consequence of this type of capacity can be positive. It becomes such when the mutual character of deterrence and its extension to the geopolitical sphere relaxes, or decompresses, the internal-political and international tensions affecting the actions of one or both parties. It can do so because the reciprocal nature of deterrence in any arena presupposes some prior movement and furthers a continuing one toward real parity. Adding parity in access to one in arms is a necessary part of full-scale integration of a late-entering power—presently the Soviets—into the international system—presently the emerging global system—as a condition, in turn, of central-systemic appeasement and major conflict avoidance.

Genuine parity and integration will affect the Soviet role in the international system as well as its status. The attendant decompression in the external environment will also influence Soviet Russia's identity as a polity and sway the decision between a stance that is more western in essence (and increasingly in orientation) and one that is increasingly eastern. If one wishes to shape this greatest of all issues positively, it becomes less important to go on offering moralizing invocations and technological inducements from the outside and more important to concede external outlets for pressures and phobias accumulated within.

Rationales for extended mutual deterrence and dual decompression: geopolitics and domestic politics

The contemporary Soviet drive for parity echoes the earlier German claim to *Mitspracherecht.* The right or entitlement is one to world-power role and status manifested in the right to speak—and, if need be, act—with authority on major questions. Its foundation is now, as it was then, an equitable if not immediately equal distribution of access to the world's strategic assets. The similarity is not undone by the fact that Soviet Russia will continue to be in some respects less like the Germany of Emperor William before World War I than like the Russia of Count Witte before the war with Japan so long as she lacks the economic means for extending her influence to the seas and overseas. She will only more strenuously overcompensate for this lack by military means—if deliberately and even cautiously now rather than, as often in tsarist times, improvidently or blunderingly. Neither will it be any easier for America and Russia than it was for England and Germany to define what an equal entitlement means and requires for parties asymmetric in both power and spirit, internal orders and geostrategic situations. Confrontations will, therefore, accompany all progress toward parity if the operational scope of mutual deterrence is to go on expanding. It was extended beyond protecting U.S. or Soviet homeland to safeguarding allies; now it must aim, past restraint on the use of the ultimate weapon, at the reapportionment of contingent influence by dissuading both geopolitical rivals from pressing unreasonable claims.

The connection between the nuclear-strategic and the geopolitical terms of mutual deterrence is a "necessary" one in more ways than one. It is causal (one ultimately entailing the other) as well as sequential (the application and implementation of deterrence in geopolitics following those in nuclear strategics); and the sequential link being logical in the common sense meaning of "logical" substantiates further the analogical connection (the requisites and the achievement of mutual deterrence in the geopolitical realm being assimilable to those in the nuclear-strategic one). Thus, as to the primarily "causal" link, so long as and insofar as the essential deterrence-defense function must be and is addressed, and actual operations related thereto occur, in conditions of qualitatively evolving military technology, maintaining nuclear-strategic parity for mutual deterrence will either entail or require corresponding changes in the distribution of access to geopolitical positions and assets; the distribution will be conceptually focused on geopolitical parity as the norm, and in practice fluctuate around that norm in deference to the parties' situational disparities as the qualifying fact. Conversely, insofar as and whenever a qualitative or quantitative military-strategic parity has been achieved between the parties at any one point in time, this state of things will "cause" the side previously inferior in access to bid for geopolitical parity less as a military-strategic, or defensive, necessity, and more as the "logical" political corollary to the prior military-technological achievement, while that side's progression toward such parity will be an equally "logical" political dividend from the military-technological investment.*

* An illustration of the causative military-strategic necessity in conditions of changing technology is the expanding range of the U.S. submarine-carried nuclear-deterrent strike force, from the Polaris to the Trident generation. The expanding range pushed the Soviet defense perimeter correspondingly outward, from the eastern Mediterranean to the Persian Gulf and the Indian Ocean, entailing (and largely "explaining"?) the widening circle of the Soviet quest for geopolitical assets securing access to naval and other facilities, first in and around the Suez Canal–Red Sea bottleneck (mainly in the Egyptian phase up to 1973) and farther south (thereafter). See Amnon Sella, *Soviet Political and Military Conduct in the Middle East* (New York: St. Martin's Press, 1981), p. 48 ff. The strictly military-security, and in the main arguably defensive, requirement—centered on the both vulnerable and valuable Soviet south and southwest—is accordingly the sufficient, if not necessarily the only, stimulus behind that particular instance of Soviet overseas expansion, underlying while supplemented by other, more positive objectives, political and economic and internal-domestic or external.

For purposes of grand strategy, the necessary—including "causal"—connection between military-strategic and geopolitical parity for mutual deterrence is the operational hard core

The geopolitical dimension of extended mutual deterrence. Long-term stability requires that graduated and mostly peaceful change be possible between the two superpowers while geopolitical parity is added as a support to the nuclear-strategic and other military dimension. When will effective parity and essential equivalence exist in critical areas of overlapping interests and legitimate access for both of the two contending powers? Only when Soviet Russia can say with equal effect as the United States: If you deny me access (whether to diplomatic role or to material resource), I have the ability and intention to deny—i.e., bar or oppose—yours. And the United States as well as the Soviet Union must assume equally: If I deny access, "they" must be expected to, and most probably will, counter-deny it, with effect. If—and only if—both powers have the capacity not only to intimate retaliatory counter-denials but also to carry them out does each have a second-strike capacity in geopolitical terms over similar stakes. Only then is the system one of mutual deterrence as far as arbitrary denials are concerned.

The counter-denial capacity is, however, short of the capability and the conditions required for the equivalent of a first-strike military strategy. Under these conditions, one of the parties could safely attempt a preemptive unilateral denial of access or resource to the other party. For such an objective to be credible, the denied party's position would have to be eroded world-wide, as well as be subverted in the critical geopolitical theater; only such a combination of vulnerabilities warrants the related apprehension of the weaker side: "they" will deny, because they can do so with relative impunity, in order to disable "us" irreversibly.

It is not necessary to know what the long-term objectives of the Soviet Union are, and idle to speculate from an ideological perspective what they might be. Only wholly inept western policies, especially in the Third World, could endow the Soviets with the risk-free capacity to be the first to deny the West access to areas of vital importance. In principle, the same kind of precautions are needed to foreclose the first-strike option on geopolitical ground as it is on the strategic-nuclear level. In practice, the required countervailing positions and capabilities must be such as to permit flexible retaliation for misuse or abuse of geopolitical assets; they must minimize the need for either nuclear response or diplomatic or economic abdication without imposing a similar choice on the Soviets.

Different perceptions are possible, and alarmist views are unprofitable, in this connection. Thus, in southeast Asia, it is possible to regard the later

within the softer circumference reducible to a like connection between the key polarities conditioning U.S.-Soviet relations at a deeper level. Just as the land-sea power schism was not only followed by the East-West cleavage in salience, but also "caused" the latter's distinctly modern material bases and politico-cultural manifestations, so the causal chain had been initiated when the secular-spiritual schism favored the coastal-maritime over the inland sectors when enlarging the scope for rational-scientific inquiry and enlarging the role of commercial-industrial enterprise.

Soviet implantation in the ex-U.S. bases in South Vietnam (Cam Ranh Bay) as intolerably destabilizing, also from the viewpoint of U.S.-friendly states in the Association of Southeast Asian Nations (ASEAN). Or, one may take into account the implications of American withdrawal from Vietnam and of American movement toward China, and view correspondingly the new Soviet geostrategic asset. It becomes then not only an inevitable if deplorable consequence of military defeat, but also a factor in a reshaped global equilibrium and mutual-deterrence system. The remaining local American or U.S.-friendly positions are then not so much targets of illegitimate Soviet expansion as items in America's wholly (but not exclusively) legitimate countervailing power.

Reciprocal encirclements and a stable equilibrium. In the real world, it will take a very dynamic equilibrium interplay for mutual deterrence to be extended and for the shared capacity to point toward geopolitical parity. There was at one time a quite stable *static* equilibrium between Russia and Britain in central Asia. It rested on reciprocal recognition of safe frontiers between the two powers. But longer or shorter spells of such stability could be achieved only by way of prior *dynamic* interaction. That pattern is likely to be repeated between the United States and the Soviet Union. Pressure and counter-pressure, penetration and counter-penetration will first have to strategically interrelate areas or regions that may but need not be geographically contiguous. In the more volatile periphery, a mobile diplomatic strategy across space will have to do what competitive armaments and intermittent crisis management have done in those central parts of the systems (i.e., Europe) where space is more limited and stakes more sensitive; it will have to make access divisible and the principle of divisibility concertable.

After World War II, Europe was the laboratory for outright division of physical space between the superpowers. This state of things has been only precariously yielding to the interpenetration of Soviet diplomatic influence in western Europe and western economic influence in eastern Europe. Outside Europe, third-world regions such as the Middle East might travel the European path in reverse toward a fixed partition, by way of an aborted spell of mobile interpenetration of superpower access and influence. They would then miss the chance of becoming a laboratory for routinizing the more dynamic and hopeful approach to regional and global stability. However, they can serve that purpose only if the local regimes either become or remain impenetrable to integral and irreversible control by either superpower, and if the superpowers themselves gradually relax their fears as well as their expectations in any one region.

Events in the peripheries increase in importance as conditions in the nuclear-strategic and geopolitical center grow either particularly tense or exceptionally tranquil. As one or the other situation arises, the process of evolving an equilibrium will shift away from the center to such peripheries, as either a derivative from central tensions or a compensation for their subsidence.

The shift will be all the more turbulent if the type of power that is relatively stable because major is distributed differently in the periphery than at the center. The often mutually hostile smaller states are then less likely to produce locally a near-automatic interstitial equilibrium by flexibly recoiling from one of the great powers to the other—as did Afghanistan and Persia between Russia and British India. Tensions will also rise when each of the great powers is unable (because of major-power distribution) to guarantee the other against threats or disturbances originating in its willing or unwilling protégé. Competition of the great powers over imperial China and her orbit began in earnest only when neither the Chinese nor any other authority was able to guarantee them against disorders in and from areas nominally under Peking's sovereignty or suzerainty.

By contrast, the stability of the interzonal frontier in central Asia was due, after 1907, to Britain guaranteeing Russia against disturbances from her de facto Afghan protectorate and to the two powers virtually partitioning control over Persia. Stability lapsed again when first postrevolutionary Russia and then late-imperial Britain weakened their hold in the area. One of the pillars on which stability could be reconstituted has been the (lately waning) American capacity to guarantee Soviet Russia against hostile intrusions from either pan-Islamic propaganda or Chinese support for such propaganda.

The failure of Napoleon's attempt to divide control only in or also beyond eastern Europe with Tsar Alexander, as well as first Hitler's tractations with Stalin, and then Churchill's similar ones, have shown that mere negotiations cannot demarcate zones of influence in the borderlands of Eurasia. Of late, a new fluidity in that area has revived the Anglo-Russian "great game" in central Asia, within a widening multiregional theater. Formerly, the strategic core areas were southeastern Europe (with eastern Mediterranean) and central Asia, extending to east Asia via the Anglo-Japanese alliance against Russia. Now, more or less directly interrelated are the Horn of Africa cum Red Sea, (northern-tier) Middle East cum eastern Mediterranean area, and the Afghan-Iranian sector extending to the Persian Gulf and the Indian Ocean. The arena with potential for interplay extends westward to instability-prone Turkey and Yugoslavia, while in the eastern direction Russia's anti-Chinese alliance with Vietnam matches the projection of Chinese presence or influence into central and south Asia.

In the past, the British strove to be able to punish Russia in southeastern Europe for advances in central Asia, and the Russians initiated or feigned pressure on the approaches to India in order to distract a Britain acting hostilely in Europe. Similarly, Soviet Russia could—and up to a point does—position herself in or adjacent to the Arabian Sea or the Indian Ocean so as to make the United States receptive to claims in the northern tier of the Middle East. In return, the United States could—and does—step up hostile action against pro-Soviet Aden from the Horn in order to gain leverage on Soviet initiatives in or from Afghanistan—and so on, across a widening field of forces, from Angola to Afghanistan and from eastern Europe to eastern Asia and the western hemisphere.

Before replacing contests with delimitations of influence by consent, thrusts and counter-thrusts will assume the acute form of reciprocal encirclements. The American-Soviet competition is replete with examples of this reciprocal encirclement. In the 1960s, a Franco-Soviet diplomatic entente was a counter to prior U.S. efforts to expel the Soviets diplomatically from western Europe as part of containing their suspected drive deeper into Europe. American councils were vocal with resentment of de Gaulle's part in the counter-containment strategy, but it soon proved to be a key incentive to procedural and nuclear-strategic détente between the United States itself and the Soviets. In the 1970s, the United States entered into a de facto alliance with a China straining to envelop Russia from the south. It may not have been the American purpose in this alliance to encircle the Soviets in Eurasia while they were being expelled from the diplomacy of Middle Eastern peacemaking, but such was the ostensible result of the new alignment. The Soviets responded with efforts to counter-encircle the United States through penetrations in the Red Sea–Persian Gulf area. An earlier Communist thrust into South Korea had somewhat similarly followed upon the Soviets being kept out of peacemaking with Japan.

Soviet actions and reactions often matched earlier ones by the tsarist government. At one stage, the forceful Russian response was to British denials of full and equal role in the diplomacy of the Ottoman question; at a later stage, to penetrations by the Central Powers into areas vital for Russian standing or security in the south (Austria-Hungary in Bosnia Herzegovina, and Germany along the Berlin-Baghdad railway and through the military mission to Turkey). Just as with the movements of tsarist diplomacy, Soviet thrusts and counterthrusts have specific objectives. But their larger strategic aim could be nonetheless to move the United States toward accepting the role-equality and access-safety that implement parity.

Third parties and managed decompression. The travail of reciprocal encirclements will signal the clarification of mutually permeable boundaries between zones of free or preferential superpower access and influence. And the encirclements themselves will tend to generate the geostrategic capacities for extending mutual deterrence from the nuclear-strategic to the geopolitical arena in both parties. All this can transpire, moreover, as part of promoting overall stability.

Working out the conditions of extended mutual deterrence in a two-power situation or perspective will lead to frictions. If the process is poorly managed, it will be punctuated by minor-to-middling conflict, as a reintensified cold war approaches the Crimean War in intensity. But misapplying pressures on the Soviet Union in the triangular setting of land and sea power will risk precipitating ultimate choices that are likelier to trigger the ultimate conflict. Adding the third power to complete the triangular complex does not fundamentally change the dynamics of reciprocal encirclements and mutual deterrence between two powers. Their identical perception of a third-power threat (possibly, but not necessarily, from the just-mentioned third power) may ideally convert reciprocal encirclements into parallel entrenchment for common defense. Yet completing the triangle—in both fact and analysis—does modify the setting of the bilateral relationship. The two-power dynamic becomes less exclusively salient even before it becomes subordinate; the range of theoretical or also practical options for one or both parties expands; and the time span shrinks within which the two-power dynamic can unfold without raising the ultimate survival question for the *globally* encircled power.

Most or all of what can be said for or against extending mutual deterrence is pertinent to managing decompression in relation to a power such as the Soviet Union—and vice versa. The two strategy strands are interdependent. However, it is in the triangular context that the decompression component of the total strategy raises issues of the most far-reaching gravity.

The fundamental purpose of the navally ambitious, would-be amphibian state (currently, the Soviet Union) is to place its relationship with the preeminent sea power (the United States) on the basis of parity in both the continental and the maritime environments. If the relationship is triangular, the would-be amphibian is increasingly pressed to do this before the continental rear power (China) can effectively exploit its entanglements with the preeminent insular-maritime state or become itself the ascendant challenger. Given these premises, the would-be amphibian's options are limited. The insular wing power, on the other hand, has a basic choice. It can set out to deny the would-be amphibian in the middle the outlets required for achieving parity by confronting it with a containing or encircling alliance with the continental rear power. Or the preeminent maritime power can make graduated concessions to the precariously placed expansionary power in its drive for seapower and overseas positions. It would then do so in order to decompress the challenger's external environment. And it might do so in the expectation of relaxing the challenger's authority structures internally.

No conclusive historical evidence supports the expectation of a beneficial internal effect. But it can be logically based on two assumptions. The first is that expansion—and overseas expansion in particular—will make demands on internal efficacy, prominently the economic. The second is that meeting the demands will foster greater pluralism in society and compel association of expert talent with the governing function—in short, that the tendency will be toward internal diversification. Such a development is not immediately attractive to an expansionist regime that is also authoritarian. But, then, neither are geopolitical concessions alluring to the defending, including a liberal-democratic, power. If at all, they will be made at least as much for the sake of diverting the would-be amphibian from an all-out assault on the central system as with a view to promoting the internal liberalization of its authoritarian base. The assault, if forthcoming, would be aimed at creating an unassailable basis for later peripheral expansion. Historically, it repeatedly followed the challenger's defeat in its first-phase pursuit of relatively moderate gains in the central continental and overseas theaters.

A second phase in the present situation would consist of an all-out expansionary Soviet drive westward and/or eastward on the continent of Eurasia. Should the assault be again repulsed, and the two-phase sequence be extended into the customary three-phase cycle, the defeated bid of a henceforth decomposed Soviet Union would be replaced with the bid of a covictorious China for parity on land and sea with the surviving or emerging insular-maritime power (if any). If the surviving power is the United States and no third power is a worthy or willing ally, America would face alone an ascendant China across an immense power vacuum—one so extensive as to dwarf the latest of the gradually expanding postempire fragmentations and postwar vacuums in Europe. Should Japan be preserved and become the preeminent insular wing power while a new power aggregate slowly regroups in China's rear, a completely new triangle would emerge. The point of gravity in world politics would then shift yet more decisively to Asia than in the first case. Neither outcome would seem superior to what U.S. strategy might achieve by condoning Soviet moves out of either west-east encirclement or southern envelopment, within limits set by the concern (among others) to simultaneously integrate China into an effective politico-military equibrium.

A mechanical containment of Soviet Russia via a U.S.-Chinese military alliance risks speeding up Russia's critical timetable; so does a systematic U.S. effort, in the tactical dimension of the triangle, to make the Soviets accommodating on issues of immediate interest by matching China's exploitation of the U.S.-Soviet rivalry with a China-biased exploitation of America's theoretical equidistance from the mutually hostile Communist powers. For a more organic process of change within and without Russia to proceed, a geopolitical access and influence will have to be reapportioned. To achieve the more stable balance, a strategy transcending mere tactics would have to mesh with an attitude, and extended mutual deterrence between the two principal powers coincide with shared deference for China's sensitivities as the upcoming power. If this means that a phased progress toward U.S.-Soviet geopolitical parity neither need be nor should ever be consummated in a condominium, it also means that China would be most effective as the background regulators of changes in the status quo—even if not eager to be thus useful. Her anticipated responses would weigh upon the territorial gains the Soviets could safely aspire to, and the extent of corresponding concessions the United States could safely make, without driving an alienated China toward the rival or to other extreme recourses.

So long as she was no more and no less than a key background factor, China was more suited and better equipped to stabilize the international system as a relatively inert ballast than as an active peripheral balancer; she is more useful as a largely passive mass that weighs down and thus limits the oscillations of world equilibrium than as a trump card that enables one of the players to raise the stakes in an international game of bluff.

Strengths and weaknesses of heartland and offshore powers. Offering a rationale for reapportionment immediately raises the question of the relative position of the two superpowers. It is far from certain that the continental heartland power has retained or improved upon the advantage that Halford Mackinder (questionably) assigned it early in the century over offshore insular or quasi-insular powers on the strength of technical progress in the means of overland communication and transportation. And even if the advantage did persist or increase, so too have the vulnerabilities in the case of Soviet Russia.

Such vulnerabilities raise the question of the Soviet "right," as well as the Russians' capacity, to shield the ethnically soft underbelly in Asia as a single-mindedly as the topographically open flank in eastern Europe—and to do so as emphatically as the United States insists on safeguarding itself to both its north and south in the western hemisphere. It is possible that Russia's Asian frontier is more directly, if more subtly, vulnerable to religiously or racially upsetting penetrations than her European one is to conventional or nuclear projectiles. By the same standard of judgment, it is possible to overstate the dangers to the West from a Soviet penetration toward the Indian Ocean if the threat is related to oil and is (correctly) connected with provoking or fighting a war so big or long as to preclude fighting it from western reserves. In all other circumstances, a Soviet presence at the Gulf might well threaten the essential security of the United States (or of western Europe) even less than the mere existence of the German High Sea Fleet in the North Sea had menaced Britain's—and, under certain conditions, a U.S.-Chinese encirclement (with U.S. nuclear submarines on station in the southern seas) could threaten Soviet Russia.

To bar all further Soviet extension beyond the continental habitat is to claim so extreme an advantage for Soviet interior lines (and inland raw-material resources) as to make world equilibrium depend on Russia's continued confinement in the regional compass. On a more permissive view, further Soviet expansion would go beyond redressing geopolitical parity and would upset it to western disadvantage only if it enabled the Soviets to bar the

United States from most (or all "vital") forward coastal or insular bases adjoining the Soviet sphere, and from similarly situated subsidiary heartlands with interior lines of their own. In other words, the expansion would have to nullify all of the remote-insular power's advantages over the heartland.

By the same token, the West would have sufficient grounds for refusing to condone *any* Soviet movement toward geostrategic parity if it could infer that any further increase in the capacity of the Soviets to deny the West access to vital areas would invariably lead to the utilization of this capacity. However, no such simple inference can be made from only local capability anywhere. To be reliable, the inference would have to be backed, both conceptually and empirically, by analysis from wider than local or regional structures of power and interests, as well as by evidence from relevant past events or tendencies.

What does this mean for a particular contested region such as the Middle East? It suggests that the configuration of power and interests to be considered transcends the structure (including the vacuum) of power indigenous to the region as one that might invite and promise easy success for Soviet incursions.

Although the situation in the Middle East permits comparisons with Europe immediately after World War II and during the early stages of the cold war, the analogy is also incomplete. Unlike the contemporary Middle East, Europe was a relatively isolated and self-contained island of U.S.-Soviet confrontation. Hence the intensity and high-risk potential of the confrontation. Matters changed once the contest spread globally along with the increase in Soviet capabilities and the extension of Soviet interests. It then became possible to shape or counteract Soviet intentions in the Middle East by action in other areas and on issues without incurring all the risks and costs of a local confrontation that had gotten out of control. System-wide offsets to any actual or presumed local Soviet capabilities and intentions could henceforth achieve in any one third-world region much of what U.S. nuclear superiority accomplished once in and beyond Europe.

Nor is this all that has changed the parameters of superpower competition over regional control or influence. A vacuum of organized and usable power in the Middle East or elsewhere in the Third World is offset by the surfeit there of intractable "forces." These are less accessible to outside coercion than was eastern Europe to Soviet Russia in the aftermath of World War II, and more impervious to external attraction on the grounds of either security needs of cultural affinities than was western Europe in regard to the United States in that same period. Finally, the wider global arena supplies not only occasions for offsetting maneuvers by one rival superpower against the other. It also generates a constraint on both insofar as intemperate superpower inroads in one area have a counterproductive demonstration effect on potential friends or allies in other areas. That factor, too, was not in operation so long as Europe was the sole active arena while the Europe-centered colonial framework debarred the rest of the world from spontaneous local reactions with geostrategic significance.

The Europe-Middle East analogy applies better to the configurations of superpower interests than of capabilities. To be sure, vital and immediate western and Soviet interests are differently asymmetrical in the Middle East than they were in Europe; the asymmetry (to western "advantage") is especially stark if oil alone is emphasized and the western need for it is treated as total while the Soviet as indefinitely nil. But, on any other assessment, the distribution of stakes and interests is such as to encourage both sides to settle in the Third World (as they did in Europe) for privileged "presence" in areas that adjoin their respective power centers most closely and are most critical for their differently conditioned security concerns. In the Middle East, this principle tends to leave the West—and inclines the Soviets to leave the West—once more in possession of objectively more valuable, and for the West more vital, parts of the contested region. To go beyond that is to ask for the impossible, an undisturbed possession of the region in its entirety.

Any other presumption—and simple inference from local Soviet military capability—would have to be backed, next to the hypothesis of total western ineptitude, by past events convicting the Soviets of criminal levity. These would have to be more widespread and conclusive than is the one possibly incriminating act: the Soviet encouragement of the Arab oil embargo in 1973. This action was suspect. But it was also a retaliation for—or an equivalent of—the nuclear alert (the so-called second missile crisis) set afoot to bar an active Soviet involvement in suspending the Egypt-Israel hostilities. It can be argued that such an involvement was fundamentally in conformity with a prior superpower agreement about the local ceasefire—and with U.S.-Soviet détente.

Finally, one basic point is clearer than any speculation. For drastic inferences and projections regarding Soviet intentions in the Middle East (or any other area of "vital" western interests) to inspire confidence in their being genuine, they would have to be reflected in actual western policy in the region and generally. This would mean the adoption, by the United States, of a posture of all-out hostility and hostile preparedness vis-à-vis Soviet Russia. That kind of posture would, however, probably turn safeguarding anticipations into explosive actualities.

Requisites of mutual-deterrence and decompression strategy: Soviet moderation and U.S. management

If it is to be of practical use, a theoretical rationale for a grand strategy will depend on the presence of fundamental prerequisites. Many of these have been already outlined or implied. Additional observations can now be made, relating to relevant aspects of Soviet expansionism and of western, and specifically American, responses to it; to the momentum and modalities of the former and the aptitudes for its management by the latter.

Stakes and suspicions in land-sea power competition. Soviet thrusts within and across regions raise questions about Russia's ability to make lasting penetrations and about the immediate and the ultimate purpose of the Soviet initiatives. In addition to questions that cannot be reliably answered, a more pertinent question is whether any one Soviet thrust can be justified in terms of such routine matters as diplomatic reciprocity or status-and-role parity, access to material resources, and geostrategic peculiarities and symmetry. If successive U.S. administrations agreed on anything, it was on denying the Soviets equal status and role in maintaining order in any region outside their control. The unifying assumption was that the Soviets could not be trusted anywhere to use their influence in favor of peace and stability. The determination to expel Moscow from any meaningful part in Middle Eastern peacemaking was only the most striking instance of acting out that assumption.

More than a century ago, the British similarly strove to curtail Russian influence in the Ottoman Empire. They did so although the Russians had freely surrendered the near-exclusive influence gained in the early 1830s (the Russo-Ottoman treaty of Unkiar Skelessi) and although Tsar Nicholas I had tried (successfully, he thought) at a London "summit" to talk the British into joint decision-making on the then Near East. The Crimean War was the consequence. When, before the October war of 1973, the Soviets yielded *their* monopoly of influence in the crucial country of the region (Egypt) without resistance, Brezhnev is on record as having reenacted Nicholas's bid for great power concert, this time with the United States.* Whether or not this or any other Soviet initiative had been rejected by one (the Nixon) administration in good faith as insufficiently "sincere," the event was followed four years later by another (the Carter) administration's hasty retreat under pressure from a short-lived joint superpower declaration on the Middle East. It is unlikely that the combined impression slowed down Soviet retaliatory probings inside and outside the area.

*According to one account, Brezhnev contended in a conversation with Senator Edward Kennedy (in April 1974) that, during his visit to the United States prior to the October war of 1973, and in contrast to subsequent American "trickery," "We had agreed that . . . the United States and the Soviet Union would work together to secure peace . . . we must act together, or there will be no tranquility in the Middle East." And, "At San Clemente, I kept Nixon up almost all night on the Middle East, trying to convince him of the need to act together. Otherwise, there would be an explosion in the Middle East. Nixon did not heed my words. . . . The Soviet Union has shown some restraint in the Middle East." See Tad Szulc, *The Illusion of Peace: Foreign Policy in the Nixon Years* (New York: Viking Press, 1978), pp. 762–63. Szulc describes Brezhnev's comments as "self-serving."

Analogous to western vital interest in unimpeded access to Middle Eastern oil in the present state of energy technology is Britain's dependence on the Indian economy in earlier conditions of world trade. Any Russian threat to the British control was then hypothetical and far-fetched when compared with the long-term threat to the British position from within India; barring Soviet readiness to provoke a nuclear exchange, western access is likewise threatened more from within the oil-rich states than from the outside. For either Anglo-Saxon power to highlight the external threat was a way of concealing an unwillingness to either admit sources or check forces of subversion indigenous to the critical region; anti-Russian agitation was a cover for passivity in areas where precautions might have done more good.

It is widely believed in the West that Soviet Russia will need more oil for herself or her eastern-European dependents than can be produced internally at some (repeatedly revised and deferred) point in the future. Therefore, it was not necessarily a hostile act against the West for the Russians to try in advance to make their access to Middle Eastern oil independent of revocable western forbearance. Nor was it consistent for U.S. critics to contest the right of the Soviets to obtain failproof access to outside oil resources and to simultaneously deny secure access to western technology for expanding domestic oil production. Supplies of western technology would make external sources of Soviet oil less necessary; subjecting technology supplies to punitive suspensions (e.g., following the invasion of Afghanistan) creates a disturbing precedent for western attitude to future Soviet access to the commodity itself.*

Neither would there seem to be a self-evident reason why a major power should be indefinitely barred from seas closely adjoining its heartland. Even the touchy British were on one occasion ready to condone Russian access to an "economic" port on the Persian Gulf. However, what is really at issue is neither the subjectively felt need to possess nor the right—inherent or claimed—to deny. Instead, what matters is the capacity of one side to seize and hold, and of the other to withhold or neutralize, the asset or position in contention. For Russia to penetrate to the Persian Gulf and the Indian Ocean by the overland route might be at variance with traditional Russian pathways of expansion to both inland and open seas along river routes. However, taking into account only the local and the conventional-military aspects, the advance would not be logistically impossible under modern conditions. The Russians might also be more effectively able to safeguard a coastal facility on the Persian Gulf now than they were in the earlier era—from, say, south Vietnam than all the way from Vladivostok. But the United States ought to be

*The list of denials has included the American (and Japanese) decision against assisting in the Soviet development of large oil and gas fields in eastern Siberia (possibly in deference to China). See Giovanni Agnelli, "East-West Trade: A European View," *Foreign Affairs* 59, no. 1 (Summer 1980): 1023.

able to neutralize such facility from one or more of its own overseas bases (including those in Diego Garcia and, perhaps, east Africa), even if not as handily as Britain would have been able to do from India.

Time and space in Soviet expansion. For the United States to concede the principle of geopolitical parity would legitimize some gains for the Soviets. Ideally, it would legitimize enough gains over a sufficiently brief period to rally the Soviets to the defense of stakes and interests common to the relatively conservative major industrial and naval powers. But a parallel effort would also have to be made to phase the Soviet expansion over a period sufficiently long to permit the evolution of regional equilibria as part of a plural global balance of power. If regional equilibria took shape among local parties, this would automatically diminish the scope of geopolitical assets to be reassigned between the superpowers and efface the impression of their indivisibility by peaceful means. If the local powers finally failed to contribute to overall stability, a genuine prior effort to reapportion great-power access and influence would not be wasted. At the very least, it would have delayed the perilous time of a serious testing for the competing alternatives of condominium, climactic conflict, and uncontrollable chaos.

Promoting decompression at the same time as stability means that Soviet globalism has to be managed, as to the pace of tolerable Soviet expansion, but also its direction and scope, with special regard for critical time spans. A key problem is how to synchronize relaxing containment with reinforcing residual constraints. A rationale for tolerating a decent quota of Soviet gains early in the new phase is one thing; another is to make it serve as the doctrinal umbrella for developing the capacity for safeguarding truly vital, narrowly defined American and western interests against the Soviets in the medium term. Over a yet longer but not indefinite time span, America's key allies ought to become able and willing to participate in measured counter-actions in the Third World, against either Soviet expansion that proved immoderate or third-world actions and conditions facilitating such expansion.

The possibility for joint action outside the NATO area would recede if contemporary, postcolonial west Europeans behaved differently from medieval Europeans. After a period of postcrusading self-confinement, the latter responded dynamically from renewed strength to the perils of prolonged passivity. A U.S. posture combining consent with constraint in relations with the Soviets will encourage active allied engagement on the American side more reliably than will unvarying rhetorical opposition to Soviet initiatives. Merely to keep protesting Soviet inroads can only perpetuate the impression of American impotence while Soviet power gradually impresses the west Europeans as an irresistible force from the east or an indispensable safeguard against a remoter East.

However, containing Soviet Russia too rigidly in her eastern and southern rear with the aid of faster-than-anticipated increase of pressures from China might make the Russians react "prematurely," likewise lessening the prospects for U.S.–west European cooperation. Tsarist Russia overreacted in 1904 to British and Anglo-Japanese advances in the Far East, and Imperial Germany in 1914 to Russia's rebound from defeat and depression after 1905. In both instances, real or feared time limits on effective self-assertion set off attempts at military preemption. The determining precipitants were geopolitically and economically conditioned. Compared with them, the strictly military advantage of being the first to mobilize was as much a secondary trigger of conflict in August 1914 as superior first-strike prospects would be in "1984."

Next to time spans, a strategy of decompression has to be concerned with the direction of Soviet expansion. If historical precedents supply any guidance, the main direction will fluctuate first along a north-south axis. Tsarist Russia redirected her expansive energies southward (toward the Black Sea) in an effort to repair initial setbacks there after securing vital security interests in the north (the Baltic Sea region). The northern overland and maritime approaches have now again been secured (against Germany as, earlier, against Sweden and Poland); the inadequacies once again responsible immediately after World War II for the abortion of tentative early probings southward have been made good. Within the south itself, free access to the southernmost regions (in the Persian Gulf and Indian Ocean) may again be sought with the help of leverages exerted from a more effective presence in areas to the north (the northern tier of the Middle East, Afghanistan, or Soviet Turkestan and Azerbaijan).

Similarly at the earlier stage, Russia pried open and then secured free peacetime passage through the Straits with levers from entrenchments to the north of them, in the Balkans and on the Black Sea. The objective of the tsars in regard to the Straits was primarily defensive. But they pursued it offensively when trying to restrict western access through the Bosporus to Russia's southern flank. For the West to now, in peacetime, too strictly limit Russia's "free passage" in and to areas south of the Straits might have a like effect. It would put a premium on Soviet attempts to restrict western access and passage in the region around the Persian Gulf from Russia's positions to the north of it; it might even tip the scales from using mere pressure to applying outright force.

A still more dramatic denouement is possible in the longer run, within an enlarged setting of a global conflict. Just as, early in World War I, the western European powers had to resign themselves to conceding to their Russian ally the very same Constantinople they had previously worked and fought to deny to a rival Russia, so the West might eventually have to surrender some of the embattled southern positions to Soviet Russia "freely"—and, possibly, too late.

As a complement to the south-north axis, Soviet global expansion—and

U.S.-Soviet reequilibration interplays—can again oscillate increasingly also along an east-west axis. The mix and even the sequence of the two directions in the earlier, continental phase of Russian expansion are not impossible to reproduce—although, to be sure, the targets of Soviet opportunity in the western hemisphere would undoubtedly lie south of once Russian-held Alaska and those in east Asia probably south of once-coveted Manchuria. There is another side to the coin. If the process is to remain in balance, reduction of external constraints on Soviet global outreach will have to be rewarded by lessened exclusiveness of access in any one region. Thus, the range of either American or west European access in Soviet-dominated eastern Europe in particular will have to go on expanding as well.

What does it mean to "manage" the direction of Soviet expansion within and between the two complementary axes, south-north and east-west? It means multiplying and diversifying the positions each party can use against the other. Only then is it possible to exert pressure in areas where the rival's access is most vulnerable, or divert it toward areas of maximum opportunity and minimum conflict potential. The purpose of such efforts is to momentarily relieve an embattled area (such as, currently, the Middle East) and thus avoid the worst. One such "worst" contingency is a headlong collision over local issues; another, a competitive on-the-spot courtship of local parties.

What, finally, about the scope of Soviet expansion? If other things (including local resistance or resilience) are equal, it will depend on which superpower knows best how to outflank or encircle the other. As the geographic scope of delimiting zones of access and areas of parity expands, it is wholly possible to routinize the competition well short of a cold war. The single prerequisite for this is that both sides recognize the dynamic process for what it is, an indispensable preliminary to a provisionally static accomplishment, to wit, to the assured capability of both parties to extend mutual deterrence to the issue of access and its denial in the geopolitical sphere. So extended, mutual nonnuclear deterrence may be preferred to the escalation of competition into delayed mutual destruction. But for the preference to be reciprocal and lasting, it must rest on objective tests and dispassionate assessments of parity. These must replace the view that one side is providentially entitled, and the other is diabolically impelled.

The actual pace and extent of Soviet expansion, even if not positively favored, will be tolerable so long as it does not trigger a last-ditch U.S.-Chinese effort to implement Russia's global encirclement, or precipitate China's secession from the American connection into enforced accommodation with the Soviets. Unfortunately, such a pragmatic criterion is liable to produce only judgments that come too late. Therefore, it will have to be reinforced conceptually. Accordingly, such Soviet expansion should be considered within safe limits if it does not preclude parity or is not about to upset equilibrium between a heartland power and an insular power asymmetrically endowed with the advantages and liabilities of, among other things, interior and exterior lines, access to coastal and offshore bases and continental or overseas allies, and differential resource assets and dependence. We have already observed and can only repeat that such disparities complicate assessments of what constitutes overall parity. But they do not prevent a bona-fide U.S. commitment to a parity-evolving strategy. If nothing else, such a commitment would act as a lever on the Soviets to think twice before reviving American intransigence and foreclosing movement toward newly flexible superpower ground rules.

Ground rules on means and uses of Soviet expansion. As the Soviets' military capacity rose, they necessarily looked for political and economic dividends. This, in turn, raises the issue of the means they adopt in securing new gains, and of the use they actually make of such gains. There has been sufficient evidence to date as to the means the Soviets have been applying on one level from Angola via Ethiopia to Aden; on another in Iraq (following Egypt) and in India under different local regimes; and on yet another in Afghanistan. The means have been variably efficacious and the accomplishments invariably precarious.

It is too early for any new rules to outlaw the more drastic of the means in all circumstances and conditions. Any effective restriction on means can be evolved between the major parties only gradually, be it militantly or consensually. This is not fatal. Spectacular as the issue of means may be, that of actual use is more critical. Consequently, the vital question for the West is: Will the Soviets use "situations of strength" to position themselves so that they can counteract any American attempt to deny them access to either diplomatic role or material resource? Or, unprovoked but still hostile, will they employ such positions in order to themselves deny such access to the United States and to the West at large?

One cannot wait indefinitely to see what use the Soviets will have made of new positions of influence. But the strategy the West has chosen can influence, and may even determine, the ultimate Russian choice.

Concern with redefining ground rules between the superpowers in ways allowing for flexibility will rise when such a redefinition's full bearing is understood. This redefinition carries an initial definition of norms for the entire global system, as that system emerges out of its prenatal state of U.S.-focused bipolarity. What and how much the United States tolerates from the Soviet Union, and vice versa, will automatically imply what residual role the major powers can go on claiming for themselves, and what must be conceded by others, to maintain minimum world order. It will also imply what behavior of the lesser as well as of major powers is consistent with a relatively peaceful and orderly gravitation of power and roles among states and regions. Within an evolving world system such a gravitation is the necessary—if not assuredly sufficient—preliminary to a genuine world community. Consequently, it will not be enough to depend on immediate tactical cost-benefit calculations when deciding what implicit definition or revision of the ground rules is unavoidable under protest; it will no longer be decisive that this or that form or extent of "unacceptable" Soviet expansion is momentarily irresistible. Reasons that are in part historical and in part hypothetical must be included if some Soviet expansion under new rules and revised constraints is to be freely conceded. It may be conceded not only to tighten the latent bonds of solidarity between two "rational" powers and endangered "empires" neither of which can really profit from efforts to subvert the other—but also as a means to decompress the internal Soviet authority structure as part of diverting a progressively attenuated thrust of Soviet power away from the central system.

Applying a static perimeter strategy to the military defense of a still-confident American empire resulted in an aborted land war in Asia. Successive administrations had previously been unable to implement and maintain the military-strategic preconditions of a more elastic in-depth empire defense and to sustain its risks. The inability of the American political elite, as well as the society at large, to sustain the stresses of the Asian war have not boded well for the readiness of either elite or public to apply the more rigid perimeter strategy unswervingly to an actually or seemingly advancing Soviet empire.

As an alternative to perimeter-type containment, can an elastic in-depth defense in geopolitical space be combined with nuclear-strategic deterrence (and produce, as a dividend, positive offshoots in the form of Soviet decompression and diversion)? And can the change be effected in ways that will moderate the scope, and mitigate the consequences, of a seemingly unavoidable displacement of world politics eastward in one form or another? It will not be possible to confidently answer the questions in the affirmative so long as the fundamental premises about Russia that inform U.S. strategy remain intact and nothing changes in the dominant perceptions of the nonwestern world outside Russia. However, the prerequisites of an affirmative answer can be illustrated by hypothetical examples.

One such example relates to the relationship between the Middle East and the Far East, between southwestern and eastern Asia. Because it raises different kinds of interaction between Russia and China, it also indirectly relates to the two overlapping dimensions of the more or less far-flung East-West relationship. Hypothetical as it is, the example entails an alternative to the strategic concept of keeping the Soviet Union out of the Persian Gulf while fostering the China connection. Much as the perimeter-type containment of Soviet Russia rests operationally on the still-accessible rimlands and key offshore islands, the China connection has become its diplomatic centerpiece. The long-term risks it generates must be weighed against the potential long-term advantages of a radically different perception of Soviet intentions and likewise different approach to the Russo-Chinese factor. There might be a way how, instead of triggering a tripartite process eventuating in global conflict, one might first recrystallize a triangular regional power structure with potentially stabilizing effects.

A start for this process would involve revising the current orthodoxy used to explain why Soviet Russia seeks access to the Persian Gulf and Indian Ocean. Does she do so in order to win a strangle hold on the western lifeline in the Middle East, be it for blackmailing or bargaining purposes? Or is she also and perhaps principally interested in acquiring a safe and assured terminal point in the southwest for overseas connection with her easternmost continental-Asian provinces? Those provinces are underdeveloped and underpopulated when compared with the adjoining core provinces of northern China. Hence, the Soviet outreach, instead of having designs on the western lifeline, would aim to strengthen Russia's own one, and to foster conditions vital for her internal equilibrium among regions and ethnic groups, as well as her external equilibrium with a populous neighbor. Just as the West has been concerned to keep its industrial and transport sectors moving (with an assured and economically affordable oil supply), so the Soviets may have been increasingly pressed to hurry the economic development of Siberia with technologically feasible exploitation of its oil and gas resources. This effort has appeared even more urgent to the Soviet elite in the face of an American and Japanese reluctance to risk offending China by assisting in the enterprise.

One affirmation may be ventured, without making it dogmatic, about the past and present place of warm-water ports in Russian foreign-policy goals. The advantage of overseas transport relative to overland transport (of bulk goods) is of long standing and continues as to both cost and efficiency; it could not but interest the Soviet leadership in forging a both safe and economical connection between Russia's economic heartland and periphery. Such a link best could be forged, if not without hazards, via the Indian Ocean from a safe economic port in the Persian Gulf area within a practicable—even if not easily negotiable—overland distance from the Soviet southwest.

Several features of contemporary world politics would change abruptly if an eastward overseas route was hypothesized as the primary operative objective behind a Soviet "drive to the south." The use issue would be transformed, as would that of Soviet means. Even forceful Soviet means of acquiring the outlet would be less alarming than before from the viewpoint of the vital interests of the West, especially if altered assumptions about Soviet aims allowed U.S. and Soviet approaches to the area to be coordinated for purposes of required order maintenance and peacemaking. An overseas Soviet outreach, originating in the Persian Gulf, toward a Soviet territory in the east, could then amount to a beneficial form of eastward displacement. A strategy that blocks the Soviets in the Middle East and elsewhere, while China grows in both the east and southwest under western auspices, is liable to displace the center of gravity of world power eastward. Only the focus of the competitive dynamic involving Soviet Russia and China directly and Japan (alongside or in lieu of the United States) indirectly in east Asia would be similarly displaced under the alternative approach.

One resulting difference might be between a military, including nuclear, Sino-Soviet confrontation and a prolonged jockeying for position only. This is not to say that adopting the more benevolent view of Soviet intentions would automatically banish the specter of the ominous sequence; the Soviets might still pass to an all-out continental onslaught if their moderate expansion on land and sea is frustrated. But it would permit contemplation of a potentially benign set of symmetries.

To begin with, the overseas Soviet east-west route would be exposed at both of its terminals and along its trajectory to flanking thrusts from both western (or West-controlled) and Japanese positions. This exposure would match that of western positions to Soviet pressure or penetration in, say, the Middle East and central Europe. The Soviet acquisition of exterior lines would reduce the advantage peculiar to the continental heartland state; this alone would materially increase the scope for an elastic western strategy.

Nor is this all. The superpowers would become more evenly vulnerable to claims and encroachments by third powers in, for example, the maritime narrows. As a factor fostering U.S.-Russian appeasement, any increase in the commonalty of superpower interests on this, an important, issue of world order must be added to attrition of Soviet resources or dispersion of Soviet energies attendant on advance. It could only reinforce the interest commonalty if Americans were to participate in developing Siberia and exploiting its riches.

Among the most critical symmetries that could be improved upon is the one between Soviet Russia and China. The primary focus here is on the two countries' extreme remote flanks. Sinkiang's closeness to Russia's heartland is for China what Siberia's proximity to China is, or might become, for Soviet Russia. Once Siberia has been strengthened, both eccentric areas would be more equally vulnerable to the other power center. They would be also more even sources of pressure against the other power. A sufficiently developed and populated Siberia could balance the economic strength of China's northeast and enhance the area's vulnerability.

The Siberia-Sinkiang symmetry would join the expanded U.S.-Soviet parallels in a multiple stalemate; Soviet immersion in a feasible land-development task via an overseas route would play a part in operationally shifting the overall stalemate eastward. The efficiency required for this development task would help to gradually diversify the sources of input into decisions that are relevant for foreign as well as internal-resources policy; progress in the task would offer a long-term guarantee against Soviet decline relative to either China alone or a U.S.-Chinese combination on a wider front. The Soviet incentive to intensify the drive to expand would be correspondingly reduced, as would pressure on western Europe caused by Soviet reactions to east-west encirclement.

Japan would be peaceably propelled beyond the thwarted attempt at continental expansion toward what has been the second stage in more than one offshore insular power's relationship with an adjoining land mass. She could more safely move toward being either a moderator or even a balancer between the two military powers on the Asian mainland. For Japan to act as an impartial restraint would differ fundamentally from Nippon's role at the outset of the century as a frontal barrier to Russia's overland advance to the Far East, along the Trans-Siberian and Manchurian railroads, leading to the Russo-Japanese War. The new role would be also vastly preferable to what the new Japan's situation would be if the Soviets reacted violently from their Eurasian center against a historical reversal in east Asia. Whereas, before, Russia oppressed China in the Amur region, it could become China's turn to exert militant pressure there on the neighboring land power were a worsening land-population ratio in China to compound continuing underdevelopment and underpopulation in the Soviet east.

Thus the hypothesis is suggested: the current end-of-century competition over the Middle East, off the European Mediterranean, is a prelude to activating international competition over east Asia, off the Asian Mediterranean-like land-sea configuration in the twenty-first century. An improved Soviet overseas access eastward might dampen the intensity of that competition, compared with either the late-nineteenth-century Russian overland drive, or the consequences of denying Soviet Russia maritime access in the remainder of the twentieth century. Moreover, the current risks are considerable that Soviet Russia will be prompted to counter-encircle a Sino-American combine globally, by methods expanding on her so far limited Vietnam connection. These risks might be greater than are the ones present in a Soviet move that would do no more than countervail China regionally in northeast Asia on land, as a defensive variant of the last tsar's Korean strategy.

Nor is the hypothesis of Soviet designs on western oil supplies inherently superior to the alternative hypothesis. Adhering to the oil-related scenario could set the stage for a nuclear war as a result of western misperception of Soviet intentions, even before a major continental war instigates the feared Soviet action. Proceeding on western suspicions is apt to engender more or worse tension than might Soviet miscalculation as to the western response to the Soviet implementation of actions that are presently imputed to them. Tentatively proceeding on the Siberia-related scenario would carry with it less ominous portents. It would set the stage for an operationally expanded, conventional maritime-continental balance of power between Soviet Russia and the West globally (as part of Soviet diversion eastward), and between Soviet Russia and China regionally (as part of redistributing pressures and vulnerabilities). This trend would increase the prospect for decompression in the southwest (contrary to the effect of a Sinkiang that has not been offset in Siberia), as well as more generally (contrary to the effect of continuing western interdicts on seaborne Soviet exits from the Russian southwest). It would not take long for relaxing effects on authority within Soviet Russia and tensions with the West to make themselves felt.

Interempire solidarity or subversion in a crisis-of-empire setting. The opposite to a policy fostering decompression is one increasing pressures on the rival empire as is, without easing resistance to its further expansion. Applying such an approach to the Soviet empire will tend to retard any further evolution of the Soviet political system into a conservative one by treating the empire itself as one that already is decaying—and as one that can be easily propelled toward deepening decay. The conservative instinct, it has been noted, can express itself in repression of upheavals within an empire, as well as by exploitation of disorders outside it. The game of combining repressive strategy with exploitative tactics can be played by both sides when two empires of internationally conservative powers, Russia and America, face one another. On the American side, the dual approach is either muted or confounded by domestic liberal residues; on the Soviet side, neither of the two expressions of conservatism is necessarily exclusive of a continuing trend toward civilian inspiration and increasingly "civilized" implementation of both empire management and further imperial expansion.

There is a condition, however. The social order at the core of the Soviet empire must not be exposed to too frequent and threatening challenges. If this contention is correct, then any possible beneficial evolution in the Soviet system at large would be jeopardized if the United States lacked discretion when trying, on the British model, to make up for defects or defaults in its own geopolitical thrust southward with opportunistic attempts to foster liberal values wherever and whenever convenient. The formula has lately entailed championing reformist or revolutionary militancy within the Soviet empire, such as Soviet dissident intellectuals and Polish workers, while losing control over forces of unrest that do or might impinge on Soviet Russia from the outside, such as the Iranian mullahs.

Intensifying the problem of empire defense for the Soviet leadership has meant aggravating its task of averting the decline and dissolution to which any empire is liable. Strains and stresses in an aging empire are due in some cases to arrested capacity to expand (e.g., the Ottoman Empire); in other cases, to an eroded capacity to export (e.g., the Italian city-state empires, the Dutch and English trading empires); and, in yet other or in most cases, to the inability to fit elements of static or perimeter military defense to a basic strategy of elastic defense (the Roman and American empires among others).

A flexible balance between central control and peripheral autonomy is indispensable for an in-depth elastic political defense. It will not be feasible unless groups other than the original core-imperial elite are meaningfully co-opted into the management of empire. The challenge of co-optation has been rarely if ever met to everyone's satisfaction. However, for a rigid imperial structure biased toward static political defense such as the Soviet, whom to co-opt into elite roles, and how, is more critical than further expansion or a rising export curve. Instead of clinging to the Soviet-ideological principle when determining eligibility for co-optation, a more realistic choice for the regime would seem to lie between either the ethnic principle (and then wider-Slavic rather than great-Russian) or an essentially societal principle. Falling back on the latter means trying to combine fresh stimulus to expansion with a vital spring of dynamic organization; it also means, as a prerequisite to either, relaxing constraints on individual-expert and social-group pluralism to the detriment of party-type monolithism. More social flexibility may be gradually revealed as the only serviceable method for solidifying the empire if the "Slavic" principle falters over intra-Slavic (notably Russo-Polish) divisions even before intensifying other divisions (European versus Asian ethnic strands), and the "Soviet" principle proves no more assimilative than the "great-Russian" one.

Western policy can be keyed to promoting crisis or to fostering creativity in the Soviet empire; the West can either wager on the long-term potential for change that is implicit in the essentially European nature of Russia, or gamble on the potential for quicker results of an anti-Russian posture implicit in the internal or external Asian factor. The choice might codetermine which, if any, of the possible substitutes for the Soviet-ideological common denominator would eventually predominate within the empire and how. Any outside effort to affect the Soviet empire's internal balance of control and autonomy will face the choice between promoting changes inside Soviet Russia first and foremost and (aiming at effects to be produced within the core-imperial polity only indirectly) encouraging prior changes in Russia's and the empire's dependent territories. Events in the two theaters are necessarily interactive. However, it is unlikely that, contrary to an always-latent and periodically resurgent belief, significant and stable results could be achieved by downgrading the Russia-first approach in favor of the more circuitous approach.

Asking questions about the present stage of Russia's evolution as society, nation, and empire, and about the directions in which she can be expected to move and be moved is hazardous. Risking the wrong answer will, however, harbor fewer perils than does the assumption of an unchanging Russian or Communist man- and territory-eating monster, unprecedented in kind and unchanging in essence. The one thing that is easier under the latter assumption is to view the United States itself as a humanistic obverse of such a Russia, a country and culture also unique, though in a radically different way. It is more useful for policy to view the United States as a fellow empire with a comparable stake in influencing the current state of the empire phenomenon—as something capable of surviving if bound to evolve, or as something foredoomed to be replaced by a different if yet unknown or unperfected organizational form altogether.

On the supposition that the present era is again one of the increasingly frequent crises of empire, the question to ask is: to whose advantage? Is it safe to assume that the tone-setting legatees of defunct empires will be middle-sized and well-ordered entities, less nation-states than national economies, more concerned with the balances of trade and investment than with those of power and deterrence? Or will the future belong to unpoliced and unpoliceable entities whose policies revolve around internal or local balances of terror rather than regional balances of either trade or orderly power? Does the future lie with a composite Scandinavian-Japanese type or with the post-colonial African or post-imperial Iranian model, and in which proportion and distribution? The best that can be assumed is that, following the reduction of the Soviet empire, western societies will improve internally upon the Scandinavian-Japanese model while they retain enough of an "imperial" vocation to guide and supervise the evolution of the unevenly rich, fragmented, and unstable-to-chaotic other parts of the world to a like terminal point. The odds of this happening are not improved if the "other parts" include the *disjecta membra* of a disintegrated Soviet Union and empire. They are no better from a matching optimistic view undoubtedly held by some on the Soviet side, if differently biased and distorted.

Those who ignore or idealize the state likely to succeed to the demise of the Occident's western and eastern imperial structures will reject any idea of interempire solidarity. They will favor instead the strategy to subvert only the Soviet empire and discount all American-Russian similarities and symmetries as too schematically simplified. Thus schematized, the upheavals at the outset of the 1980s in central America (El Salvador, more directly affecting the United States) could be seen as comparable with those in southwest Asia (Afghanistan, closer to Soviet Russia) in one respect, and disturbances in eastern Europe (Poland, more critical for the Soviets) as not unlike those in the Middle East (Iran, more critical for the West) in another. The first of these pairs involved an irritating but not lethal upheaval, officially (if not always reliably) alleged by the nearer superpower to have been actively furthered by the remoter superpower against the other's interests and security. The second pair raised a much more critical threat to the vital interests of the most directly concerned imperial power and a much more critical question of how the other would react to the former's forcible or other efforts to reestablish empire cohesion.

Because Poland and Iran are undoubtedly the more serious problems, any (even superficial) parallels that throw a light on the predicament they cause for themselves and others are more noteworthy than is the similarity of position between El Salvador and Afghanistan. Just as Persia, so Poland was a major empire at one time; an autocratic leadership in both countries resumed regional power ambitions more recently (Pilsudski Poland in the interwar period, Pahlavi Iran in the latest postwar one). Although not immune to the desire to dominate, both peoples have shown a limited capacity to govern and discipline themselves for prosaic ends; they have repeatedly triggered more widely ramifying upheavals from this posture. Both at times paid the price of being partitioned. At vastly different costs in wartime suffering, Iran and Poland were, in terms of capitalizable resource or valuable real estate, among the winners of World War II. But the gains only fostered waves of social perturbation, initiated or supported by a combination of modernist impatience and persistent traditionalism. The impatience has been to consume material goods before producing them; the traditionalist desire, to conserve ideal (including religious) values—while the two desiderata fused in social groups owing their very existence to the differently inept "socialist" or "capitalist" modernizing efforts against which they rebelled. Finally, in both cases, the latest explosion was fueled by an effort to reject the tutelage of the imperial power and to either repudiate or reshape its local court- or party-clique surrogates.

At the point of explosion, there was a difference. In 1981, Polonophile romanticism was again injected into western reactions to Russia's Polish dilemma (as it had been in 1793, 1831, 1863, and, perhaps, 1939). No such emotional element seemed to enter into the more discreet Soviet reactions to the western embarassment in Iran. Yet on both occasions the immediate world-order issues were the same: whether the incumbent imperial power would be able to mix flexibility with firmness in a way reconciling the minimum needs of rebels and rulers alike; and whether, if "firmness" had to prevail, the rival empire would condone an empire-maintaining effort of last resort, or act to either frustrate or penalize that effort.

In the event, American forbearance or passivity in Iran did not give a chance to Soviet Russian leadership to show its hand in the matter; the present state of the Soviet mix of interempire solidarity and subversion has remained unclarified as a result. But, however doctrinally inexplicit or camouflaged, the U.S. attitude on Poland and (in different ways) Afghanistan has been clear enough in its basic message. It comes dangerously close to practicing against the Soviets the kind of interempire subversion the latter have been accused of engaging in indiscriminately against American imperial interests around the globe (including El Salvador and the Persian Gulf).

On only one assumption could U.S. foreign policymakers consider inter-empire symmetries nothing more than structural abstractions: if material and value dissimilarities are held to be all-important and wholly favorable to the United States. A policy inspired by this assumption was bound to overrely on the remaining economic superiority of America and on superior U.S. capacity to attract sympathies. Its proponents could not but discount the role of will or spirit, of the determination to cling to domination. Therein the shrinking American world empire has proved inferior to the still largely regional Soviet one. One reason is that, if the former was essentially accidental, obtained by inheritance from the Europeans, the latter one was built by organic accretion and conquest—as had been also America's regional empire before spreading and thinning out.

The prototype of the accidental empire by inheritance is the sixteenth-century global conglomerate of the Habsburgs. That kind of empire may be reinforced up to a point by a dynastic or a comparable transnational principle. If it is not, it will be all the more vulnerable to the principle of "easy come, easy go" when faced with trends to segmentation and symptoms of dissolution. Organic empires included the Byzantine, Ottoman, and Russian ones in the east. They will put up a stubborn fight before succumbing to secession and disintegration. An intermediate type of empire originates in conquest, but is buoyed up by fortuitous factors. Thus, the conquering second (India-centered) British empire was boosted by the accidents that added fuel to England's industrial revolution, and it was kept going, beyond its natural lifespan, by interstate competition on the Continent. Such an empire will struggle to hold on to its assets until a different arrangement emerges, one that meets continuing needs at less cost and effort. In the British case, such a different arrangement was the U.S.-upheld liberal world economic system.

As matters stand in the world at large, it is daring to assume that other and less onerous means have already satisfied the security and welfare requirements that induced the United States to accept succession to the European empires and even to enjoy it while the burden seemed easy to bear. Unlike the British, Americans cannot yet rationalize thus the descent from empire. The Soviet empire's globalization is in theory premised on a not so accidental inheritance from a decayed world-capitalist system; in practice, its managers are unlikely to accept secessions from its regional base without a fight. They will behave much as did their predecessors in the Byzantine and Ottoman empires. It mattered greatly for both of these empires at one stage or another how pressures and forces from the east (Anatolia for the Greeks, Persia for the Turks) would tie in with pressures from the west or, at flood tide, with opportunities westward. Their crises were near when gains in one direction could no longer compensate for losses or setbacks in the other; or when reacting either defensively or offensively in the two directions alternately proved too much.

It has been Russia's lot to incur early thrusts by the Varangians from the northwest and the Mongols from the east; to clash at midcareer with the

Anglo-French coalition in the Near East and with the Japanese in the Far East; and, most recently, to enter World War II by way of assault from Germany and to turn to Japan only at war's end. Thus, even if one admits partial exceptions—from the converging exactions by Teutonic knights and Mongol tribute collectors to Britain's complicity with Japan—truly serious hostile pressure rarely if ever came simultaneously from Europe and Asia; nor were Russia's offensive actions or counteractions in the two directions typically coincident. A coordinated U.S.-Chinese squeeze would thus face Russia with a novel situation, broadly analogous to Byzantium's dilemma between Crusaders and Islam and to the Ottomans' situation between Spanish or Austrian Habsburgs and Safavid Persia. The resulting "encirclement" could be relaxed either by conscious policy or by a failure of power or nerve on the part of America or China. If it was not, it would sharpen the choice for America and Russia between interempire solidarity and subversion; and it might add the option of surrender for the west Europeans caught up in a tightening vise of their own between a rash ally and an aroused adversary.

Interception in depth versus perimeter defense against rival empire. Joining outside pressure on the Soviet empire to internal pressure is the obverse of a strategy designed to decompress the environment of Soviet foreign policy within and without. However, to favor relaxation is not to propose resignation. It is not to imply that a permissive grand strategy does not have a grand-tactical component for both risk- and damage-limitation; that a basic commitment to turning the Soviet and the global dimension of decompression and diversion to positive internal and external effects rules out specific counterstrokes that exploit the attendant dispersion of the Soviet efforts.

Indeed, the decompression strategy implies and necessitates such counterstrokes against the adversary, not least if he is to be mollified by a combination of advance and attrition rather than stiffened by a passive or static defense impeding his internal, social and functional, diversification. Checking thrusts will be in order when the adversary either overextends himself or is drawn into vulnerable positions; whenever it thus becomes opportune to intercept the spearheads or interfere with the flanks of an expansion that is impossible to interdict at the rival system's immediate periphery. For efficacy, a western strategy can afford to be permissive at the fluid margins of overlapping superpower influence if—and only if—it is also elastic in depth; just as, for consistency, it can afford to be tactically mobile only if it is conceptually rigorous. Moreover, only when free concessions alternate with forceful constraints in the full range of effective U.S. options and operations will surprise become part of a settled strategy. Conflicting intramural evaluations of a disconcerting American policy will then help diversify inputs into Soviet policy within an externally decompressed environment of that policy.

The fundamental need is to replace an asymmetrical confrontation with a two-sided mobility of maneuver. The asymmetry has been in evidence whenever the current of one side's (the Soviet) expansion gathered speed while the other side impotently sought to stop fissures in the dam from widening and the dam itself from bursting; when one (the western) side has groped for the most risk-free single device for turning the tide while the other side was busy turning the positions of the defender. The defending side is at its most inept when, in different or the same parts of its domestic political spectrum, inflated language replaces impactful leverages and build-up of matériel substitutes for in depth strategic reflection.*

Strategic mobility is present when the geopolitical space is put to use as a vast field of operations, diversified in many respects but unified in a crucial respect. That strategic area is—and is treated as—one, where losses in one place cannot be always prevented, but may be compensated for by gains (or losses for the other side) in other places. An aggregate "net" balance of gains and losses will then often have to be the result of both parties to the central conflict being alternately kept or thrown off balance. But a minimum of world order will also require that the countervailing to counter-encircling activism of the rival great powers occasionally intersect in joint action against third and lesser parties, because no rigid or permanent line can be drawn between major- and lesser-power sources of disorder.

It looks sophisticated to deny the effective unity-in-diversity of the global force field. The likely consequence is to argue for a discriminating politico-economic strategy in regard to the several sectors or units of the third-world periphery; the corollary, to maintain an unbending politico-military strategy against a too-active resurgent great power at the system's center. A corresponding earlier, and now impossible, pre–World War II tendency was to ignore the global size and scope of the relevant balance-of-power arena with inhibiting effects on the strategy of appeasement. A restrictive conception of the possible range of basic modes of action with regard to the main adversary—complementing limitation with latitude, restraint with relaxation—has since replaced the restrictive conception of the arena. What has remained intact is an approach to the land-power challenger that is tactically reactive and strategically unimaginative to the point of being historically reactionary.

There are risks in shifting policy to a more dynamic conception of

*The verbal overkill was applied not only to Soviet movement into Afghanistan but also—by Republican as well as Democratic political aspirants in the 1980 election year—when criticizing the one proposal for a strategically mobile response (by Ronald Reagan) that suggested the "option" of a retaliatory blockade of Cuba. The merest possibility of an effective strategy was squeezed out between official worry over how to prevent U.S.-Soviet cooperation and alarms at the mere hint of flexible U.S. counteraction. A political culture that places a premium on publicly proclaimed alarms about audacious initiatives, and a professional establishment paralyzed by private worries about the implications of differently daring initiatives, is not likely to retain anything approaching command over events.

equilibrium and setting more positive goals than was characteristic of the strategy of containment—and would be of its watered-down "selective" variety. There are also good reasons for assuming the risks. The main one is that anchoring stability in more foreign-policy movement and greater internal (domestic-Soviet) depth points to a situation wherein peace is more likely than war between Russia and the West. To describe that state as appeasement is to use for lack of a less compromised term one that translates the original meaning of *apaisement* as inadequately as *détente* is transposed into "relaxation of tensions."

Yet before being a condition wrought by policy, appeasement must be among its objectives. As a policy poised between present risks and prospective rewards, it is burdened with the experience previously made—incurred as well as generated—by the west Europeans when facing Germany. But the west Europeans have since acquired an even greater stake than the United States in rehabilitating the policy vis-à-vis Russia, without venturing to revive its denotation. This diversity of outlook cannot but complicate intra-Atlantic relations and pit the need for maintaining the essential parts of the western consensus against the ideal of restoring, element by element, Europe's wholeness. The circumstances in which the second try at appeasement would take place are both novel and, in some striking particulars, comparable. As before, material interests and substantive values contend for attention and influence over policy with more formal or procedural principles; ultimate community of fate with Russia in Europe and in the Occident at large can variably outweigh or leave untouched the contrasting western and Soviet views and practices centered on force as an instrument of expansion outside, or oppression within, Russia's regional empire.

The dispute between the western and the eastern wings of the Occident is not superficial, being embedded in both time and space. Among the least deeply running sources of controversy are issues occasioned by parties that are both nonwestern and non-European; are either contestants in the world arena themselves or objects of contention between the world powers. Any diplomacy in and for the Third World will find it difficult to come to grips with native demagogy and antiwestern demonology. It is there that Russia is most apt to disown her westernness so long as she is not made to feel part of the West; it is there that the Soviets are most likely to violate the procedural rules and incur western rebuke, if not reprisal, so long as Soviet Russia lacks the efficacy for a wider range of influence and a subtler mode of seeking influence. But it is also there that the western powers themselves can unfailingly observe their preferred rules and restrain their own use of force only at a price in the currency of a different kind of effectiveness.

VI

TOWARD DECOMPRESSION.

Intra-Soviet and East European

Peace within the greater West—comprising Russia—is largely preferable to war. But genuine appeasement, as a conservative purpose implementing conservative perceptions, must be sought by a strategy that can be combative; the more philosophical is the conservative in temper, the more must he be defiant rather than defeatist in action when managing transactions in a world prone to revolution or upheaval. Genuine American-Russian appeasement requires, therefore, the activation also of the "defending" side if coordinated U.S.-Soviet action on the side of order is to be a realistic prospect. Co-optation of the potentially order-supporting, but immediately upthrusting, new actor does unavoidably entail concessions; but a concessionary strategy in geopolitical space automatically creates opportunities for counterstrokes into the exposed flanks of the forward party. Such opportunities must be used at appropriate times and in the proper places if eventual coalescence is not to be a misnomer for capitulation. This means that for a shift of power eastward to be offset by a mutation in its quality pointing westward, the erosion of traditionally triumphant American mass must be compensated for by refining the less congenial arts of mobility in political action and strategies.

If the rival is a continental heartland power, as is Soviet Russia, a way to reduce the tensions with it without abandoning competition is to divert its thrust away from the center of the system to the geopolitical periphery and overseas; if the rival is an authoritarian or totalitarian regime, the problem is to foster a measure of convergence of internal orders that entails a substantial measure of the regime's liberalization. A doctrine is present if the interlocking issues of geopolitical diversion and many-faceted convergence are addressed in explicit premises and propositions; a strategy, if they are brought together in and promoted by a policy best suited to foreclose major war without sacrificing essential values.

The strategy of decompression is targeted at both power distribution and value hierarchy, at both the external and the internal constituents of an appeasement that, as a condition, is the obverse of both nuclear Armageddon and subconventional anarchy. A major war is the proximate cause and ultimate controller of anarchy; its causes can be attributed either to appeasement as a misguided policy from weakness or to a provocative configuration of strengths. The former is a process and the latter a matter of structure; the degree and form of prior East-West convergence will influence the direction and thrust of either. The United States has a principal role to play in adjusting process to structure in behalf of peace in the larger West; but, because the core of the East-West conflict lies in Europe, and the values to be either protected or given a new lease on life by East-West appeasement are either European or Europe-derived, so too do the west Europeans have a part to fill.

Outlines of U.S.-Soviet convergence: social values and policy strategies

The question regarding Russia is whether a continuing growth of her power is compatible with the survival of truly essential western values; whether renewed percolation of these values eastward can serve as a corrective to an eastward drift of material power and political influence. The issue bears upon the erosion of Soviet ideology and the conditions for liberalizing the Soviet system. It can be dealt with in terms of the degree of convergence between the West and the East, the American and the Soviet systems, that is or seems possible.

Integration of values and co-optation of actors in political systems. If power were actually to shift eastward, but the mode of exerting it increasingly followed the western mode, the evolutionary direction would still be toward convergence. However, convergence as a process implementing an only seeming contradiction would have to come to terms with a two-faceted problem. Each facet has kept the western and the eastern branches of the Occident apart. One facet concerns the different ways of mal-integrating "power" and "spirit"; this bears on the mode of exercising power. The other facet involves the several ways of conservatism in statecraft. It bears on the mode of perpetuating and transferring order-maintaining power, as opposed to liberalism that is chiefly concerned with the transformation of power.

Both East and West have their peculiar ways of mal-integrating power and spirit. As to power, the bias in the east has been to escalate it into violence whenever a major nation, Germany or Russia, was on the rampage; to sublimate or negate power in the act of transcending a failed policy when the polity was on the ropes, or was recuperating between rounds of battle. The situation that conditioned the oscillation in Europe's east was one of dichotomy. Power was either fully present or fully absent, pointing to in-gathering aggression or to alienation from actuality. The western parties were by contrast almost invariably possessed of some power. Therefore, in lieu of dichotomy, typical for them has been the mere discrepancy between active and passive power, power in the ascendant or power in decline.

The realm of spirit is still more heterogeneous than is the universe of power. A typical way of mal-integrating the two in the east has been to oscillate between excesses of physical force and of intellectual fantasy about history and society. The relationship has been more elusive in the west. When any nation's power was active and ascendant, spirit was manifest as moral energy, whereas a passion for moralizing attended passivity or decline. The "typical"—and especially Anglo-Saxon—western nation was not to be rushed in modern times into deploying spirit to tame rival, and sustain faltering, power. It had to be cornered by a life-threatening crisis into replacing praise of its superior virtue with practice of stern *virtù*. The western tendency to complacency acted as either a depressant or an irritant in the east: it either aggravated the latent sense of powerlessness or exacerbated the use of briefly overflowing power. It rarely acted as a constructive stimulus.

The intrinsically different, but superficially coexisting, ways of mal-integrating power and spirit in west and east bred a predisposition to East-West conflict. Because, in addition, assertive power's rise and decline in the west and its presence or absence in the east were frequently poorly synchronized, conflict tended to translate into alternate catastrophes for one side or the other.

The pattern has had in recent times only intermittently antiliberal domestic effects in the west. It fostered the more thoroughly illiberal bias in the east. Reinforcing the problem have been the likewise different flaws in the conservatism typical of each part of the greater West. America has shown the way to the limitations of conservatism in the liberal-pluralistic western society overall. In Russia, the Soviet regime has been reverting to the other, authoritarian-bureaucratic forms of deformed conservatism exemplified by the tsars.

Thus, America has prefigured the impossibility of genuine, philosophical conservatism in and for a society that stresses individuality over community (and its institutional mold, the state) and equality over rank hierarchy (while substituting for it money- or skill-based stratification). Hers is a society that couples discontinuity between the objective conditions and the values of an early rural social order and the late-industrial one with the absence of an innate sense of continuity with the past and its link to the future. In Soviet Russia, at least one—the organic—dimension of philosophic conservatism has been latent in the regression to patterns of thought and behavior reminiscent of tsarist Russia. Its chances were jeopardized by efforts to neutralize the organic base and traditionalist bias of nationalism by fitting it into the institutional strait jacket of party-dominated statism. A simultaneous regression toward bureaucratic careerism inside and through the party was giving rise to a bastardized form of hierarchy. Soulless routines could not but dilute the peculiar historical sense and prophetic thrust innate in theoretical Marxism.

The rebirth of statist-bureaucratic conservatism reflected a decline of leftist ideology inside the Soviet Russian body politic and fostered its further decay. In America, communal-organismic conservatism lost out long ago to its corporate-business variety; it has also faded lately in western Europe before a species of neocorporatism. A conservatism that is confined to the cultivation of free enterprise is socially sterile on an emotional level. Thus it has been inevitable that efforts to express a revitalized conservative thrust and temper in U.S. policy would branch out ebulliently into foreign affairs, in the form of newly militant commitment to the world-wide defense of "freedom" from its enemies on the political left. Somewhat similarly at the end of World War I, the New-Freedom liberal reformism searched for a new lease on life through institutional-normative globalism, under the guise of collective security of the Wilsonian brand. It merely succeeded in setting off a reactive confluence of left- and right-of-center isolationism. The right-wing anti-Soviet neorealism has reacted more recently to the debacle left behind by an exhausted "new left." It replaced what had been a reaction to American imperialism with a new-right revolt against the implications of a previously unresisted retreat from America's world-wide unilaterialism. It was unlikely that one reactive lurch would improve on the continuity and coherence of policy achieved by another.

The difficulty of connecting social reality and values to genuine conservatism has contributed inside both West and East to a false and unproductive convergence between ideological and pragmatic approaches to foreign policy. The but superficial narrowing of the gap occurred in the west when the process of updating a residual conservatism led to reideologizing a customarily pragmatic approach to foreign policy; in the east, when an originally dogmatic *modus operandi* was partially deideologized conjointly with resurrecting traditional bureaucratism. A more productive convergence can take place only if tenets of philosophical conservatism are imaginatively directed to the interstate arena instead of being debased there. They may have to be wholly relegated to the international arena as the last remaining stage of political action still suited to the perceptions and practices of genuine conservatism by its hierarchical structure and continuity of historically evolved and vindicated essential procedures and processes. The world at large is a stage that more than ever, and more than any other arena, requires the distinctively conservative qualities of sympathetic appreciation of power dynamics and a politic disposition to ease evolution by discriminating co-optation.

A discriminating co-optation is not targeted at all and sundry. It is more narrowly focused on political activists or activated powers that are genuinely able and, if accorded a proper role, conditionally willing to help perpetuate the essentials of a marginally revised system. Their claim to a role will have to be conceded if it cannot be safely denied or deferred without heightening the risk of disruption. To be co-opted are, thus, actors who have been raised to prominence by something new; who can infuse fresh life into key elements of the old; and who might help preserve the revised order against forces that are unappeasable either inherently or for the time being.

To be preserved in an inchoate international system are the essential rules for the exercise and transfer of power among social or territorial actors capable of displaying the elementary means-ends rationality on which hinges the system's survival. Such essential rules are known, unlike the exact shape and form of the compromise unavoidably entailed in co-opting parties with an independent basis of strength. The unpredictability of the synthesis of old and new is real, but it is not radical: it need not comprise the system's uprooting from its base in instrumental rationality. Yet again, only a very special kind of policies will reduce the range of unavoidable uncertainty.

Ideally, if "power" and "spirit" are to shed the peculiarly western and eastern forms of their mal-integration, the (only theoretical) opposites of liberalism and conservatism must each make its special contribution. They will make this contribution if and when the superior concern of liberalism and the superior sensitivity of conservatism inform and correct one another. The peculiarly liberal concern is with improving the method for identifying the terms of consensus on what constitutes either interclass or internation justice; the especial sensitivity of conservatism is to the historical dimension of especially the latter kind of justice and to constraints that must be respected at all times if political adjustments are to work. Such constraints can be the most routine of limitations on what is practical in politics, or they can be vested in the most protean of mystiques—including that of historically validated rights or conferred entitlement. Reducing the gap between East and West from the sides of liberal procedure and conservative perception would ease the effect of differences in provisionally irreconcilable values. But for such an easing to be at all realistically postulated as a possible incremental growth, the notion of what constitutes convergence must be toned down. Convergence must be viewed empirically as a process of evolution that is open-ended as to duration and indeterminate in outcome—or, determinable only in retrospect as to the net thrust and balance of changes occurring unevenly on both sides of the divide.*

The scope and the limits of convergence relevant for policy. The question transcending immediate policy issue is whether and how a liberal-conservative integration of power and spirit, adjusting liberal mode to conservative mystique and liberal procedure to conservative perception, would be fostered by co-opting Soviet Russia into the leadership of a greater West. Practically, part of the answer lies with how to manage or modify the western strategy of containment; theoretically, another part lies with the attitude toward convergence.

It will not do to either preach or practice containment as a strategy that must be invariably rigorous as to criteria and rigid in execution if it is to be effective and productive (of Soviet "mellowing"?); nor will it do to relax containment on grounds of its momentary or local infeasibility only. It will be no more helpful to set up, only to more easily demolish, the straw man of both rapid and radical convergence—one, that is, which transforms polar opposites overnight into a pluralistic identity, and is the easy product of reciprocal magnetism rather than the delayed side effect of concertedly extended mutual deterrence. East-West convergence in strategic perceptions must precede one in societal foundations and institutional forms; both kinds can be at best the staggered outcomes of a rivalry over geopolitical (and other)

*The general temper underlying such views must be philosophico-historical in perspective at least as much as, in intention, socio-scientifically predictive. This is not quite the case in the otherwise masterly dissection of U.S.-Soviet similarities and differences in Zbigniew Brzezinski and Samuel P. Huntington, *Political Power: USA/USSR* (New York: Viking Press, 1964). As to direction, the book's concluding sentence, "The evolution of the two systems, but not their convergence, seems to be the undramatic pattern for the future," does not do justice to the (secondary?) features of growing similarity that the authors detail, and it begs the real question: Will the "evolution" be toward more similarity or more dissimilarity—and which in what, functional or fundamental, features of the two systems? As to duration, the possibility that the authors' perspective is too short is suggested by the following comment: "Today both China and India are at similar levels of [economic] development—yet no one would seriously argue that their political systems are becoming more alike" (p. 420). The proposition is hard to sustain from a longer perspective, capable of looking past Mao to Teng's pragmatism in China and at the (provisional?) culmination of a similar trend from Mahatma Gandhi to Nehru in Indira Gandhi (briefly interrupted by the Desai regression to the original Gandhi-ism) in India. The convergence seems to be toward a bureaucratic-authoritarian developmentalism more in line with the tenets of philosophically "realist" or "statist" traditions than with the tradition of ethical or other revolutionists or humanists in either country. Analogizing from, and setting up a contrast with, this apparent point of (ultimate?) Sino-Indian convergence in two subvarieties of "oriental despotism," the (ultimate) convergence point for the West and the East operating within the European or Europe-derived political culture would be in a nuanced, intrinsically more humane or "soft-minded," as well as more historicist, political realism than is the oriental one.

parity that has been moderated. Convergence neither will nor need lead to identity any more than the parity-evolving process itself will or need culminate in equality.*

As in the case of co-optation, something new and different will emerge in either case. In the parity-evolving process, this new element will become evident as "third" parties preempt part of the force field while the process (itself fostered by their emergence) is under way; in the convergence process, as both parties to it undergo some, if not necessarily equal amounts of, change as part of their competitive interaction. The unequally distributed sum of the two-sided change will represent the degree of the "ideal" synthesis that can be actually realized at any one time without mobilizing resistance to too abrupt changes—changes threatening to encompass each of the competing sociopolitical systems in its entirety.

Summarily put, for convergence to keep going as process requires initially no more than that the Soviet political system move on in the direction of "pluralism" and "pragmatism," while settled doctrine disciplines American foreign-policy making and shields it from changing moods and ideologies. Properly downgraded, progress toward pluralism means no more than multiplying specialized "inputs" into policy; it does not mean that the polity itself becomes more democratic. Deconcentrating authority in Soviet Russia does not require Americanizing the Russian polity into a free-for-all interplay of overtly codetermining interest groups contained by either settled or official doctrine only loosely, if at all. Authority is being deconcentrated and convergence is under way if, for reasons of efficacy, increasingly diversified political and technical elites become able to inject their specialized rationalities into the shaping of policy, and have to be taken into account within a political-administrative apparatus that is ever less homogeneous and rigidly hierarchical.

Insofar as pluralism is a response to efficiency requirements, it is congruent to pragmatism. Pragmatism begins to play a role within a political system when the system first reacts to the needs that are strongly felt and subtly communicated by the society; definite limits may continue to be set to such reactions by either officially perceived "state necessity" or presumptive imperatives of an official ideology. In foreign policy, pragmatism means primarily that the positive objective and the corresponding *modus operandi* of Soviet statecraft have shifted from world revolution to the pursuit of world power. Western statecraft follows suit when it shifts from an ideological rationale to a reason-of-state perspective: from the Soviet hypothesis that Communism is the wave of the future (in accordance with historical materialism) to the common-sense hypothesis that Soviet Russia is the power next in line in the bid for role parity or preeminence (in accordance with the historically evidenced trajectory of power migration).

*On the parity-evolving process, see the author's *Quest for Equilibrium* (Baltimore: Johns Hopkins University Press, 1977), ch. 9.

Both of the hypothetical perspectives are shaped by a keen sense of history and of Russia's place in the predicted future. But the difference between the two perceptions is great nonetheless, as is the difference in prescribed or preferred rules of conduct derived from them. The differences are too great to be disposed of by a western species of ideological revisionism, variably allocating most of the pretended residual or continuing role of ideology in Soviet policies to either the domestic, the east-European regional, or the global-peripheral, sphere. The insights such speculations produce do not persuasively rival the perception of Soviet Russia as a conventional anti–status quo revisionist power. That all too familiar posture supplies an adequate key to the interpretation of Soviet conduct, more so than any similarly well-defined conventional posture shapes American foreign policy most of the time—or illuminates the role of various ideologies in formulating U.S. policy.

In theory, the interpretation of Soviet external conduct based on ideology is weakened whenever Russia's strength is on the increase. The reason is that leaning on doctrinaire ideology will be less a function of a conflict's intensity than of the actor's ability to engage the opponent. In other words, recourse to ideology expresses either an insufficient ability to resist an effective wielder of power or one's own exclusion from exercising effective power. Neither condition applies any longer to Soviet Russia as a world power; or at least, not enough for her to compensate for the disparity between fact and fancy by confusing rhetoric with reality. This is true also when appearance or argument suggests that objectives or targets of Soviet policy are shaped by ideology. Thus, Soviet statecraft—as distinct from sloganeering—addresses the Third World ever less as the one remaining arena with revolutionary potential, to be nourished by public messages on the subject of (western) imperialism and exploited by subterraneous manipulations of its alleged objects; it deals with it ever more as one of the several arenas of crisis among incumbent regimes of all kinds and ideological denominations. In the conventional perspective, a crisis can be utilized for immediate advantage in the competition between the superpowers, and then as part of a vocally advertised difference between them; or a crisis can give rise to explorations of the momentarily feasible scope of cooperation between the great powers—and the purpose will then have to be somehow camouflaged as an insurance against the uncertainty of outcome.

Neither inside nor outside the Soviet Union is there an objective standard and impartial tribunal for judging ideological orthodoxy, least of all in foreign policy. Moreover, the conventional approach will be more effective, safer, and less costly than an ideological one in promoting a long-term success of the Soviet (or any other) regime, country, and appropriately modified creed. It will be so perceived soon enough and most of the time. For example, Soviet conduct in the Middle East conflict generally, and during the Iraqi-Iranian warfare in late 1980 specifically, fitted the conventional-pragmatic model of conduct closer than the revolutionary-ideological one. By contrast, the American official attitude vis-à-vis the postulated Soviet threat in the region displayed a highly ideologized perception of the Soviet objectives. An at least partial reason for this was the lack of materially based and doctrinally buttressed confidence in the efficacy of U.S. means to deal with the threat, be it in general or in the setting of warfare between two Islamic states (Iraq and Iran) in particular.*

If the process of change is to continue toward convergence, the American system will have to infuse a more unified doctrine into diplomacy even as the Soviet system continues diversifying the inputs into the policymaking process. The process may call for some institutional changes in America, but it is even more a matter of firming up social discipline. Such a discipline places society in a viable relationship to the state and, when necessary, subordinates societal pluralism to the authoritative locus of primary responsibility for defining policy priorities. In foreign affairs, this condition requires that internal desiderata are adjusted to fit the ultimate primacy overall of foreign policy in both doctrine and operations; it also means having a national strategy that warrants the concession of such primacy.

The cold war was a brief period of strategy-supported foreign-policy primacy in the United States. Since then, the erosion of the strategic consensus assisted the reassertion of domestic priorities in bringing America low in her external performance—and down to a common denominator with her western European (and Japanese) wards. That kind of convergence among the western allies in the ways of evolving policies has made for more rather than less numerous or serious divergencies in substantive policies. It spawned a crisis of leadership inside the coalition and postponed to Greek calends the prospect for effective common action outside its narrow perimeter. In short, the wrong kind of convergence in the present has undercut prospects for a different kind of confluence in the future. The strategies of allies need not be identical at all times. In some respects they may not usefully be such.

*Even a casual reading of the daily press in late September 1980 disclosed three features that bear directly on the analysis and argument. In a situation of well-documented fundamental military incapacity, the United States was unable to influence the belligerents significantly and keep them from freely destroying, in a contest over local stakes, the energy assets the West has not dared to touch forcibly in the face of a system-wide need. Unable to back diplomacy with the threat of effective interposition between the belligerents in the last resort, the U.S. administration seemed equally unable to induce its major allies (West Germany and Japan) to pledge participation in even a comparatively innocuous naval-military demonstration in the event of an academic contingency (the closure of the Strait of Hormuz by Iran). Finally, it panicked at the mere hypothetical prospect of the Soviets proffering a joint intervention to stop the fighting and confine the material damage and political instability resulting from the combat in different ways and degrees for the region and for the superpowers. See the *New York Times* series of articles on U.S. military unpreparedness, 21–27 September 1980; 27 September, p. A4, on the allies' reluctance; 25 September, p. A17, on White House national security aides' "worry" about a possible Soviet offer of cointervention; 26 September, A7, on Soviet self-restraint in the Persian Gulf war.

However, this is true only if they are responsive to changing world conditions at least as much as they reflect domestic conveniences or presumed compulsions.

For the American and Soviet foreign-policy-making systems in particular, convergence will prosper whenever the growing pragmatism in the latter is offset by the former's more doctrinal approach to strategy; when the growth in Soviet bureaucratic routines is matched by greater U.S. professionalism. While the autocratic regime becomes increasingly responsive to fundamental needs and demands of the society when external stakes permit, the elective one must be more often insulated from volatile public moods when external stakes so demand.

Advances in convergence will increase the chances of co-optation. The two together will augment the likelihood that a formal peace will continue between Russia and the West and will be gradually transformed into more than formal appeasement. And both convergence and co-optation will in turn depend on whether greater pragmatism in Soviet foreign-policy will be attended by domestic changes broadly describable as "liberalization."

Main core of convergence: erosion of ideology and relaxation of authority

Whenever a partial and temporary concert takes place between the Soviet and the American foreign-policy-processing systems, convergence in action keeps alive the trend toward (and hope for) convergence in kind. For such a movement to gather speed, the proper course was not to replace "static" containment with "roll back," one day targeted on eastern Europe by means of psychological warfare and another day on southwest Asia as an aid to a warlike psychology. The surer way than a policy of "liberation" of any hue and in any quarter is to discard a containment that continued to be static and became obsolete in favor of a strategy aimed at liberalizing first and foremost the Soviet core system itself.

Decompression, détente, and dogmatic ideology. There are reasons for expecting a measure of East-West convergence to come out of greater latitude for Soviet expansion. The background is relatively unequivocal. Historically, Russia expanded more efficaciously by gradual accretions over land rather than over water, or toward remote seas over great distances. This fact was related to internal authoritarianism as both cause and effect. However, unlike unified Germany, Russia did not so much force herself upon the international system with unassimilable overweight as she was repeatedly pulled into that system by its various disruptions. Within that general context, even as Russia's energies oscillated between Europe and Asia (without her ever disowning prime concern with Europe), setbacks in either theater tended to provoke redoubled self-assertion externally. The latter might be preceded by an internally reformist pause or coincide with the regenerative effort.

More difficult to document historically is the question of how a domestic political order adapts to an active foreign policy. The issue invites speculation about the relationship between predispositions rooted in ideology or culture and the political exigencies and instincts closer akin to felt necessities. It is a relationship as problematic as is that between material capabilities and policy intentions. To posit expansionist intentions on no firmer evidence than the adversary's apparent and locally usable material capability will go far toward stimulating the suspected intentions, by placing the adversary under pressure—verging on necessity—to deal with the imputation lest he appear to abdicate before a hostile presumption. When this happens, the negative attribution (of reflexive expansionism) frustrates the positive potential (of instinctive caution and practical expediency) for moderating ideologically or culturally magnified incentives to expansion. As positive inducements to greater pragmatism, caution and expediency may even foster a degree of liberalization in situations where ideology or culture make for an absolutist concentration of authority.

In the Soviet case, the erosion and politicization of ideology began when the goal of world revolution, to be achieved by conversion or subversion, yielded to the objective of world power to be realized by expansion. This meant, in extreme cases, substituting the duress of conquest for declining capacity to either retain or impart dogmatic conviction. However, the erosion of ideology will also continue if external diffusion of the power to influence, control, or coerce produces a stalemate with a rival power, and if that stalemate is sufficiently tight and even to compel a variable mix of diplomatic détente, geopolitically centrifugal diversion, and a restriction of military competition to armed deployments; and if, in addition, the diffusion of power abroad brings about a deconcentration of power internally as either a condition or the consequence of external efficacy.

Whether a central authority becomes less monopolistic because politics is deideologized or because ideology is politicized does not matter much. What does matter is that a more realistic approach to the world follows when the wielders of power have become responsive to a widening range of factors outside the body politic even if not—or not yet—either responsive or responsible to growing numbers within the polity. At the same time, ideology will erode steadily or cyclically by way of either rivalries or opportunistic transactions with diversely alien powers. Erosion is cyclical when the ideology's loss of potency is repeatedly punctuated by its resurgence, while in each successive phase ideology is less of a belief and more of a make-believe; its expression is less spontaneous and militant and more ritualistic and defensive; less coercive and more compulsive and conservative.

Thus, when it was spontaneously coercive, religious ideology carried Christianity into the crusades against Islam; at this point it was also a mechanism for draining off likewise spontaneous internal conflicts. When Christianity had been routinized by Rome and divided by Reformation, part of the reaction to declining fervor and cohesion was a second, compulsive, phase of ideological revival. Its external thrust, though impeded by tactical (Protestant-Ottoman) collusions, was directed to an Islam that had been similarly rigidified in the Osmanli caliphate. And finally, after the French Revolution, yet another religio-ideological revival, but one that was conservative this time, set in to defend the established order against a combined socioeconomic and secularist challenge. It found a secondary expression in missionary contests with Islam over proselytizing in remote places such as Africa.

Soviet ideology has evolved in a comparable rhythm. A coercively militant creed came first; then, in essentially defensive and increasingly compulsive responses to dangers of uncontrollable erosion, orthodoxy was ritualized; an overall conservative, regime-legitimizing role came last and survived all regressions longest. Were a virtually unopposed Soviet expansion to reopen the prospect for an induced world revolution, the ideology might retrace the evolutionary path all the way back to coercive militancy. But a compulsive reaffirmation of ideological orthodoxy is more likely to be triggered by a protracted exposure to severe stresses and setbacks. A regression could then be much less routine and more radical than have been the periodic efforts to turn back ideological erosion as a remedy to cleavages within the Communist movement or an offset to challenges (in the form of both rising and declining tensions) from the capitalist "camp."

Both stress and need for every possible defense would grow if Soviet Russia were increasingly confined within an ideologically and racially heterogeneous triangular context. An intense Russification could then readily reinforce the Soviet ethos. It would do so as the latent suspicion of a West ever ready to ally with Asia was mobilized into hatred against the West for actually weakening its own shield against Asia. A so reinforced Soviet regime would gain lasting legitimacy for the most illiberal internal order so long as it was plausibly needed to implement (in the words of a major pan-Slav poet-diplomat) "the law of [the Russians'] existence as a tribe and as an Empire."* The law is alleged to require Russian statecraft to offset latent or overt western hostility, and gain strength in what is now southeastern Europe and the Middle East, by exploiting all existing divisions in Europe—meaning, in our time, the Atlantic West.

The obverse is a relatively stress-free Soviet ascent to parity in world power. Its requirements and opportunities would tend to inflect political instincts

*Tyutchev, cited in Frank L. Fadner, *Seventy Years of Pan-Slavism in Russia: Karazin to Danilevskii, 1800–1870*, p. 289.

toward pragmatism. An ever more ritualized ideology would have the mainly conservative function of formally legitimating the Soviet regime. Even if unpopular on all other grounds, that regime would be materially vindicated by raising Russia's standing abroad at a bearable cost to living standards at home. Ideology could then be indefinitely adjusted to the internally relaxing effects of externally secured new latitudes. Increased pragmatism would progressively attenuate the sporadic relapses into ideological orthodoxy serving as a residual check on too abrupt a dissolution of internal disciplines following upon external decompression. It might do more and help mute another transitional tension within the Soviet system: The symptoms of progressive deideologization (including spells of reideologization) are unlike the symptoms of regressive Russification; without some help from pragmatism, the two sets of symptoms would not necessarily merge in a materially liberalized synthesis.

Expansion of power and deconcentration of authority. At this point the perspective moves from the patterns and stages through which state ideology and foreign policy become more pragmatic to the internal order and its possible liberalization. While the historical precedent becomes almost wholly subservient to the hypothesizing temper, the relevant time span extends to a yet longer term. However, the issue is no less central to present strategic choices for being speculative: the grander the strategy and the graver the stakes, the more tactical cleverness and tactically informed guess must yield to inspired speculation. Yet, for such speculation to be serviceable as well as inspired, it must deduce principles of politics from recurrent tendencies of power and integrate both with historical precedents into a doctrine that is more than momentarily opportune and thus more than ephemeral.

An increasingly pragmatic foreign policy can long do without increasingly "liberal" domestic policies. Effective liberalization is similar to an eroded ideology formalized into a conservative function: both enhance regime legitimacy. But they do so in different social depths and over different time spans, even if they may ultimately depend upon one another for lasting results. Similarly, notable military capabilities can long exist and have an effect without notable economic and political efficacy. But just as foreign-policy intentions can be only dubiously inferred from capability without taking into account wider power configurations, so too physical capabilities will not be either secure or effective for long without wider-ranging efficacy. Yet again, different kinds of domestic efficacy will be required for different kinds of expansion. A coercively imposed, autocratic type of efficacy will be both required and fostered by an all-out expansionary drive for hegemony, induced by compelling patterns (including triangular ones) of power and carried out mainly overland and with military means against opposing major states. A more spontaneously generated efficacy will be better suited to the other type of expansion, one gradual, moderate, and—because it is undertaken in both continental and overseas theaters—mixed. Such expansion will depend on economic means at least as much as military ones being projected abroad and applied indirectly mainly to the lesser powers. It will have to take into account the normatively constraining state of world politics, as well as take advantage of the more relaxed structure of world power.

In the transitions from the late Bourbon era to the first Bonaparte era in France and from the emperor-type of rule to the *fuehrer* regime in Germany, the change was from a relatively liberal to a more coercive regime, the first engaged in first-phase continental-maritime activism and the second undergoing the strain of an only-continental but escalated, second-phase expansionism. Had the global outreach of Imperial Germany been flexibly managed by England, rather than being blocked by the Entente, the essentially liberal (even if "national-liberal") economic and political forces behind the Wilhelminian naval and colonial program would have undoubtedly gained progressively on the dominant rural and reactionary (Junker) forces. The shift would have implemented a close connection, nearing complementarity, between incipient overseas imperialism and early-stage domestic liberalism, first exemplified by the Athenian democracy.

Newly revealed external outlets may not divert the energies or the attention of lower classes or repressed groups from their grievances either immediately or sufficiently. But they do compensate ruling-class interests for whatever concessions to lower-class demands have become politic or proved necessary. Interclass transactions that revolve around outlets abroad for energies, and around compensations at home or abroad for self-restraint, are crucial for phasing social change over time. The change is least upsetting if it appeases the less privileged group, because the change is sufficiently liberal in kind or thrust, and if the most conservative among the elites accept it as one that is liberally offset by compensations including the consecration of the retained function or privilege. Because an unfolding imperialism preserves and expands the foreign role of such elites, they will find in it a most convenient mechanism for coming to terms with the reduction of their domestic authority consequent upon internal reform.

Fully manifest in a country like Britain, the interplay was not wholly absent or ignored even in Russia. Typified by Nicholas I, autocracy at its peak opposed overseas ventures. But forces interested in internal reforms (e.g., the so-called neo-Slavs before World War I) were aware of the connection between effective reform and successful outreach abroad. In the event, neither outreach nor reform materialized in either the late-tsarist era or the initial liberal phase of the revolution. When the Soviets became active overseas, an internally rigid domestic structure continued to handicap these activities relative to either Soviet action on land or to the nonmilitary efforts of Russia's maritime rivals. The regime has thus come up against a quandary. It can either relax domestic controls or let the direction of expansion be indefinitely determined by the waning advantage of the overland route. Worse still, it can disregard the declining marginal utility (or increasing disutility) of additional continental gains relative to initial efforts undertaken overseas (or internally by the overseas route) and precipitate thus the dreaded power configuration impelling a risk-maximizing all-out overland drive.

Overseas expansion interacts causally with domestic political and economic liberalization. It does so whenever expansion promotes liberalization, and liberalization supplies new incentives to continue expansion or new methods to consolidate it. Tsarist Russia's largely military expansion came to a halt when the initial predatory drive was exhausted, when the preclusive response to foreign (British and Japanese) rivals in the Far East proved no more forceful than local challenges to the imperial frontier in other areas were compelling, and when the outcome of the Russo-Japanese conflict reopened the question of the traditionally vital connection between wars and internal economic growth. Domestic conditions had previously stimulated expansion. But they did so mainly as a diversion from unproductive internal strains, except when an embryonic capitalist middle class acted as a stimulus to economic expansion—a rare exception, fostered by an unusual policy such as Witte's before 1904. For the West to accept overseas Soviet expansion as a continuing process may be henceforth the price to pay for an eventual common good: the linking up of positive domestic incentives to such expansion with the relaxation or deconcentration of internal Soviet authority structures.

In a "classless" socialist society, technocratic elites and foreign-assistance specialists have a major stake in overseas expansion. They can expect some rewards, at first chiefly material, for their indispensable part in making the expansion effective. In a general theory of imperial expansion,* such elites take the place of a middle class gradually ascending over a landed aristocracy that fades along with its capacity to compensate the former with economic gains and social status gains at home for delaying or lowering its pretensions to effective political power. In the Russian context, a reorganized political autocracy leaning on the military remains the "ruling class." The social origins of its leading members are less middle-class than are those of the technically specialized elites. Although the latter elites' support for expansion might be functionally identified with the one-time landowning interest's when it backed penetrations into central Asia (for the sake of securing the Black Sea exits for Russia's grain exports), the specialized elites' more direct

*I refer, again, to the framework developed in *Career of Empire.*

line of succession is to Russia's turn-of-the century city-based interests. Whenever they favor or foster overseas expansion, the technocrats and the specialists take over where the traders and the capitalists left off when governmental inefficiency and insufficient popular support had undermined their stake in protected east-Asian outlets for noncompetitive manufactures.

Political liberalization need not depend on a capitalist middle class, nor will it necessarily generate such a class. It will do so least of all in a "socialist" society. Nor need an expansion that has initially coupled economic growth and war evolve into a full-fledged "informal" or "free-trade" imperialism, more reliably predicated on peaceful conditions than it perpetuates them. Yet even so, if expansion attains global scope or is keyed to global ambition, it may still propel industrialization toward a level that will compel an ever less rigid regulation or centralization of the economy. This is important in the Soviet case if penetration into the global (third-world) peripheries is to be more successful than it was for any prior Russian regime, and more lastingly successful for the Soviets than it has been so far.

To this end, the Soviet regime will have to reduce and diversify dependence on military or paramilitary instruments, including military aid. In the best of all possible worlds, such an imperative would set off a virtuous circle. As world policy pushes the Soviet system into the quest for more efficient economic organization and policy, an increased dependence on western technology and other forms of economic aid would help regulate the rate and extent of Soviet world-wide activism. Moreover, as the potential and the needs of Soviet industrialism grow, so would the Soviets' perceptions of the Third World as a source of threats to Soviet economy, as well as of opportunities for Soviet diplomacy. The least signs of U.S.-Soviet solidarity vis-à-vis third-world pretensions or disorders would make it more acceptable for the West to see the Soviets advance toward more symmetry with America, also as a naval power.

It would consolidate U.S.-Soviet solidarity and symmetry if they coincided with even a token convergence of internal political structures. Such convergence gets under way in a practical fashion whenever political influence in the Soviet Union drifts ever so little toward middle- and upper-level technocrats due to the shift from military to economic instruments of world policy. The least such drift will narrow a gap between Russia and the maritime West, which is far from new. The gap originated in the consequences of the Mongol invasion and solidified when mid-seventeenth-century internal dislocations and the Petrine administrative revolution arrested the renewed growth of the Russian mercantile class. The atrophy of that class turned the military into the main impetus behind modernization and also transferred to it the mandate to open, as well as protect, Russian access to trade.

Russia's military-economic-political dialectic may or may not be in keeping with the theoretical tenets of economic determinism. It has nonetheless made her gradual economic and political modernization largely a function of the military factor. The trend began when the seventeenth-century gunpowder revolution impelled a measure of initial modernization. The military-technological innovation even set off a short-lived primitive democratization, as the unfamiliar weapons system shifted the grounds for preferment from noble birth (of the cavalryman) to technical expertise, at first foreign-mercenary. When military excursions abroad had exposed the Russians themselves to the outside world, the early nineteenth-century Decembrists were the first to go beyond abortive quasi-democratization to sociopolitical revolution as the consequence of this exposure. For this reason, if for no other, it would be risky for the Soviet regime to go on depending on military strength for relief from the consequences of either economic backwardness or political stagnation. Nor would the regime find remedy in leaping from war-related economic growth directly to employing the military-strategic assets of empire for the protection of a regressive economy. Such a leap would bypass, within a regional compass, the normally intermediate state, taken up by more liberal global-imperial economics. Attempting such an overleap would be to accept as final for Russia a condition that historically was the stigma of declining post-liberal empires and a source of trauma for the empire-building and empire-managing ruling class.

Russia's record of time lags suggests instead that she would in due course follow the western prototype into an imperfectly liberalized imperialism on a global scale. Under the tsars, various delays behind western models preceded other instances of sociopolitical change toward greater liberty, including the abolition of serfdom and incipient constitutionalism. The same record also permits, to be sure, less auspicious propositions. Thus, the relatively liberal past departures can be seen as somehow connected with military defeats, as also were instances of autocratically imposed modernization, including the Petrine and the Soviet. Or, contrary to the more hopeful speculative hypothesis, it may be noted that Russian expansionism coincided with political reaction: under Nicholas I in the Caucasus (in the 1840s); under Alexander II in Central Asia (in the 1860s after the rightward turn due to the Polish rising); under Nicholas II before 1905—and, most recently, under Brezhnev regressing from Khrushchev's globally expansive domestic "liberalism."

However, it is equally true that authoritarianism accompanied instances and forms of expansion that were by and large of the overland, military-bureaucratic kind. They differ from overseas penetration, which must be also economically efficient if it is to last. By the same token, for the government to tighten its grip on dissolvent domestic repercussions of a relatively outgoing, expansive foreign policy from time to time as in, say, the Brezhnev era, is one thing; the net effect of overseas outreach over the long term is another thing. The latter is apt to be internally relaxing, all the more if contrasted with the cumulative effect of imposed or self-imposed isolation. It is, furthermore, equally necessary to distinguish between noncomparable entities when considering any coincidence or connection between reform and defeat. Intended as remedies to military setbacks were abrupt and shallow reforms. They presaged political instability without hindering renewed military self-assertion. Such reforms are poles apart from the more gradual and enduring modernization. Although its closest tie is to economic proficiency, such modernization also grows out of steadily increasing military efficacy. The military kind of efficiency, although increasingly insufficient for a lastingly rewarding expansion, is still required to underpin even an economically slanted overseas drive. The military and the civilian sectors have continued to be segregated to a large extent in the Soviet political and technological economy. However, they neither can nor will long continue in that state of separation once a well-rounded world policy has become a peacetime ingredient of strictly national-defense policy.

It will take time before incompatibilities and corrective tendencies become fully manifest. But it is unlikely that, before gradually constraining the Soviets, modern conditions would favor a western strategy keyed to the connection traditional for Russia—a strategy that would set out to create occasions for inflicting military defeats on the Soviet Union for the sole purpose of promoting political or social reform inside it.

It was initially correct and effectual to contain a quasi-Asiatic, Stalinist despotism with a view to its internal mellowing. In a politically inert and economically retrograde society, an invariably forcible expansion will be the only possible one; it will impress the leadership as either useful or necessary if the need is to intimidate subjects or facilitate adjustments among competing elite ambitions and fears. Forcible expansion may then be the only available alternative to an ultimately self-defeating repression of the subjects or rifts among the elites; blocking it from the outside will sharpen the regime choice between growing stress and immediate efforts to gradually alter the conditions that make eventual decay inescapable. When, by contrast, positive and potentially productive social and economic energies have developed, their internal compression will increase the need for diverting them abroad. This, too, will impel expansion. But, because the expansion need not then be invariably forcible and will not be, as is the other, as inherently limitless in the underlying drive as it is limited in its instruments, it can foster internal relaxation as well.

An authoritarian-totalitarian regime will undoubtedly impose ad hoc constraints from above on degrees and forms of "liberalization" that are neither authorized nor immediately controllable; but some residual, and on balance cumulative, loosening up of the internal authority structures will occur nonetheless. The parallel expansion may be usefully circumscribed from the outside, but it neither need be, nor must it be, wholly blocked. Only if its global outreach is inhibited but not prohibited, is the global expansionist himself free (in terms of the requisites of domestic stability) to be forced (by the requirements of external efficacy) to unblock economic and political processes within the country. A policy committed to diverting an expansionist power to targets and objectives that promote decompression within, as part of diminished constraints from without, can, therefore, follow without much fear and trembling upon a containment that, while among the factors inducing the rival regime to "mellow," has stiffened its resolve to expand the range and improve the results of national self-affirmation.

If it has become possible to adopt a foreign-policy strategy keyed to promoting the maturation of Russia as more a European-type industrial society and state than an oriental-type despotism, it is equally possible that more policy pragmatism will make the revival of cultural nativism comparatively benign. A long-term erosion of Soviet communism by Russian nationalism, with the aid of regime-legitimating successful world policy, is different from employing artificial techniques to make the regime appear national. But, although the distinction is important, its constituents may in fact follow one another in a productive sequence. Ideological erosion rooted in political success may build upon and make irreversible selective revivals of the Russian heritage—in specific institutions or generalized myths—that were at first opportunistically engineered under the stress of various kinds of survival crises by either a single autocrat (Stalin) or a transient "collective leadership" intent on conquering personal or safeguarding regime power.

Official nationalism differs as much from spontaneously expressed patriotism as a despotically frozen system differs from an extraneously compressed dynamic society. Both distinctions have connecting links with the inherently controversial difference between rising and declining powers. A declining power will try to pursue an expansionary foreign policy in order to offset the atrophy of internal social dynamism. The compensation will be mechanical and contrived; the political regime will have run out of the capacity to either generate or tolerate social forces of creation and regeneration. It will only retain some capacity for forceful compulsion abroad, a compulsion all the more assertive for being feeble and waning. This interplay between foreign and domestic politics is different in a rising power, and it will tend to be the reverse one. Marrying a continuing rise in power potential to foreign-policy efficacy will demand initiative and innovation: this will call for releasing the social forces that the regime has previously reined in during the delicate phase of generating the material conditions of an initial ascent from a low starting point.

The related question is fundamental for any contemporary foreign-policy doctrine and strategy. Is Soviet Russia an intrinsically declining or an initially rising power? If it is the latter, the issue for strategy is whether and how to implement the assumption that conceding a leeway for actualizing the potential will work to reduce the ultimate scope of expansion and soften an either hostile or disruptive use of intervening gains. The implied risks are matched by the risks of treating, and trying to block, the Soviet Union viewed as externally expansionist because internally stagnant and irreversibly declining.

It will take insight and courage to wager on a tolerable outcome of the rising-power hypothesis; it will also require patience to win the wager. And it will take these same qualities, bred by the historical temperament, to resist the temptation to adopt the short-range view, the negative presumptions, and the elementary mechanics of containment as guides to both interpretation and response. It may be that a conservative doctrine is more attuned to seeing liberalization grow out of an intrinsically limitable geopolitical expansion than is the liberal doctrine. The conservative's faith in organic change may be more pertinent to the issue than is the liberal's inclination to attribute beneficial change mainly to participation in infinitely expansible world trade—or cooperation within its contemporary institutional equivalents.

A westward-inclining East-West convergence in political structures is bound to be problematic and may be questionable. But it may also be the only long-term alternative to its opposite, an eastward-inclining convergence toward militarism or even authoritarianism (in the West) as part of a continuing and escalating conflict. A prolonged conflict *always* narrows the initial gap in the makeups of the contestants. The chief question is which way and on what level of sociopolitical reality the narrowing takes place.

A secondary and related question concerns the scope of arenas involved in the convergence process. When a polity such as the Russian is also a regional empire, the metropolitan and the imperial arenas will of necessity interact and communicate to one another impulses toward either greater or lesser centralization of authority. It is one thing to (correctly) believe that the decisive and lasting changes for better or worse must and will first occur in the domestic arena of the imperial polity; it would be a different (and wrong) belief to hold that what happens within and to the dependent empire is without effect on the internal developments. Nor would it be correct to assume that because internal liberalization of authority is tied to the extension of power or influence overseas and to freedom from world-wide encirclement, it is unrelated to relations within the narrower compass of the land power's continental habitat—in Russia's case, the European as distinct from the wider Eurasian. This means, simply, that Soviet Russia's liberalization is inseparable from her Europeanization; that East-West convergence has, next to its U.S.-Soviet dimension, a strictly European one that might call in conditions of stress for a form of collusion.

Regional oppression and intra-European accommodation: easy principles and irreplaceable values

A global Soviet outreach will outgrow its regional base in the established Soviet empire in eastern Europe in the search for an additional security rampart and resource base. Yet the wider periphery will eventually cause the inner core to dissolve. The imperial ruling or managerial class will have to direct its attention ever more outward; the challenge of coordinating the disparate requirements of world-wide appeal and regional ascendancy will be increasingly perplexing; and the contradiction between the need for central control and the pressures for local autonomy will become fully manifest. Incoherences will result and begin to flow sooner or later inward, deranging the control mechanism and interfering with whatever might be or become its base in consent.

The solvent effect of the grand empire on its regional support system and domestic core will normally assert itself only in the long run. One method for accelerating the loosening up is to enhance, another is to try to reduce, the external pressures or internal needs and compulsions that were coresponsible for the empire's coming into being. The safer prescription for a peaceable transition is for controls to be relaxed gradually until they are converted into consent. However, decompression in the global setting and from the outside must be the means to this end before it can be the outcome intraregionally or domestically.

The Russian empire in Europe and western principles. Whereas the United States has the primary role in managing Soviet Russia's global outreach, western Europe (whether she wishes it or not) has a primary role and responsibility in helping relax controls in the Soviet core empire in eastern Europe. There, not in the Third World, is the foremost stage on which the west European middle powers can recover the full statehood forfeited in and through World War II; it is there that they can find, that is, a meaningful engagement on a politico-military issue of high policy, one that is as directly related to their individual survival as it is critical for the global balance of power and world order.

Eastern Europe surpasses the Third World as a west European priority in terms of both importance and timing. If they correctly evaluate threats from different sources, the west Europeans will usefully differentiate their diplomatic and economic policies on the European issue from those of the United States even as they get ready in attitude and ability to act politico-militarily with the United States in the global peripheries. Their contributing thus to East-West accommodation first on the European plane and thereafter on the global will justify any intervening frictions with the United States over tactics. Reinforcing the underlying differences of geography and history are the Euro-American divergences in material interests, themselves due to an essential similarity or even identity in economic structures and needs. In themselves inevitable, such differences and frictions can be progressively reduced and eventually absorbed only if the awareness of identical goals on the dual East-West issue creates a basis for tolerating complementary approaches; if the concern to coordinate every step is qualified by the awareness that what matters more is to synchronize desirable outcomes over a longer period of time.

Over the same quarter of a century, the challenge that the Soviets offered to the United States has included a series of probings in the global peripheries (from, roughly, the Suez crisis via the Cuban issue to Afghanistan). The simultaneous challenge to western Europe has been punctuated by a series of Soviet repressions staged in or rehearsed for in what is, seen from the west, Europe's periphery. The two sides of the problem created for the West by the Soviets were linked by the temporary impacts each had on East-West tensions and their relaxation, arms control and arms competition, as well as on different forms of intra-alliance cooperation in east and west; the deeper interconnection was in the fact that Soviet actions in both arenas were expressing the same combination of regime determination and ineptitude that is the natural offspring of a transition from an industrially backward and military-continental system of power to an economically more diversified if not necessarily efficient, and politically expansive, if not necessarily limitlessly expansionist, one.

This tormented metamorphosis added world-wide interests to Soviet regional concerns, while its ramifications within the Soviet-dominated region introduced additional sources of domestic upheaval, especially in the less-developed parts of eastern Europe. The latter followed the industrializing third-world countries into the "revolt of rising expectations" on the mass level, with manual workers increasingly ready to add their sheer weight and ideologically embarrassing identity to the aspirations of intellectual elites chafing under the rigidity of a *laager*-type orthodoxy. The confluence of the material-organizational and the cultural-professional desiderata of these two key groups made it possible to subsume both under the unifying rubric of individual freedoms and human rights. The resulting ferment and intermittent upheavals faced the once-revolutionary Soviets increasingly with a highly conventional problem of empire management: that is, how to blend central control and local autonomy in an enduring and endurable system of authority that would be at once diversified and dovetailing, susceptible to marginal changes but immune to basic challenge.

The problem is one that no empire on record, including the American, was capable of solving satisfactorily for any length of time. It is also one that the west Europeans themselves solved only late in their career by divesting themselves of formal imperial authority overseas and settling for economically underpinned informal ties. The problem has been made worse for the Soviets by an unusually severe ideological constraint and by a less than average amount of situational leeway. The ideologically posited irreducible requisite, of leadership monopoly for the communist parties, has made political adaptation difficult; the root cause of mass disaffection, the inadequacies of socialist economies, has made the need for adaptations ideologically humiliating. Thus, the ideological factor has placed the Soviet Union at a disadvantage relative to more pragmatic past or present imperial core powers, to the same extent as the factor of economic organization disadvantaged it relative to more productive ones.

An empire thrives on blending administrative compellence or forceful coercion with material and psychological inducements to consent. The insular or otherwise insulated core powers—most conspicuously the "Anglo-Saxon"—dominated mostly remote dependencies from a large margin of metropolitan security and material resource. They could afford to be pragmatic and even liberal. Not so the continental empires all the way from counterreformation Spain to national-socialist Germany. Like the Soviet one, they all tended toward ideological dogmatism and administrative tyranny. Extraneous pressures on the continentals were both contiguous and remote sea-power supported. They made the security or control margins correspondingly narrow for the core powers, while the rebellious reactions of dependents to actual constraints, or their secessionist defections toward outside sources of hoped-for relief, made the imperatives of both security and control seem all the more compelling—only to see the resulting repressions either invite or legitimate additional self-interested pressures by outsiders.

In the setting of regional empire, the authoritarian-to-totalitarian dynamic is as much due to geopolitically conditioned power structures as it is to historically conditioned sociopolitical group structures within national settings; it is more commonly due to either of these than to any peculiarities of culture or ideology. The ramifications of such a dynamic were always easy to exploit by powers whose safeguarded situation permitted more freedom at home and, conjointly with the resulting political culture, was compatible with respect for a measure of liberties in the dependencies abroad. However, as one form of oppression in the east followed another, from the atrocities actually or allegedly wrought by Turk or Tsar to later ones, the objects of the not always disinterested solicitude did not invariably benefit from the liberal concern.

Nor was solicitude invariably converted into effective action against the "oriental" oppressor when the more liberal western power lacked easy access or pressing interest: the nineteenth-century Polish risings and Bulgarian or Armenian suffering met with a different and less potent kind of western response than did the Greek revolts. Matters have not fundamentally changed by the late twentieth century, when the endemic Russo-Polish crisis resurfaced in 1980 as the focus for East-West relations in Europe. The basic conditions, considerations, and complaints in the west were not unlike those in 1831 or 1863; they differed from those in 1920–21 (the last time a Polish regime sought eastward expansion under the cover of Russia's "time of troubles") even more than from those in 1939 (when the situation was back to its modern norm).

There have been some changes, to be sure, from one century to another. But the determining difference has not been between feudal-agrarian and industrial stages of civilization, between a multipolar and a bipolar international system, or between a pre- and postnuclear military balance. The crucial difference is in the slate of primary actors. The west European states, once the main competing actors, are now only subsidiary ones in world politics. The related transformation of Europe as a whole is from the center of a global balance-of-power system into a fragmented part of a wider balance—a part, moreover, in danger of being further downgraded if some form of continental or regional solidarity continues to be absent. Relations between Soviet Russia and eastern Europe remain an object of concern and a source of crises in the new circumstances. But they are also an opportunity. The challenge for western Europe is how to help defer or defeat the final supersession of the continent as a power center; the question, whether this can be done by displaying for the vulnerabilities of Europe's last-remaining great power an understanding, if not necessarily sympathy, that does not translate into disinterest in the lot of its dependents; the dilemma, how to fit a morally distressing partner (Soviet dictatorship) into a politic purpose (a gradual and safeguarded attenuation of the controls that dictatorship deems mandatory for its security and survival) without the suspicion of moral insensitivity compounding the absence of political or military strength.

Western Europe between America and Russia. So long as they were being suspected, Soviet preparations for the invasion of Poland had repercussions in the west similar to those of the accomplished Soviet invasion of Afghanistan. The questions were whether talk about U.S.-west European cooperation to deter or punish a Soviet invasion would evolve into close complicity in action; whether lopsided warnings prefigured lopsided sanctions—many warnings to the Soviets not to intervene and few, if any, to the restless Polish workers not to provoke an intervention; sanctions economically and otherwise more onerous for the west Europeans (and the Soviets) than for the United States. The scope of stressful complicity among western nations was limited by the west Europeans' greater fears of Soviet reactions, rooted in geography. It was further reduced by policy dissonances created by the wrong kind of Euro-American convergence (toward shared primacy of domestic politics) and the consequently reinforced competition (over comparative economic gains from East-West détente in Europe, and gains and losses from alternative strategies in the Middle East).

A West self-satisfied on value issues to the point of relapsing into moralistic westernism looked to changes on the Soviet side in Europe that would be virtually cost free and nearly effortless. Extreme domesticism and economism, whenever gaining ground in American foreign policy, prompted the desire to retain the favorable position in the world at large with equal ease—except for intermittent reversions to hardware-obsessed militarism entailing mainly fiscal, when not also intra-alliance political, costs.

A west European strategy that would seek a corrective to these several -isms, denoting excess or deformation, would have to offset the three Atlantic *c*'s: complicity (anti-Soviet), convergence (toward domesticism), and competition (economic), by the policy of two pro-European *b*'s. West Europeans have first to act as *brokers* between the United States and the Soviet Union, as well as between the Communist regimes and their oppositions in the Soviet bloc. On the strength of this brokerage they could serve as a *bridge* on which Russia could begin to cross westward as part of her role-integration into the international system as a whole. Neither function could be successfully performed previously, when tried too soon and from too weak a position. The west Europeans might succeed if their moving toward the role of coguarantors of stability in eastern Europe with Soviet blessing coincided with Soviet Russia becoming a coguarantor of order in critical regions outside Europe with American blessing. All the parties would have to accept the complementary "partnerships" as a state to be attained gradually and concurrently. To do so, they would have to restore primacy to foreign policies keyed to defusing the propensity to unrest and conflict that was aggravated by, when not lodged in, manifest bipolarity and latent triangularity.

For the west Europeans to be acceptable as brokers between Soviet Russia and the east European peoples, they must be perceived in the east as honest brokers; but for them to act as coguarantors of the Soviet order in eastern Europe, they must be accepted as coregulators of a widely acceptable rate of change there. The rate must be compatible with Soviet Russia's security in the region and ambitions in the world, while meeting ever more of the elementary needs of national patriotism, material prosperity, and general well-being in the region's smaller countries. Even as the west Europeans acquired material (i.e., economic) leverages in eastern Europe, they would have to be reliably evenhanded in discouraging excess both in demands for change and in repression of moderate aspirations. The initial objective is to flatten extreme fluctuations in revolutionary (or, in Soviet parlance, counter-revolutionary) demands and reactionary repression (or, in Soviet parlance, acts in defense of socialism); the longer-term object is for west European infusions of credit and technology to help inflect the interactive effects of Soviet-bloc economic industrialization and Soviet political globalization toward stability of the regional empire, as a greater and growing material proficiency permits Soviet rulers to incur "freely" the risks of liberalization in order to further increase efficacy through enhanced legitimacy.

Material links have been forged and have grown between western Europe and both Soviet Russia and non-Soviet eastern Europe by way of western credits and advanced technology and eastern energy sources and trade outlets. But the economic cross-dependence would lack an appropriate complement in political evenhandedness so long as the west Europeans sacrificed long-term stability to self-indulgent emotionality, token sanctions, and celebrations of Atlantic solidarity at critical junctures in relations between rulers and ruled in the East.

A broadly based long-range *Ostpolitik* for gradual change in eastern Europe and for the confluence of the two Europes is not a neat matter of nice adjustments as part of a good-neighbor policy. It does not mean trading a piece of East-West détente for a commensurate piece of western-style democracy in eastern Europe at every point; nor will economic and technological infusions from western Europe and resulting links with eastern Europe necessarily promote improvements there in a smooth, gradual, and linear fashion. The process of change cannot but be fitful and even dialectical, as intraregional events and developments occur for a time in ways contrary to either intra-Soviet or world-wide ones.

The dialectic will give rise to paradox whenever the west Europeans must betray the cause of freedom in the abstract if their commitment to orderly increases in liberty in eastern Europe is to have practical results over time. The paradox will take on the shape of a moral dilemma whenever a too-urgent east European push for instant liberalization brings the strategic concept into open conflict with sensitive conscience. Demands for more freedom have been—and can again be—so pushed by either illusionist *littérateurs* or materialist laborers, by dissenting intellectuals who have lost the sense of what is politically possible and disgruntled proletarians who have acquired a feel for what will make economically infeasible demands politically legitimate. Events in Czechoslovakia illustrated one side in 1968; those in Poland, the other side in 1980 and 1981. How the two strands might be linked was first illustrated in Hungary in 1956. An initially tactical link is easily converted into explosive fusion in the pressure chamber of widespread disaffection made up of the Soviet system's inherent flaws, its materially and psychologically inadequate ends-means ratio, and the incidental ruler-ruled frustrations. Irony supervenes, as does national if not wider calamity, when publicity for dissent and dissenters' demands heat up together and decrease the chances for stabilizing freedom's gains at any one lurch forward.

A west European strategy toward eastern Europe that amplifies *Ostpolitik* is aimed at reconciling contrary rights and necessities. It occupies a middle position between alternative extremes. It replaces the preplay of tactical diplomacy for more leverage across the East-West divide; and it stops short of seeking greater strategic latitude through an organized or organically growing west European bloc.

The preplay got underway when de Gaulle sought, and up to a point found, leverage on Soviet Russia in diplomatic relations with China, and on West Germany by means of a subsequent rapprochement with Russia—a rapprochement that in turn increased pre-détente Russian leverage on America. The West Germans followed suit in stages. While they were getting ready for their own opening to the east, the hardliners among them were briefly intrigued by the possibility of a China-based squeeze on Soviet Russia. A Sino-German vise might progressively generate sufficient pressure on East Germany to ultimately pry her loose; a milder version might meanwhile offset a Franco-Russian diplomatic reencirclement of (now only West) Germany, itself a potential counterpoise to a coincidental tightening of a U.S.-West German alliance-within-alliance. Maoist China's more modest contribution, following upon her ideological backing of dissent from Soviet "social imperialism" in eastern Europe, was to incite the west Europeans to firm up their defenses against Soviet global "hegemonism."

Even when not grounded in real possibilities, this checkerboard diplomacy broke up obsolete postwar rigidities. It thus served as a useful preliminary to a western European *Ostpolitik* that would be more solidly founded in the economics of credit than the preplay was in the internal economy of effective cabinet or conference diplomacy. Token diplomacy lost luster in western Europe once consistent statecraft lapsed with de Gaulle's collapse and the resulting vacuum of diplomatic initiatives was filled with economic problems. Among other things, the latter forced France into a marriage of necessity with West Germany that was too close to allow for the conveniences of serious diplomatic flirtation with Russia. Nor could France resist a too-close alliance of Bonn with Washington by means other than sharing the Germans' disaffection with a U.S. administration or moving to out-atlanticize them. The preplay also lost luster in eastern Europe when Soviet diplomacy veered from Paris to Washington even as de Gaulle defied Moscow in Warsaw; and, no less importantly, when, after Mao, the China option lost ideological legitimacy for Soviet clients conjointly with the Chinese rediscovery of the superiority of practical efficiency over doctrinal innovation and revolutionary purity.

The alternative, although currently only a theoretical one, is an organized western European bloc approximating an organic union. It could, for economic reasons, take place only under more or less overt West German leadership. So long as its economic base held good, that "hegemony" could be only transparently camouflaged by a Franco-German special relationship, or only inadequately offset by a revived Anglo-French *entente cordiale*. Neither pairing would be sufficiently solid to safely involve Soviet Russia in even a token triplice under the circumstances; nor would so organized a western Europe that has become materially coequal with the United States and Soviet Russia (and, as *she* grew stronger, China) assuredly realize the potential for equilibrium inherent in structural multipolarity. Instead of squaring actor mobility with system stability, unity under German auspices would tend to repolarize the world system and perpetuate Europe's division as Soviet Russia recoiled in one direction or another. Russia would be under pressure to seek accommodation with China if the consolidated west European ensemble itself remained within the Atlantic orbit; with the United States, if unified western Europe sought strategic independence in the west and set out to restructure the Eurasian balance in concert with China.

Even as a speculative possibility, the simple multi-power equilibrium would carry with it serious risks. It would be more apt to destabilize world politics than would a more complex, many-sided balance of power. Moreover, the latter would also be more likely of achievement in the next phase. The role for the west Europeans (and the Chinese) in such a balance will be more modest, more subtle, and in some ways less satisfying. But it will also test and qualify the new-type, if old-culture, middle powers for whatever might be in store for their restoration and rehabilitation in the future.

In the complex balance of power, a western Europe of states is neither an internally subdivided segment of a global diplomatic checkerboard nor is she a coherent power bloc in politico-military equilibrium. Viewed schematically, she is instead an intermediate zone occupying the elastically expanding or shrinking convex area of overlap between two circles. One of these circles is centered on the United States, the other on Soviet Russia. The U.S.-centered circle rests primarily on economic power (and attraction); the Russia-centered one, on military power (and political will). But western Europe's connection to the former is at least as much due to the military protection she enjoys from the United States, whereas her occupation of a segment in the Soviet-centered circle is largely due to the dynamic factor of actually or potentially mutual economic utility (next to the static geographic factor).

If the west Europeans are to act as honest brokers between the two power centers, they must move flexibly toward one and away from the other. And they must do so in response to conduct by either superpower that they judge injurious to the west European stake in East-West equilibrium in Europe and to progress toward European and greater-western unity. This will require two basic types of movement. One is toward the United States for more military protection if the scope or rate of either world-wide expansion or regional coercion by Soviet Russia becomes inconsistent with the west European objective: that is to say, is inconsistent with a gradual progression toward geopolitical parity world-wide and a gradual, if regression-prone and intermittent, evolution toward a freer (even if not institutionally formalized) social pluralism in eastern Europe. The other basic movement is toward Soviet Russia, in the form of intensified economic and diplomatic links with her. This would have to occur whenever Soviet expansion or coercion construable as legitimate elicits U.S. sanctions liable to threaten the west Europeans' all-European objectives, along with their security and material well-being. There is a built-in contradiction here. A long-term strategic concept is the only valid basis for defining the criteria of legitimacy by which to judge Soviet behavior. However, actual acts or events and actually perceivable trends will be on a much shorter time scale, and they will have but an ambiguous relationship to the envisaged goal, basic to the strategic concept. However, this contradiction is not practically insuperable if it is approached with a willingness to incur risks commensurate with the stakes, and the risks themselves are approached with a sense that they are more likely to be redeemable, before they become irreversible, than the prize at stake is likely to be indefinitely retrievable from contrary developments.

It might be useful for west Europeans to act in concert with Japan when practicable. However, their role as an honest broker on one side of Soviet Russia physically and of the U.S.-Soviet relationship operationally would more perfectly complement the role of China as a ballast on the other side in both respects. Whereas China is likely to be insufficiently active and mobile to initially act as a balancer, western Europe would be too actively engaged to be merely nonaligned. Moreover, she would be too intent on moderating the superpower competition to qualify as its neutralist exploiter. Western Europe would tend to stabilize the international system as both superpowers avoided propelling her too far toward the rival, while they took care not to unduly activate China prematurely in any way. Largely independently of one another, China and western Europe would both regulate the amount of gains Soviet Russia could aspire to make and keep without triggering the undesired movement. American desire not to antagonize China would itself regulate principally the amount of concessions the United States could make to Soviet Russia in the global peripheries, while the same concern in regard to western Europe would regulate the type and extent of constraints American policy-makers could attempt to impose on Russia globally and in Europe's eastern periphery.

The result in the next stage would be a quadrilateral system of checks and balances, oriented toward stability through evolution. It would replace a tight bipolarity as the manifest structure of world politics and would alleviate instabilities implicit in the complex of a major triangle and the several subsidiary triangles as its latent structure. A plurality of significant parties to the equilibrium process would not be tantamount to multipolarity among near-equal powers; neither would the alternately active and passive regulatory role of western Europe and China automatically terminate or pacify the U.S.-Soviet competition over the meaning and scope of parity. There would be present, however, the basic conditions for relating the three levels critical for world equilibrium in a mutually reinforcing fashion: the global level, the regional (and interregional: from eastern Europe via the Middle East to northeast and south Asia), and the intranational (critically and directly Russian, perhaps also indirectly and unpredictably Chinese). Finally, the west Europeans would have a clear and definite policy role in spanning the gap between the economic and the military constituents of world equilibrium in a critical area. These constituents have been lately disjoined by America's simultaneous if unequal regressions from the leadership role in both aspects of world equilibrium. Active diplomatic brokerage and bridging efforts would do more for bringing the two key functional elements back into some kind of coherence than if western Europe merely grew stronger economically relative to the United States while Russia grew stronger militarily.

It will not be easy for the west Europeans to act as honest brokers—either between Russian and American interests or between Soviet masters and Russia's subjects—amidst complexities bequeathed by the intractable structures of heterogeneous power and related sentiments. Honesty is not always the best policy between states or between people mistaking interests for either divinely or historically ordained entitlements. Brokering between competing powers will always pull the mediator in opposing directions; the twists and turns of a split political personality may be required for reconciling the rulers' view of necessity with the notion of justice of the ruled. In undertaking the task nonetheless, the west Europeans would have to rely on their present position even more than on the political wisdom saved from their history's vicissitudes. Their location is a propitious one in the wider configuration of political-military and economic power. It allows them to make up with widened options for lost omnipotence, with diplomatic mobility for mass, and with political flexibility for force.

For the United States to behave as if the West could be returned to politico-military superiority over Soviet Russia by either massive build-up or masterful diplomacy has been a recurring inclination; it will need to be overcome. So will acting as if either method could return the western alliance to a unanimity on foreign policy antedating both East-West détente and American decline in both the politico-military and the economic balances. So long as this is the American position, interallied contention over means would obscure the basis for the common goal; the resulting interallied frictions will intensify suspicions that the Soviets might be tempted to exploit a developing western European economic dependence on Russia (notably, if not only, in energy supplies). Overstating the danger that economic interdependence will hatch one-sided political dependence ignores the certainty that any Soviet attempt to foster such a trend would be self-defeating. It would overthrow all prior assumptions behind alternatives and force the west Europeans back into unquestioning conformity with, and energy dependence on, America. The one exception might be a Soviet economic blackmail that is a proportionate reprisal for politically motivated western-European economic sanctions against Russia. Short of such a provocation, any Soviet effort to misuse the economic link would defeat both Russia's own economic needs and Soviet political purposes in western Europe. It would also frustrate one consequence of the economic link: the continuing Europeanization of Soviet Russia, first if not only in diplomacy, conjointly with her westernization in matters of technology and economic rationality. Such a consequence has implications beyond diplomacy and economics which the Soviet rulers may not desire but cannot wholly avoid. Much will depend on whether the west Europeans can phase and shape their diplomatic Finlandization—if there is to be such a thing—so that it will remain more than one step and degree behind Soviet Russia's Europeanization, while increasing its speed.

A steady, if only gradually growing, Euro-Soviet economic interdependence would also have a stabilizing political effect on East-West relations on the global plane. It could help equip Soviet Russia for economic forms of extraregional influence by means other than a military conquest of west European economic and technological assets. The prospect would tend to divert Russia from forcible responses to global encirclement on the continent; it would also weaken any tendency to react drastically against the intraregional consequences of a too one-sided western economic engagement with the lesser east European countries. A guarded Euro-Soviet engagement is likely, therefore, to be both safer in the short run and more promising in the long run than are intermittent made-in-USA efforts, or scenarios, of a different kind. These were premised on the possibility of employing politico-economic inducements to third parties in order to isolate the Soviets. At one point, notably late in the Johnson administration, the strategy was targeted at the east European satellites; at another, early in the Carter administration, at potential targets of Soviet opportunity in the Third World. Intra-European détente is bound to dampen such unpromising U.S. initiatives. It raises the (less theoretical?) possibility that instead of isolating Russia from whomsoever, too much zeal in this direction would open a breach between American statecraft and its west European associates. Moreover, a safeguarded Russian connection with western Europe will check a latent, but likewise periodically surfacing, tug-of-war between two tendencies—or temptations—affecting American foreign-policy making. One is to give the Russians what amounts to a free hand in eastern Europe in anticipated exchange for their free (i.e., globally unrequited) aid in perpetuating U.S.-type order everywhere else; another, to challenge the Soviet position in eastern Europe all the more stridently when there seems to be a reason to retaliate for a lack of Russian cooperation world-wide or for interference in the Western Hemisphere.

Costs and benefits of intra-European convergence. The least and most immediate benefit of the brokerage-and-bridge strategy is for the west Europeans alone. The strategy is superior to present, and likely near-future, alternatives. One such alternative is an uncoordinated détente policy or *Ostpolitik*, always on the verge of degenerating into competitive *détentisme* among the west Europeans; another is Atlanticist loyalty, always liable to serve as either a cover for submissiveness on a global issue or a compensation for disappointments or disaffections on a purely west-European issue.

Alternating between competitive *détentisme* and competitive Atlanticism has entailed the risks of disunity mainly between France and West Germany on the continent; compensatory submissiveness is likelier to afflict the policies of the British as they vacillate, like late Renaissance Venice, between the terra firma and a new, scaled-down version of oceanic destiny.

The British pattern may hold the greater possible pitfall. England can do much good in mediating, and some harm in confusing, the issues between both parts of the Continent on one side and the United States on the other, as she looks across the Atlantic to America and across historic time to her lead role in dealing with Germany. She encompasses the widest range of experience among all west Europeans in dealings with Russia as either partner or peril over the centuries. But she is now unevenly divided between residues of a sympathetic understanding of the logic of raw power, peculiar to the reformed past sinner, and a vicariously "American" toughness on the subject of specifically Soviet brutish power. The empathy of the island-state's last, foredoomed hero-statesman for Russia's travail expressed an epic sense of history and the desire to go on acting on it as an equal of the newly great; the since dominant antipathy for the Soviet Union in many places has been too shrill to be commensurate with the available will-to-act in the crucible of real crisis. It does little more than compensate for such a will's limits or its absence. Be it as it may, what British statecraft does to help ensure that Russia stays European in essence and does not become Asian in defense of existence will weigh heavily on whether Britain becomes wholly European herself or remains Atlantic; this will, in the long run, matter more than do the material concessions Britain makes to, or extracts from, western Europe's own community institutions.

A wider and longer-lasting benefit would follow if western Europe's acting as a broker and then as a bridge would help conclude a long series of land-versus-sea power conflicts. These conflicts historically pitted England against a succession of continental rivals before abasing western Europe into an auxiliary role and an essentially postpolitical social mentality in the face of a reshaped continental-maritime conflict between Russia and America. If the west Europeans have been made sufficiently wise by the so-far transpired conflict series, they might suitably react to its continuance beyond a historically unavoidable (and in some ways creative) lifespan. They could then assume a genuinely political role and identity as agents for finally resolving the tie-up between the East-West and the land-sea power schisms in the global setting. It is a setting more latitudinous and variegated in both effective power and socioeconomic forces or functions and cultural values than was the ever less spacious and adequate European one.

If it were internally appeased, Europe as a whole might yet become the centerpiece to which would fall a key task in accommodating the larger, global and intercultural, East-West issue. However, before helping consummate traditional European history, and reset the course for the more inclusive western one—all with due concern for internation as well as social justice and for feasible liberty as a way station to fundamental freedoms—the west Europeans will have to bear the onus of brokering the quarrel between the ruling and the ruled in the east. This is a quarrel less artificial than the one between Russia and America is rapidly becoming. And it is aggravated whenever the issue it raises is posed most sharply in Poland.

This issue is posed with some inner logic in a nation that, at the start of its unending quest for a greater role and power, was the earliest catalyst of Russia's alienation from the Europe west of her. More than any other nation, Poland sowed the early seeds of the East-West conflict in Europe as now constituted. Portentous questions arise out of this background. Could Poland not spare herself, if only to enhance the prospect of Europe, yet another crucifixion at Russia's hands? Or could she, with outside help and inner self-denial, become a catalyst in a crucial step toward a propitious finis to the interminable quest for East-West conciliation? The prospects were dim as long as Poland remained what she always was, and they will be dim as long as the Poles remain what they are. A nation that, seeing itself through the eyes of the poet as the Christ among nations, is also unpurged of daemonic pride when she raises her heroic banner for freedom—and risks martyrdom for goals tainted by their origin in desire for material goods; a people that both wills itself to be and is foremost among the western Slavs, but is also the most backward-looking among them; a race of believers most religious, but also blasphemous when they seek to incarnate Him; and, least helpful of all, a collective consciousness smarting from having been saved and enserfed at one stroke by the hereditary enemy.

The testing of the west Europeans' ability and resolve in the face of tension and turmoil in eastern Europe comes at a time when their independence as a group from America is only a secondary objective, subordinate to the promotion of trends toward all-European unity. That priority is even greater now than it was in the days of de Gaulle's ascendancy and of Gaullist promise. The west Europeans owe it to their past and future alike to resist losing themselves in domestic and economic concerns; they need to recover the capacity to actually employ more than token (and, however skilled, near-mercenary) military force, as well as merely deploying it, where it is needed in order to keep the future open outside Europe. But, at this stage, western Europe as an entity must shackle her power (just as Russia must enlarge hers) if she is to help achieve freedom elsewhere. She can retain greater leverage on American policy in behalf of long-term liberalization in eastern Europe if west European military power remains intertwined with America's at the necessary cost in independence. She can then better hinder U.S. unilateralism and serve as an inducement for the Americans to do their share for East-West appeasement as a matter of prudential intra-alliance calculations even if not at first as a matter of conviction.

If the west Europeans accept a limit on their corporate independence for reasons other than to prolong petty hedonism in postpolitical decadence, if they help decompress the environment of Soviet policy-making for reasons that are not limited to simply averting the thrust of Russian power and do not result in issuing a blank check for its exercise in the Soviet orbit—if they do this, they will strengthen their mandate in regard to the non-Soviet east Europeans. They can then set a strict limit on the increase in individual freedoms in eastern Europe that they would be prepared to support at any one time by sanctions against the regional hegemon.

So long as a west European recommitment to integral Europeanism has a chance to mesh creatively with nascent Russian globalism, and so long as there is not a fundamental conflict of objectives between the two shores of the Atlantic, any likely measure of allied disunity over priorities and procedures will be dwarfed by western Europe's great stake in the outcome. This psychological advantage over America has its moral price. When acting on Europe's East-West issue with serious purpose, the west Europeans can and must avoid sharing in the emotional luxury of indignation over Russia's abuses of power. But they will also have to accept the moral obloquy of colluding in the crime of necessary Russian repressions. Such is the west Europeans' special act of contrition. It will help even out the scales of historic justice between Russia and Europe; and it responds to guilt inherited from history.

The guilt goes back, if no farther, to the all-European failure to deal without outside aid with the problem caused by late German entry into great-power competition. The obligation was to resolve the ensuing crisis in ways that would not accelerate the inorganic flight of power westward and eastward before either America or Russia were fully ready to exercise it, and in ways that would not entail human and material costs for Russia that give her—

rightly or wrongly—the feeling of the right to ignore the costs to others of safeguards for her future safety. The guilt at issue is not of the individual or subjective kind associated with war-guilt theses. It inheres in being part of the nexus among states competing at different stages of their being over near-indivisible stakes. Consequently, the duty to make reparation is not apportioned only or chiefly according to who was the more active instigator of conflict at any one point. It is incumbent equally or more on those who suffered less, or less lastingly, the full measure of the punishing consequences of enacting the partnership in guilt. That partnership is an element in the community of fate between Europe's western and eastern parts. This community survives any temporary division, because it derives from a common responsibility both for and to what was—and for what must yet be if the future is not to be reducible to a derisive dismissal of all that was of value in the European past.

Empire and liberty reconsidered. Unrestricted freedom for individuals and a regional or world community of fully independent and equal polities are the extreme, ideal poles of a vast continuum of intermediate shapes and forms of either. They are, like universal peace, the stuff of which dreams are made. Their full realization would carry with it all the dangers implicit in the ancient recognition that if and when the ideal best incurs inevitable corruption, it turns into the worst. Practical policy for men as they are, by men as they should be, will aim at only partial, contingent approximations. Therein, the conventional "worst" will often have an amending effect on the actual or potential excesses and debilities peculiar to the normatively "best"; or, at least, the one will not be seen as mutually exclusive with the other. Foremost among the impugned evils has been (next to totalitarianism) imperialism in relation to individual or group freedom; so has been, and will continue to be, a conflictual state system in relation to either regional or world community. The image of both of the arraigned phenomena improves most markedly if the search for freedom (or equality) and for a community free of coercive force becomes an excuse for anarchy.

The slogan *imperium et libertas* is not wholly deceptive if it suggests the possibility of a positive relationship between empire and freedom. A positive link will be present whenever overseas imperialism in its early stages reinforces the role of middle-stage or middle-level industrialization as an engine for liberalizing procedures (if initially no more than procedures) in domestic politics. Industrial growth in itself may not be sufficiently compelling. However, the extra impetus toward greater freedom emanating from overseas activism will fail to materialize if a prior beneficiary from the conjunction between economic and political-military expansion imposes frustrating inhibitions on the latecomer; external constraint will invert the potentially beneficial inner connection into reactive internal responses fostering repressive authority instead. This is what happened with and to Imperial Germany and might again happen, *mutatis mutandis,* in and for Soviet Russia.

An early imperialism cum industrialism may be usefully restrained from the outside, so long as it is not repressed. Its tendency to foster social and political pluralism will then have a chance; it will also be at the opposite pole from the tendencies peculiar to imperialism and industrialism in their late stages, before the solvent effect of grand empire has done its work. These will tend to be illiberal or even antiliberal. An early dynamism with liberalizing effects will yield to restrictive defenses against incipient decay and the threat of dissolution. Foreign policy will be influenced by attitudes that are protective or protectionist in economics and institutionally or procedurally formalist—and ethically moralistic—in politics or diplomacy.

The mid-term stage of empire is likely to be one of assured dominance, congenial to a free-wheeling approach all around. Economic liberalism ("free trade" and "free enterprise") is then typically coupled with conceptual and institutional informality in devising and executing foreign policy: muddling through attends preference for informal or indirect control. Because Great Britain originated the industrial revolution, she was well-advanced in overseas expansion before her imperialism could interact with industrialism to propel the empire's domestic base in a liberalizing direction. She fully exhibited the characteristics of mid-stage dominance. However, she displayed only ineffectually the economically protectionist, and only tentatively the institutionally formalist, features of the final stage. The United States was not only the first, but also the only privileged, major late entrant into the modern industrial-imperialist system. As such, America is inconclusively poised between the middle and the final stage. If she cannot reassert dominance but adjusts in time to the loss of ground, she can still draw on late-stage devices with moderation and discrimination.

The proposition that Soviet Russia might benefit by the liberalizing influence of initial overseas expansionism (before the growth of empire has spawned more freedom or bred anarchy in the fullness of time) would be utopian, and prescriptions for the West to moderate obstruction only hortatory, were it not for the two-part paradox of power and freedom.

One of its parts primarily applies to a rising authoritarian power whose ideology is rooted in scarcity and survives by the urge to absolve this condition. As that power expands and increases its capacity to influence outside developments, its capacity to exercise control or influence indirectly will also increase; there will be less reason to coerce nationals or dependents and to constrict the range of participants in the making of major decisions. Put more strikingly, the expansion of freedom within the Soviet Union and its empire is in part contingent on others' freedom of action being for a time reduced by continuing Soviet expansion.

The second part of the paradox chiefly applies to a declining liberal power whose belief system was rooted in the perpetual expansion of both economic prosperity and the congruent social and political rights. Such a power's decline will begin with the failure to note the erosion of the customary resource margin. For such a power to forestall the decay that precedes or attends decline, it will have to inject more intellectual and professional rigor into previously "free"—self-consciously pragmatic or actually haphazard—choices in the planning and execution of both public and foreign policies. Only then will the liberal power at least partially offset the reduction of the margin of safety previously enjoyed. In summary, safeguarding the diminished freedom of action abroad makes it imperative to restrict its scope in choices made at home.

The two-faceted paradox of rising and declining power and different aspects of freedom thus points to a partnership between power and necessity; a practical one for the Soviet Union—to enhance efficiency in routinized operations; a philosophical one for the United States—to enhance consistency in and by a conceptualized strategy.

It is impossible to delve into issues of the most pragmatic strategy without running up against issues of principles and values. A grand strategy for the West must reconcile stability with flexibility in balance-of-power politics, and minimize the medium-term risks to truly fundamental western values. Not the least of these is, and not the least of these arise out of, the creative tension between diverging world views and perceptions of self rooted in a common subsoil. In the process of evolving and applying a grand strategy, it may be necessary to take a broad view of how essential it is to observe and sponsor secondary principles focusing on either aggressive or oppressive force. These are too often placed in the forefront of a strategic approach that, while not insensitive to fundamental values, treats them as indistinguishable from procedural principles and both of them as interchangeable with very specific interests of one party. The thus highlighted principles are not negligible, but they are too costly if fixating attention on them blocks a real peril from view. This is the risk of precipitating prematurely and, in the final accounting, perhaps unnecessarily, a terminal conflict within the already narrowing orbit of a culture or civilization that is still an identifiable and differentiable whole, however divided it may be internally.

When this is the case, it becomes imperative to be patient, to take the longest possible view, and to adopt the most comforting assumptions about one's own staying power and the other side's susceptibility to beneficial change. Only thus will it be possible to negotiate the necessary transitions—from rigid polarity to flexible parity, from a static to a dynamic balance and approach to equilibrium; and be possible to promote the desirable extensions—from nuclear-strategic to geopolitically adapted mutual deterrence, from international-economic to internal-political liberalization.

On the basis of such a long view, looking to progressive appeasement of a central conflict will not spell integral abandonment of either principles or interests on the easy excuse of defending the absolute meta-cultural value of peace in the abstract. Nor will it mean that accommodation in one place will sufficiently warrant displacing antagonisms to other, more congenial or less readily removable, lines of division. However, because pragmatic statecraft must take into account the operational requirements and implications of all policy realignments, all conflicts along all lines of manifest or latent cleavage will not be appeasable at the same time. Just as it is impossible to uphold formal, or procedural, principles at all times without jeopardizing more substantive values, so it will not always be possible to safeguard values common to a culture or civilization without some detriment to more broadly inclusive trans-cultural or pan-human values. In the difficult and rarely satisfying compromises to be groped for—without hope of their ever being permanently struck—one sustaining belief may legitimately be that the proposed or applied strategy has a good chance, in principle, to enhance the prospects for one set of values; another, that any temporary cost to other values entailed in a trade-off need be only temporary while a provisional one is practically necessary.

Nor is the need for trade-offs limited to values, occidental and other or larger. It may be also necessary to hazard actual concessions to a rival party (Soviet Russia) in the area of foreign policy on the mere expectation of gains in the area of (Soviet) domestic politics; it may likewise be necessary to countenance augmented power before celebrating enlarged freedom. Meanwhile, safeguarding a civilization will require nurturing every sign and source of civility between Russia and the West—or even, short of that, great-power rationality between the Soviet Union and the United States.

VII

APPEASEMENT OR ANARCHY.

The Two East-West Dimensions

Whereas containment and decompression are alternative strategies, convergence is a controversial process. The issues they raise come together in hypothetical scenarios. Crucial scenarios revolve around war and peace especially between the major powers, order and anarchy involving especially the lesser and less-developed states, and expansion and constriction of regionally or culturally defined larger entities. All affect the chances for appeasement between rivals and for restoration of a functioning international system out of revolution. Restoration of an orderly system of power between the revolution- and rebellion-prone "southern" regions and the order-dependent but regression-prone "northern" regions is a necessary prelude to the transformation of a conflict-centered international system into a world community. As part of such transformation, interactive regeneration of each culturally distinct region or area is the ideal outcome of a conflict series that links together differently defined East and West. But European and western history may have to first run its course in relation to Russia before any of the normatively desirable consummations become practically possible.

Sources of war and peace: policy process and power structures

Of the two main sources of war inherent in geopolitical dynamics, one—

associated with World War II—is familiar under the label "appeasement." The other—associated with World War I—has been related in these pages to the land-sea power triangle and has no comparably popularized label. However, it is closely associated with a particular implementation of containment applied to the central power in the triangle.

War and order in normative and theoretical perspectives. To stress the war-peace issue is not necessarily to argue for "peace" against "war" in the abstract. Nor is it to conceive of either condition as the paramount analytical focus any more than the normative pivot of international relations. Quite the contrary: war is only one device, if the major or ultimate one, for adjusting relations among states whenever it repairs prior derangement between asserted interests and available power; and peace is only one value, and not the absolute one, in political man's concern with not only physical but also moral survival. But again, a particular war may be a critically negative event in a developing future. A war between America and Russia would be one more fratricidal war in Europe, and it might well be the last one for Europe as a seat of independent power (Russia's) and for the West as the seat of preeminent civilization.

Such considerations are rooted in cultural preference. Not so the near-certainty that such a war, nuclear or not, would gravely injure the evolutionary potential of the international system. It would fracture, and might indefinitely set back, the previously existing degree of ends-means rationality by weakening or destroying the two powers capable of shaping the expansion of the international system into a genuinely global one in minimally orderly conditions. It is in this connection that a degree of U.S.-Soviet convergence is necessary. Only if conceptual disciplines are enlarged in American politics, and dysfunctional domestic and regional constraints are relaxed in the Soviet orbit, will the two powers be able to contribute to such an order; they will be able to define and also police the outside limits of tolerable conduct by third parties that are unready to apply internal restraints and unwilling to incur external checks.

It is not enough to rule out third-party use of nuclear weapons so long as the superpowers themselves avoid their employment; equally objectionable is the violent destruction of vital resources by local agents so long as the resources are needed by the industrial world and are being spared from retaliatory or otherwise motivated seizure by the superpowers. So is, as the most general category, any third-power initiative liable to intensify conflict between the two major powers. When smaller states seem to inveigle greater powers in acute conflict, this is commonly the sign of the giants mismanaging one another rather than of the lesser breed skillfully manipulating one or both of them. So much is true most of the time. Yet the rising prospect of the superpower's mutual mismanagement is among the circumstances that favor the elimination of all contributing factors by all possible means.

A minimum world order depends on a rationally competitive comanagement by established great powers. Before it could evolve into a more accomplished—egalitarian and interdependent—world community, two processes would have to be completed. "Power" would have to complete the cycle of world-wide migration, as nation-states of different sizes take shape and more of them achieve transient salience; "spirit" would have to consummate the full range of depoliticization, as the drive for power abroad gives way in ever more places to the desire for domestic prosperity and is blunted by satisfaction of that desire.

Circulation of power and a certain form of depoliticization of actors will have to gradually engage all of its viable constituents before the world community can cease being a legal fiction and be more than an academic fancy. It is safe to assume that the yet latent forces at large in the world, and the yet unqualified members of a potential community, will follow the pathway already marked by others. They will not overleap the stepping stone to self-awareness that consists of self-assertion within the narrowest possible frameworks. Meanwhile, the parties previously saturated or appeased must not restart a new cycle of developments injurious to the wider community, as a reaction to events attending the formation of states among the latest of the latecomers. The middle stage of such state formation (following upon formal independence) is likely to coincide with the earliest, and most explosive, stage in citizen politicization. Inordinate pretensions and disordering perturbations attendant on both stages could easily provoke earlier-matured polities into recidivist reactions.

For these and other reasons, the elementary global system that is already in existence will not ensure a spontaneously synchronized development worldwide, independently of deliberate strategies by key members. Such strategies must aim at managing, however crudely, intermediate developments so that they eventually flow together into desirable "ultimate" outcomes. Strategies keyed to this end will find support in a more optimistic assumption than are the preceding ones. An elementary world system exists to the extent that compartmentalization between areas and cultures is offset by conditions making for connectedness. Mutual dependence in economics, and at least some defenses against interdependence, have been having that effect across individual differences in stages of development; so has the so-called demonstration effect of actions in politics across great spatial distances when it produces imitations or provokes inverse reactions.

To combine the belief in gradualness with the insistence on the special duty of greatness in the world arena is to apply philosophical conservatism to its last redoubt and principal testing ground. Even glacially slow convergence between the hierarchical oligarchs can survive spells of heightened competition and foster similarities (short of identity) in external influence and internal liberties so long as the pace of convergence is no slower than are the structural transformations that point toward conflict. A slowdown in such transformations has been in evidence underneath surface agitation; but it need not be indefinite. Using the interlude productively means resisting the temptations of an instant utopia and escaping deferred nemesis. Utopian is a world community that would painlessly absorb the rebellious or revolutionary bout of the decolonizing global periphery with both modernity and traditionalism. Nemesis lurks behind the part played by U.S.-Soviet competition in the waning central-systemic revolution, set off long ago by the impact of capitalism, anchored in colonizing seapower, on feudalism, rooted in land and surviving longer in the continental than in the maritime societies and powers.

The issue of war and peace is never far beneath all other considerations and is always central to both doctrinal and strategic concerns. A broadly political approach to the issue will investigate the structures of organic power and the pressures of operative politics. A more narrowly technical approach is by way of the theory and practice of arms races and armed capabilities. There are points of similarity and difference both within and between the two distinct approaches that either persist or are sharpened in the nuclear setting.

Fears of war in the nuclear situation center on the possession of first-strike capability, liable to propel the use of force by one side in order to preempt the adversary's. In differing from this perspective, a more general theory of arms races and the theory stressing political competition in general have one feature in common: they substitute for the incentive lodged in the capacity to strike first the incentive deriving from concern with weapons of last resort. However, beyond that important point of similarity lies a lesser difference. In the context of an arms race, what precipitates war is the inability of the materially weaker side to maintain indefinitely a weapons advantage it had won at an unrepeatable cost, let alone recover the advantage after losing it. That party will face the choice between escalating political into military conflict and dropping out of competition when its materially stronger rival is about to nullify its headstart by accelerated (if belated) rearmament. The factor detonating war in the wider context of political competition is basically similar but also broader. It consists of the spasmodic reaction by one side to an overall situation that deteriorates to its disadvantage in one way or another, but always in a degree that threatens to worsen irremediably over time.

Changing conditions have made war socially and materially costly among powers that are also intricate societies. The key incentive to war in both the nuclear and the conventional military contexts, and in both the narrowly arms-related and the wider political contexts, tends thus to be preventive. This means that any war will be defensive in the self-perception of even the party that has initiated hostilities. Having a first-strike nuclear capability may coincide with last-resort necessity for reasons due either to the state of the arms race or to special features of the rivalry's geopolitical setting; and the possession of such capability may then set off a war-initiating act. But, unless there is such a coincidence, it will be longer-term assessments of wider power structures and trends than those pertaining to the nuclear arsenals that will activate the preventive instinct. It seemingly simplifies matters and concretizes reflection to fix one's attention on the preemptive compellent or "trigger" residing in a momentary relationship between two sets of rival military, including nuclear, hardware. Isolating such considerations of military strategics from a larger setting disencumbers the logic of a highly specialized and ostensibly rigorous speculative science. Stripping bare the logic cannot but enhance the magic of that science as the master key to unlocking the door to both understanding and pacifying contemporary international relations. However, giving way to the attraction is also to run all the risks present in the substitution of technological know-how for historically informed know-why.

The pitfalls and potentialities of appeasement. As the "cause" of World War II, the political side of appeasement by the western democracies was complemented by the arms race acting as a detonator of hostilities. Rearmed Nazi Germany would have been unable to maintain her arms superiority had the western powers forged abreast or ahead of her from behind—and from their larger resource reserve and both political and economic hinterland. On the other hand, military hardware played a lesser role when containment of Imperial Germany by the Entente powers is viewed as the principal political source or "cause" of World War I. First-strike capability acted as no more than a precipitant, in the guise of the presumed advantage for the side first to mobilize its conventional military forces; and even the most conspicuous naval and land-army elements in the prewar arms race were but secondary or derivative. They merged imperceptibly with the overall distribution of activable power, which was likely to turn over time against the Dual Alliance in favor of the Anglo-French-Russian combination (and its U.S. and Japanese backups or sympathizers).

In view of these antecedents, is a policy designed to appease the East-West (or U.S.-Soviet) conflict a dangerous one? Is it less, more, or no more perilous than it was in the only very partially comparable setting of the 1930s? Is it likely to reduce the prospect of warlike contention or only defer the outbreak of violence and then aggravate its scope and intensity?

The theory of appeasement as a cause of war holds that the failure to contain (i.e., "stop") an aggressive-expansionist power encourages its ambitions until the defensive side is impelled into a war-precipitating response (or overresponse?), which comes too late and is initially backed by little effort. The appeasement—or Munich—analogy was always fashionable in the rhetoric of hard-line approaches to the Soviet threat. It is bound to resurface whenever the public-relations image of détente is eclipsed.

As a matter of fact, a post-détente series of events has fitted the sequence of events associated with pre–World War II appeasement remarkably closely, if in most part only superficially. In such a sequence, the euphoria of the meeting in Vienna between the American and the Soviet leaders in mid-1979 equals the Anglo-German, Chamberlain-Hitler summit meetings of mid-1938, which preceded Munich. As with the earlier agreements, the terms of SALT II were widely considered onesided. The subsequent Soviet invasion of Afghanistan, in December 1979, equals the Nazi German invasion of rump Czechoslovakia and entry into Prague in March 1939. Both events dispelled the confidence of the principal western statesman in the power of a personal rapport to contribute to peace in his time. The extent of prior euphoria determined the intensity of the reaction: the Chamberlain government's guarantee of Poland and the U.S. guarantee of the Persian Gulf, initiated under the so-called Carter doctrine.

Thus the sequence Munich-Prague-Poland matches the sequence Vienna–Afghanistan–Persian Gulf. The potentially war-precipitating characteristics of the last-stage western commitment have also been similar. As part of attempts to "stop" the expansionist power, a guarantee pledge was issued in both instances to a volatile local power or set of powers without adequate military capability to back the undertaking. The guarantee recipients were actually (in the case of Poland) or potentially (in that of the Persian Gulf states) disposed to usurp control over the *casus belli* on the strength of a western commitment that was either an empty gesture or a blank check, one that was either conceived or represented as being not so much the first word in a serious effort to clarify competing interests as a last stand.

Nor do similarities end at this point. The guarantee to Poland was issued either too late or it came too soon in the drama of revising the status quo. Nazi Germany ought to have been stopped when remilitarizing her Rhenish "backyard," or the appeasement policy ought to have been given a chance to prove itself in a longer run and over a larger geopolitical stage than was to be actually the case. The formal independence of post-Munich rump Czechoslovakia could not be expected to survive the amputation of the frontier regions essential for defense; the revision of her status in 1939 was thus not far from carrying out the agreement between the lines of the Munich accords. Poland's exclusive control over the land corridor inserted between the bulk of Germany and East Prussia by the Versailles settlement was a situation clearly incompatible with "greater" Germany's new standing in east-central Europe—or indeed, with Germany's status as a great power.

It is not necessary to argue, and impossible to prove, that the demands on Poland were Hitler's last. But the demand was the first that was reasonable and very nearly the last he could reasonably make in behalf of formal-territorial revision before proving himself insatiable—and running up against the vital interests of Soviet Russia. The western guarantee to Poland was issued and implemented on issues that were wrong both substantively—the intangibility of the "Polish corridor"—and procedurally—the overt military means of reducing rump Czechoslovakia to dependency status. This guarantee set off, if not the wrong war, then a war begun under the wrong circumstances. As a result, the active response to German revisionism failed to activate the reserve powers on the side of the defense of irreducible conditions of stability. The obverse would have been the case for Soviet Russia in the short run, if Germany's regional expansionism continued at a rapid rate and by violent means. It might well have been also for the United States in the longer run, if a gradually and organically expanding German power began to also weigh on the global equilibrium. Instead, a seemingly last-resort western resistance brought together the rival (Germany) and the potential ally (Russia).

A suddenly militant U.S. stand in the Persian Gulf could be seen as no less misplaced than was England's in Poland. It, too, failed to activate a major third power (notably India) farther to the east; it risked frightening allies (west European and Japanese) into de facto alignment on the rival's side (if only for the limited purpose of defusing the crisis, preliminary to a joint approach to the oil problem). It terminated the appeasement process implicit in détente on the untested assumption of the rival's boundless objectives.

Even less plausibly than in the 1930s, that assumption became an article of official faith well before allowing the full range of the conditions of an effective appeasement to be proven present or absent. Like British statecraft before it, American statecraft was as a result on the verge of entrenching itself too soon, while stirring too late. Too late, if one holds (as one may) that the counterpart of Germany's unopposed reoccupation of the Rhineland in the mid-1930s was the political reentry of Russia into the Middle East in the mid-1950s, eased rather than barred by the American handling of the Suez crisis. Too soon, if the United States was stampeded into a last-ditch stand in the Persian Gulf on an unproved and so far unprovable assumption as to the "real" scope of the rival's objectives, while underwriting that stand by an unrealistic (because yet unarmed) guarantee. Once more the too broad and only formally clear issue of procedure, the use of miliary force, has outweighed in the scales of decision-making judgment the substance of an ambiguous local issue: the rival consolidating his hold over a satellite previously conceded de facto, now Afghanistan as before post-Munich rump Czechoslovakia.

National-socialist Germany sought an extraterritorial connection with a detached eastern province, East Prussia, across the "Polish corridor" and a safeguarded maritime link by way of Danzig. The Soviets may be seeking via the Persian Gulf a more efficient connection across a much larger distance with a similarly situated and in effect "detached" eastern province—Siberia. They might be helped therein by a naval base in southern Vietnam, wrested from hands friendly to the West, on the Danzig model, by local forces encouraged by the revisionist great power to do the wresting. This may be the most trivial or far-fetched comparison of them all, but it may also be given substance, as might the others, by misjudging the fundamentals.

Is there a more fundamental comparability behind the superficially plausible similarity of events and attitudes? There are several prerequisites of an effective strategy for appeasing an ascendant revisionist power. The strategy must be conducted from strength and must unfold in spatial depth. On the basis of strength, it is possible to risk a considerable advance of the revisionist power, whereas for the success of the strategy, conceding moderate expansion will be necessary. The underlying beliefs are, one, that the advance will cause dispersion of the resources and attrition of the forward thrust of the gradually saturated if not softened expansionist; and two, that the advance will activate so far unengaged dormant forces or uninvolved reserve powers. For both assumptions to be validated, a strong core must coordinate resources from a relatively narrow base and make fundamental decisions for the defense. This is the leadership from strength factor. And, making up the complementary factor of latitude for expansion, the field of both active and potential forces—the arena of the relevant balance of power system—must be viewed in the broadest possible compass.

When such conditions exist (as they do presently up to a point), it will be possible to aim safely at one of two interdependently beneficial effects, and be likely to achieve the other. One is the displacement of the focus of competitive dynamic within an enlarged balance-of-power theater to areas and issues that exhibit the lowest possible level of pressures, that dispose of the largest reservoir of previously untapped power, and that are at the greatest distance from the center of high-technology civilization. When this happens, competition shifts to stakes with the longest time fuse for detonating acute conflict.

The other desirable effect, next to displacement of conflict, is decompression of the expansionist power. One aim—and hopefully, result—is to assure that such a power's intentions become ever more a function of a widening configuration of power in the relevant force field, rather than a reflection of the "size" of chiefly military capabilities. Another is that the power's goals and intentions progressively become a function of internal skills and capabilities that are peculiarly suited to consolidating the newly won peripheral positions.

The effect sought by displacement is bolstering the efficacy of defense; the desired effect of decompression is to reduce the need for defense; the assumed effect of combined displacement and decompression is, finally, to diversify the conflict relationship between the "offensive" and the "defensive" powers by adding an expanding common stake. Such a stake is most likely to be found in joint opposition to either separately active or parallelly activated third forces. These might be other great powers with global reach; assertive middle powers seeking to crystallize around themselves regional balance-of-power systems exclusive of the presence, and impervious to the influence, of the great-power rivals; or wholly anarchic conditions of small-scale disorders and small-state pretensions injurious to the interests of both or all major actors.

It is a moot point whether an effective appeasement strategy of Germany from strength and in depth was thwarted mainly by the objectively given distribution of power and geopolitical configuration of stakes, or whether responsibility lies with the subjectively evolved perceptions and assessments of western European and chiefly British statesmen. It ought to be less a matter for dispute whether the failure of appeasement in one setting disqualifies the strategy in all other settings. One certainty is that, in the 1930s, key westerners perceived the relevant balance of power in its most narrow and static continental scope; another, that they essayed the diversion of the German drive eastward (against Soviet Russia), when at all, in the crudest possible manner with, as their aim, a frontal collision between the two totalitarian powers.

There is, therefore, much room for difference between then and now as to policy-determining perceptions. Likewise different are contemporary "objective" conditions on such major aspects as the scope of the international system and, within it, the configuration of power and geopolitical stakes; the internal constitution of the key offensive and the key defensive power wielders; and the availability of reserve powers to be activated or the quality of third forces to be guarded against. But the main difference is one that comprises perception and conditions and relates the geopolitical stage to the critical actor on it. It resides in the evolutionary phase of the expansionist power. The Nazi regime, as the inheritor of its imperial predecessor's frustrations, was predisposed toward the second, all-out continental phase of a land power's expansionary drive. Soviet Russia's is only the first, more moderate stage of continental-maritime expansionism. Consequently, both opportunities for and incentives to the indirect, elastic approach, although not absent in the 1930s, are clearly less in evidence in the German case than they are in the Russian—even if "other things" (i.e., conditions not directly deriving from the basic difference) were more equal between the two periods than they actually are.

As commonly stated, the analogy with World War II stresses the failure of an attempt at appeasement and its war-provoking effect. But, despite surface similarities, an analogy from a pattern of events may be falsified, among other things, by the factor of evolutionary sequence related to structure. In our case, this is illustrated by the fact that Germany and Britain labored in the 1930s under the delayed consequences of the failure to manage effectively the triangular configuration in the phase preceding World War I. Unless provoked, a Soviet Union operating within the framework of the first phase was unlikely to challenge overtly or massively the U.S. commitment in the Persian Gulf under either the "Carter doctrine" or, its sequel, the Haig doctrine of "strategic consensus." But Russia was also likely to direct any second-phase thrust consequent on rigid frustration of her first-stage ambitions (also in the Persian Gulf) toward areas better suited to the resources appropriate for an all-out assault.

Being swayed by differently simplistic views of appeasement as policy and its actual or presumed past applications has made the West balk at relaxing resistance to Soviet moves outside Europe while making the Soviets resist relaxation of controls in their protective *glacis* in eastern Europe. Even but partially wrong images can thwart appeasement as a condition resulting from the correct application of the policy. Warped perceptions of one-time processes might even precipitate the two superpowers into warlike conflict before they help in completing Russia's encirclement in a triangular setting. Latent in that setting is currently the more dangerous, structural "cause" of major war. Managing appeasement instead with flexibility as well as fortitude would tend to defer and might well reduce the dangers to peace emanating from the so far only emerging configuration.

The primacy of structure short of tyranny. It is possible, indeed easy, to overdo an analogy from patterns of events—that is, from processes—that obscure differences in structures (including those related to evolutionary sequence). Is it not equally possible to exaggerate the possibilities of an analogy based on structures—especially if the present "structure" is not, or not yet, fully identical with the historically evidenced one?

When the emphasized structure consists of a land-sea power triangle, the query will be answered affirmatively if both of the defining features are questioned. First, stressing the land-sea power differentiation will be questioned when changes in the technology of weapons and communications are believed to make henceforth unimportant the configuration of space globally and the physical environment locally. However, we do not know enough yet to determine what will finally matter more in shaping anxieties, ambitions, and thus, basic patterns of behavior in relations among states—whether technology or topography, high-flying airplanes and missiles or deeply embedded attitudes and mind-sets. It is not as if the predictive record of technologically disposed analysis and arguments from discontinuity has been good so far.

Second, stressing the triangular aspect of the emphasized structure will be questioned most when the well-established fact of bipolarity and its implications for superpower strategy and global stability is regarded as wholly controlling. The argument then is that the clear predominance of two powers over other states continues to define—and is likely to go on dominating—the structure, and thus the politics, of the international system. Moreover, the argument continues, the existence of only two major powers is inherently stable; the structure's essential simplicity (and/or the powers' physical and material size?) permits reciprocally compensating adjustments to possible sources of instability on both sides.*

Bipolarity may be safe and stable so long as both sides perform perfectly. However, when one side falters, a big war ensues or unipolarity sets in without resistance. Multipolarity can better absorb occasional failings of one of the parties, even when (though less when) it is polarized by rival alliances. If the risk of wars it entails is greater than in the bipolar situation, the wars are typically smaller, while the potential for reequilibration is greater. The existence of several great powers stretches a many-meshed net underneath the international system and its equilibrists, whereas the jousting limited to two powers—on or off the "brink"—takes place over a gaping void. The situation of three powers is intermediate as to numbers, if not necessarily otherwise. Even in pure theory, one that ignores qualifiers such as land-sea power diversity and disparities in terms of relative rise and decline, a three-power system ranks as the most unstable of all due to the temptation it generates for any two of the three powers to combine against the third, only to re-create antagonistic bipolarity between the previously allied winners.

The case for bipolarity falters completely when the practically (and theoretically?) inseparable factor of "process" is added to that of "structure." We have just had occasion to observe that a two-phase sequence with consequences for structure (and strategy) weakens the analogy from process (as to "appeasement") when it reveals the incomplete relevance of a past pattern of events. Likewise, the two-power interaction process weakens the argument (for peace and stability) from bipolar structure because the process assures the structure's impermanence. Bipolarity is impermanent for the simple reason that it is pregnant with multipolarity. Each of the two competing major powers will either father or raise smaller powers as part of the short-of-war competition with the other major state. Or else, such third powers will grow more spontaneously thanks to the immunity bestowed upon them by their quarreling seniors' inability to check abuses and keep the juniors in their place. Thus, most recently, China was raised by both of the competing superpowers in succession to a place in the system still undeserved on any other grounds. The same competition has lifted a range of other lesser states above their natural station.

To be sure, initial multipolarization need not be completed before the

*The argument has been made by Kenneth N. Waltz, most recently and extensively in his *Theory of International Relations* (Reading, Mass.: Addison-Wesley, 1979).

obverse tendency sets in and a gradual and peaceful, or sudden and violent, erosion of several of the plural powers again reduces the number of effective players. If the number is back to two, it may be the original or the different ones that reassert themselves or newly emerge within a retightened and further militarized bipolarity. The hypothetical end comes only when the cycles of alternately waxing and waning numbers of major competing organisms give way to something structurally and psychopolitically different from (and better than?) the system of ultimately self-dependent states breeding permanent competition and intermittent equilibrium.

Meanwhile, warlike conflict remains possible, and may become likely. It may be due to a reemerged triangular structure (or, more precisely, configuration) among the major states; it may be due to conflict-triggering internal structures (or compositions) of the national power of a greater range of critical states. The interstate feature differentiates parties conspicuously (if not solely) along land-sea power and rise-decline axes; the intrastate factor is made operative through interlocking surpluses and deficiencies. Among possible surpluses are those of population and pent-up social or moral energy, as well as, or more than, investment capital; deficiencies comprise those of land for feeding the population, as well as raw materials, technological energy sources, or markets—next, again, to social and moral energy and will.

To the extent that it is analytically possible—and for policy purposes necessary—to segregate the two, an interstate structure such as the triangular configuration (e.g., U.S.-Soviet-Chinese) is a more predictable cause of war than are intrastate structures. It is easier to project tendencies and probabilities from easily verifiable past configurations and their consequences than to predict outcomes from structures and stresses within developed and underdeveloped, agriculturally or industrially unevenly productive, participants in the world economy. At least in principle, internal social or economic conditions are neutral when it comes to fostering conflict or producing complementarity between states. If anything, it is the way the interstate (two-, three-, or many-power) structures and related scenarios unfold for mostly other immediately operative reasons that will influence the outward thrust of social and economic forces. Even where national and global socioeconomic structures become conspicuously intertwined in potentially explosive land-population ratios, thus especially in Asia, the state of relations between the two contemporary, but not immortal, superpowers will primarily determine whether they can stay aloof from resulting conflicts and moderate them or will be drawn into them on different sides of this or that cleavage.

To say so much is to imply a more general point. Stressing the determining effect of interstate structures is not the same as proposing unqualified determinism. A correct foreign-policy doctrine keyed to appeasement can correct for a history that was largely written by conflict. But it can do so only if such doctrine inspires and rationalizes a grand strategy that corrects for the manifest structure by correctly assessing a latent structure—one that will surface and itself become manifest if the compulsions emanating from the extant one are blindly followed; if, concretely for the present, the apparent dictates of the two-power structure and competition prompt policies that complete the creation of an inherently unstable and explosive three-power structure.

Instead, latent structures may be perceived and acted upon before they become manifest. Policy is then creatively related to the future, even without seeking to implement radical transformations in that future; without, that is, aiming to substitute a community for a conflictual system, and universal peace for a containable propensity to major war. When the necessary adjustments are made and the more modest effort succeeds, the primacy of structure in interstate politics has been respected without incurring the worst tyranny of structure; should the tyranny be conceded, to project from past configurations would be tantamount to predicting outcomes. Projection does not then merge with prediction because a structure that reoccurs is identical—rather than merely comparable—to a past one, but because current strategies conform with past policies. So long as mere primacy is in force, past and present structures will be seriously searched for comparable aspects, but the projection of past structures and outcomes onto the present will serve mainly to inspire a strategy that would invalidate the projection if it points to an undesired outcome. The task is then to inflect the course of events toward a different and preferred outcome on the strength of a prophecy of doom liable to ensue from repeating past behavior. Yet, again, such prophecy can be a persuasive mentor to strategy only if it convincingly dramatizes the latent structure. It will be unpersuasive if it merely deplores the lethal outcome that occurs if the manifest structure is allowed to monopolize the determination of policy.

Presently, to repeat, the manifest structure consists of two powers that vastly exceed others as a challenge or perceived threat to each other. They face each other in a field of forces that only begins to evolve toward a diffusion of power, conflict, and threats. All of these, as they spread, make the two superpowers into a possible source of mutual comfort and are themselves the raw materials of a future multipolarity that a relaxed superpower relationship would first make possible and then help make relatively stable (while, in the extreme case, an all-occidental concert including Russia would be sufficiently dominant globally at first to be effective without ceasing to be pluralistic). The latent structure is only an emerging motif in the global texture. As a taut triangular structure, it will fully surface and dominate politics if and when the habitual instrumentalities of unchecked competition between two powers have been sharpened to the point of benefiting the rising third power (alongside unruly lesser parties); if, specifically, a contentious approach to U.S.-Soviet bipolarity has been translated into a policy of close U.S. alignment with, and material assistance (including military) to, China.

The logic and the dynamics of competition for power are reducible to simple laws or tendencies that interrelate structure and process; the evidence of history is reducible to the illustration of such laws and the interrelation. Both the logic and history point toward a recurrent conversion of a latent into a manifest structure by strategies that failed to anticipate the change. Such a conversion—of loose bipolarity into tense triangularity—is fraught with the danger of supplanting minor or manageable conflicts with a major catastrophic one. Such major conflict may be delayed for decades. It may be—and is even likely to be—only conventional-military when it occurs. It nonetheless portends the trials of one more system reconstitution out of intervening destruction and chaos; any further movement toward it would suffice to overshadow the commonplace routines of maintaining or adjusting regional balances of organically evolving, migratory power and artfully displacing the foci of competition when possible and desirable.

Among the conditions that help ill-advised strategies set off the wrong kind of developments are hidden faults in the existing structure or configuration. In the ongoing seesaw between the (manifest) bipolar and the (so far only emerging) triangular settings, such hidden faults are the weak links in the several lesser triangles. The latter are parallel with the global triangle but subordinate to it; too tight a U.S.-Chinese containment of Soviet Russia will be prone to putting intolerable pressure on them. The maritime and functionally, if not geographically, "western" sub-triangle comprises Japan along with the United States and western Europe. There are two eastern ones. One, the farther eastern and continental-maritime, comprises Soviet Russia, China, and Japan; in the relatively nearer eastern and strictly continental one, Japan is replaced by non-Soviet eastern Europe.

In the maritime-western triangle, too constraining a Sino-American vise around Soviet Russia would tend to impel western Europe and Japan toward defecting from the U.S. policy line or alliance leadership into a policy that would relieve Soviet isolation and with it the pressures for an all-out Soviet reaction. In such a case, the allies' security concern might also be a medium for expressing economic interests divergent from America's. The weak link is different in the specifically far eastern and continental-maritime Sino-Japanese-Soviet triangle. Therein, a Japan that continues to augment material wealth by means of a lowered political profile might find it necessary to mark a distance from the United States and China if a Sino-Japanese alignment against Russia threatened to polarize the region along racial lines, or if Japan's help in eliminating one of the rival Communist powers altogether polarized it along ideological lines.

The weak link in the nearer eastern triangle centers on the uncertain degree of policy independence from the Soviet Union, and related western contacts, that the lesser eastern European states can safely enjoy. A U.S.-Chinese alliance might seem to neutralize Russia's capacity to react punitively. Trusting in this protective umbrella, at least some of the states might keep expanding their (unequal) amount of autonomy and contacts, or at least their aspirations for these. However, a tightly encircled Soviet Russia would be least likely to be accommodating. She would be certain to impose the strictest limits on both the contacts and the autonomy in order to keep the disintegrative process from quickening. She would run all the risks necessary to extinguish any "deviation" biased (on the Albanian or Rumanian pattern) toward China. And she would not retain any incentive to orchestrate intra- with inter-regional relaxation, however conservatively and tardily, in relations with the West. Western Europe would acquire one more reason for differentiating her policies from America's if she wished to preclude any such potentially uncontrollable developments. It might become urgent for the west Europeans to qualify as the more acceptable partner for the east Europeans, if necessary at some cost to their own internal orders as well as to their alliance orthodoxy.

If too fixed or rigid policies strained the weak links, they would foster movement toward partial dealignments or realignments along the different primary lines of potential cleavage within the Atlantic-Pacific West and in continental Eurasia. The lines are primarily generational, in terms of political history and culture, between Americans as the relatively new-state but senior-partner component and western Europe (and Japan?) as the old-state but junior-partner component in the West. They are primarily geopolitical, in terms of culturally and ideologically neutral political physics in Eurasia, with the lesser states alternately repelled from the contiguous greater power or powers and pulled back to them as a refuge from one another or on a rebound from insufficiently supportive or responsive remoter powers.

If one or both of the Atlantic-Pacific and the Eurasian key segments of world politics were to be destabilized, neither would be able to positively influence the divisions within the Afro-Asian or third-world segment. These are chiefly functionally determined in conditions defined by nearly each country or unit having a different resource endowment and capacity for development. The resulting pulls and counterpulls are constantly on the verge of degenerating into disaster-prone disorder. Adding to the suspense about third-world evolution, the final alienation of Russia would tend to fill the narrow West with rising alarm, while the physical disintegration of the Russian-dominated East would make it feel too secure at least for a time. Neither an overawed nor an overconfident West is likely to muster the material weight or to display the moral stamina necessary for helping steer developments in much of the Third World toward substantiating the largely formal character of independence and away from compounding the consequences of a largely unearned decolonization.

Stabilizing further the already existing relations is more urgent than transforming the essence of world politics. Aligning major power to that end on the central chessboard of high policy is more important than is a world-wide coordination of the steadily multiplying subordinate activities, actors, and functions; keeping key alignments within the limits of great-power tolerance is also inherently more feasible. The feat is, however, not within the range of virtuoso tactics self-consciously free of theory any more than of virtuous intentions. And performing the feat cannot be significantly aided in the west by a theory that is devoid of attention to the historical antecedents to present policy dilemmas, any more than it could be in the east by an ideology so single-mindedly revolutionary as to repudiate traditional dilemmas along with rewriting history.

Conjuring the ominous consequences of a particular latent structure, and thus avoiding their realization, will require theoretically inclined policy-makers to conjure up in their imagination the long-term implications of that structure in advance, as if the structure were already fully extant in the present. If this calls for some temerity, authority for it will flow from a comparable structure having transpired in the past. It will help further if the structure's posited implications make sense in terms of tendencies repeatedly corroborated as part of the physics of interstate politics. If correct conclusions are drawn for policy, a theory of war causation and a strategy of war avoidance that postulate the primacy of power structure while resisting its tyranny will have thrown out a bridge to the irreducible area of free will without which neither technical skill nor ethical responsibility is meaningful. The correct blend of ingredients will be rare. When they do fuse, a special kind of *virtù* in the form of the human spirit struggling for autonomy will have wrested from sagacity about power-rooted necessity the weapon for reducing the dominion of fortune; he who is concerned more with adjusting drives for power than about abolishing war in his time will have joined the ranks of peacemakers for other, uncertainly happier, times.

Sources of order and anarchy: comanagement or self-containment

The arena for testing the chances of U.S.-Soviet (or narrowly defined East-West) appeasement is world-wide. This does not mean that all and sundry in the world can or should be appeased for the sake of peace and quiet, at a cost to order and to the benefit of anarchy. Whereas the strategy of containment turned the United States into a global policeman, abandoning that role means that it should also stop advertising itself as the principal victim of

Russian break-ins in the Third World. It will be easier to deal with Soviet outreach in strategic depth if lesser local parties are exposed to the need for countervailing measures of their own and in their own interests. Avoiding a stampede in the direction of irresistibly advancing Soviets is not the same as stomping around in a vain or expensive quest for military facilities abroad. Demonstrating the capacity to act effectively requires not only physical strength but also strategic stamina; the latter implies the ability not to act so long as inaction is manifestly a matter of choice. Proof of its being this is supplied by effective (if nonnuclear) past responses at times and in places of one's choosing: across space (determined by accessibility), as well as in one's own good time (governed by discernible priorities).

Toward a new configuration of power in Asia. Suppose that, even under revised ground rules, the Soviet invasion of Afghanistan was correctly decreed inconsistent with a controlled movement toward geopolitical parity. The United States could then have reacted in different places at different costs and risks over increasingly extended time spans. It could have responded in places where the Soviets were vulnerable and either the United States or one of its allies had military access (e.g., to Aden or, farther afield, Cuba); places that were of considerable interest to the Soviets and accessible to American economic instruments (e.g., Vietnam); or in places where the diplomatic contest was wide open and the existing distribution of power and alignment could be changed (e.g., in and between India and Pakistan).

For instance, normalizing relations with the exenemy in Hanoi by virtue of assistance to postwar recovery would have hindered the Soviet counterencirclement of China inside Vietnam. But to take that line, U.S. policymakers would have had to conclude that anything like a de facto alliance with China could wait; that forging ahead in Peking would have a more beneficial effect in Moscow as a reserved sanction than as a consummated event. Instead, reinforcing China internally by technology or also externally by arms is a strictly mechanical approach through outflanking alliance. It has allowed China to remain largely passive vis-à-vis the Soviets in anything but rhetoric and left it to the United States to coerce or compress the Soviet Union into a nonaggressive or nonexpansionist posture. Not much will change until—but change suddenly and dramatically after—China has become powerful enough to step up pressures on Russia in ways and places including the traditional access route of Asiatic invaders, the so-called Great Gateway of Nations.

A more dynamic U.S. strategy with a stronger stress on organic transformations would let China countervail Soviet power on her own within the Chinese sphere of interests. While China learned how to act jointly with as many other local powers as possible, selective U.S. interventions at times and in places usually different from China's would provide only indirect backing. Relaxing the U.S.-orchestrated global constraint on the Soviets would indirectly foster changes within the Soviet Union while China continued to grow at her own pace. She could eventually join the relatively conservative superpowers against an extraneous threat that had meanwhile become manifest, unless she herself became a threat to both and finally defused the bilateral U.S.-Soviet conflict. Contrary to the mechanical approach, the changes would be slow and the adaptations to them could be gradual.

The more detached U.S. approach to Soviet expansion might be expected to encourage the Chinese to move closer to India and come to terms with Vietnam. Their choice would be to either incur all the costs of muting the threat the Soviets posed to China, and make the necessary concessions to the northern neighbor, or cease being themselves a threat to India. Only then could the Indians stop looking to Soviet Russia for counterpoise and begin to see in China, if not a firm friend, then an interchangeable partner in a semiautonomous continental-Asian triangle, on a par with Russia. India's new orientation between the two Communist powers would be even more solidly based if she acquired a common frontier between her own and a Soviet sphere of control. Acquiring a protectorate over an autonomous or independent Baluchistan (a separatist province of Pakistan), adjoining as well as matching Russia's protectorate over Afghanistan, might produce the required degree of territorial contiguity. It ought to suffice to dispose of the present asymmetry, with India directly exposed to Chinese pressures but insulated from Soviet penetration.

For the Indians to take thus over the counterweight role that the British performed under the raj exceeds in simple realism elaborate multilateral schemes for neutralizing Afghanistan as a buffer free of Russian influence; it may be a precondition to the scheme becoming realistic. Any Soviet move toward the Indian Ocean through a Baluchistan protected by India would challenge the latter in her de facto possession. By contrast, the same Soviet move in the present situation would only open the way to the virtual absorption of rump Pakistan into the essential core of a reunited Indian subcontinent—and empire. Such a gain to India would tend to soften opposition from New Delhi to a new deal in southwest Asia. American policy failed in the past to back Pakistani integrity against neutralist India in ways necessary to build up the Islamic secessionist from subcontinental unity into a viable factor in both the local and the all-Asian balance of power. Regretting the failure is not the same as refusing to accept its consequences; their acceptance would clear the way for the United States to condone Pakistan's continuing—or final—disintegration. To attempt to reintegrate instead the faltering country into a (pan-Islamic?) anti-Soviet strategy, and refloat Pakistan as ally, will inevitably push India further into the Soviet fold to the same extent as the salvaging effort is effective—and beyond the extent encouraged as risk-free by India's present structural immunity to Soviet power.

A Sino-Indian bloc would bar Soviet advance in the south even as the

United States abstained from unconditionally blocking overseas exits elsewhere and as the U.S.-Chinese vise around Russia was relaxed. Were Soviet ambitions to keep growing nonetheless, the bloc would in due course become a continental subheartland accessible to sea- or air-borne U.S. capabilities for northward projection overland, from concentration points in the south, along lines as "interior" from there on as are those available to Russia for southward projection from the north; this would more than match any intervening maritime or overseas gains of the Russian heartland power. For the U.S.-in-India to replace Britain-in-India as a watered-down replica might be read by some as meaning that India was in some way recolonized. However partial and overshadowed by an alliance tie, the reversion would not be wholly imaginary. It would express the impossibility of totally decolonizing at one swoop a Third World manifestly threatened by full-fledged colonialism made-in-U.S.S.R. It would then be only fitting for the demonstration to take place in the country that pioneered decolonization and first invented and then legitimated the antiwestern type of nonalignment.

Awesome responses to anarchy in the Third World. A different incentive to recolonization would be a growing anarchy in the Third World that invited joint or parallel U.S.-Soviet reaction. A recolonization that is only partial and provisional, second-degree but two-pronged, would match third-world regressions in concept, and would in fact aim at managing them. Foremost among the regressions have been the wrong (from the western viewpoint) kinds of traditionalism, defeating the continuous modernization that was anticipated as the counterpart of a likewise progressing decolonization. Insofar as it is keyed to U.S.-Soviet reapportionment of access and influence, partial recolonization would implement a major realignment from the old military-ideological East-West axis, via the late South-North political-economic one, into a redefined and expanded politico-cultural East-West axis.

Thus, resurrecting the 1907 Anglo-Russian agreement on the Persian-Afghan area would come close to joint recolonization in Asia. Even as ways of implementing great-power influence were updated, proportions in the zones of influence could change. An increase in the American zone over the past British one in Iran would compensate for Russia's having moved into Britain's former predominance in Afghanistan. When Soviet efforts to stand aside or ride the tiger of third-world rebellions are conclusively shown as doomed to failure, the ground will be cleared for such modified redivisions on the Soviet side. From the American viewpoint, the mere possibility of such a development would be a useful check on Iran-like insurgence before or after the event; it might become an indispensable one.

So long as the superpower contest over areas of actual or potential anarchy continues and periodically intensifies, it weakens the trend toward a thermidorlike rollback of the potentially last, U.S.-Soviet rebound of the grand-political revolution that has for centuries engaged the ever more western with the increasingly eastern powers of the greater West. Instead, the U.S.-Soviet rivalry risks fusing the so far separate third-world rebellions into one more world-wide, sociocultural as well as politico-economic, revolution—and moving it toward the terror stage. Only a hard to resist joint U.S.-Soviet containment of such a trend could afford to be benign. Because neither of the major powers, except perhaps an again radicalized China, could lead the revolution, neither can effectively control it with assurance on its own; either is more likely to capitulate step by step before the ensuing chaos.

A single-handed attempt by the United States to stem the tide within a fluid medium and demonstrate power and will to act *in extremis* would be no more cost-free than would be the steps toward a U.S.-Soviet comanagement. The need to make the attempt tell could easily force this country into its own acts of terror. An act of counter-terror may already have become the only effective recourse when the anti-Shah upheaval in Iran had degenerated into an anti-American provocation. It raised the question whether to resist and, if so, how to defeat a manifest intent to abuse and abase the leader of the West. Only through abasing traditional "masters" can the rebellious former "slaves" hope to recover at one stroke collective dignity and delay tackling the harder task of rehabilitation. Only an intrinsically condescending sympathy for their plight, or a mistaken sense of safety, could blind the West to the need of keeping the internationally significant manifestation of that plight in check.*

The West under siege and the costs of American self-containment. The Third World has been the source of multiple threats to the United States and the West at large, both within and without. With only minor exaggeration, it can be said that whereas the Soviet Union is becoming encircled, the West is besieged.

*In the early phase of rebellion, the most humane effective response to antiwestern violence might well be self-inflicted pain with a delayed deterrent purpose. Thus, a way of responding to the Iranian seizure of the U.S. embassy in Teheran might have been to employ air strikes so as to destroy the embassy piecemeal after a brief warning, and in a way giving the captors the option to either evacuate the hostages or trigger more extreme reprisals. This or a similar act of controlled terror would politically inflame the region at large less than any other use of force, but do more than many another response to inspire awe while manifesting the will to keep even but fictional national territory (the embassy grounds) inviolate. All parties would note what they might suffer from a nation that will not shrink from jeopardizing its very own, were provocations to persist. It would undoubtedly take even greater moral than political courage for an American leader to initiate an action potentially fatal to individual Americans. However, qualms would fade and critics be silenced when reflection and results showed that some such acts are on critical occasions necessary within the economy of self-preservation for a political civilization. (It is even possible to interpret the subsequent electoral verdict on President Carter as suggesting that the people's unformed political instinct is different from—and wiser than—the all too humane instincts of the self-consciously non-Machiavellian prince.)

Thus, superimposed on OPEC's economic aggression, the impact and exploitation of the Iranian revolution deranged the political process in the United States and strained interallied cohesion in the West, in addition to stimulating regional turmoil. The Palestinian issue sharpened when not creating interracial (Black-Jewish) tensions inside the American body politic; oil-rich Arabs outdid *nouveau-riche* South Koreans in the use of financial resources to influence if not suborn American social and political elites; peripheral turmoils joined to a misguided sense of imperial or humanitarian responsibilities generated an inflow of unassimilable refugees at the bottom of the social pyramid; and outlandish pseudo-spiritual messages with or without covert policy intent were turning growing numbers at all social levels away from their cultural and religious heritage. At the same time, with help from America's hereditary liberal ethos and a surviving sense of guilt (original or by association with European colonialism), third-world immunity to reprisals was turning into a sense of impunity.

Much as it owes to a vague American liberalism, the impunity is also a partial compensation for a decline in American liberality. There has been less material aid to dispense than before and little willingness to concede third-world demands for redistributive change in the regimes governing the world economy. Meanwhile, immediately less costly or less avoidable ways of courting the forces of social change could be employed at the peripheries in order, supposedly, to thwart an alliance between communist-type revolution and (viewed comparatively) Soviet reaction in the Third World. The courtship would flourish whenever different kinds of Americans pined after either spiritual rejuvenation or a strategic panacea, and west Europeans after a semblance of cultural, economic, or diplomatic independence from America.

By ignoring the possibility of initiating a virtuous circle in U.S.-Soviet relations—to be closed when the two superpowers have closed ranks against global disorder—U.S. policymakers stumbled into an array of vicious circles in the U.S.-Soviet-Third World interplay.

A vicious circle was exemplified by attempts to keep the Soviets out of the Middle East. Only a made-in-USA peace between the Arabs and the Israelis promised to keep the Soviet Union out altogether as the openly admitted coguarantor of a settlement, while it reduced the Soviet Union's chances to act as a disruptive infiltrator in a continuing or escalating conflict. If peace was to be secured by America alone, key Arab states had to be accommodated at all costs, including the cost of unresisted escalation of oil prices.

However, whereas the energy crisis weakened America and still more her industrial allies, the propeace cum anti-Soviet priority helped overthrow a key Middle Eastern ally. Tailoring the Shah of Iran's armaments policy to fit a hypothetical assault by the neighboring great power ignored the needs of protection against the more probable internal upheaval tied to forced-draft modernization. The consequences of misdirected attention were compounded by a domestically provocative commercial policy. Supplying oil to Islam's chosen Israeli enemy may have been a partial offset to the shah's leading role in the first oil price increase; it is at least as plausible a hypothesis that U.S. policymakers condoned the lead role because, and so long as, it generated funds for Iran's armament against the Soviet Union. When the shah's fall made the price of oil rise further, parallel if uneven American and European shifts toward the Arab viewpoint on the Palestinian issue, conjointly with Israel's adverse negotiating posture, produced a conflict of perspectives. The simplest way to obscure this conflict was to highlight the Soviet threat as one common to all, and the United States and Israel in particular. An intense enough threat would submerge all lesser differences in national interests; and it would suspend calculations of what the existing state of affairs cost the two countries in terms of their respective dependencies—American on Middle East oil and Israeli on the United States.

Unless the Arab-Israeli conflict is in due course superseded and made obsolete by alternative (inter-Arab or intra-Islam) salient conflicts, a more than partial, transient, or long-deferred peaceful settlement in the Middle East will require U.S.-Soviet cooperation in "imposing" a settlement. Therefore, it has not helped matters that a minor or subsidiary vicious circle intensified the operation of the major or principal one. Whereas the United States would not cooperate with Soviet Russia for purposes of peaceful settlement whenever the Russian position in the area was strong, the same Soviets would not and could not do more than pay lip service to both regional peace and superpower cooperation in arranging it when their position of influence grew weak—for example, after the changeover in Egypt from Nasser to Sadat and Sadat's from the Soviet to the American connection. Thus, if the United States was not really serious at any point about the procedure that would implement the principle of Soviet participation in peacemaking, Soviet Russia was not serious in regard to the substance of her proposals for the terms of settlement: American concentration on the tactics of maneuvering the Soviets out of the region was matched by Russia's rigid support for extreme radical-Arab bargaining positions.

If Soviet radicalism supplied a justification for American reluctance to include the Soviets, the weakness of the Soviet position in the region supplied an excuse for Soviet radicalism. Soviet diplomacy had to anticipate the unavoidable erosion of Russia's influence in the Middle East in the period following a peace settlement, when her military assistance became secondary to America's greater capacity for economic and technological assistance to local parties. She had therefore to make every effort to enter the peace era with the maximum of (erosion-prone) credit with a substantial portion of the Arab world, as well as with the capacity to regain some access to Israel. Such access could originate only in Israeli resentment of U.S. participation in the degree of coercion inseparable from a superpower comanagement of the peace process in ways acceptable if not satisfactory to the Arab, or Palestinian, side; only the combination of peace and anti-American animus could terminate Israel's imperviousness to any positive contact with the Soviets, until then inconsistent with unqualified Israeli claim on unconditional U.S. support. Finally, the relationship of forces in the area made it necessary for the Soviets to extract from the United States concessions of peace conditions that would implicitly convey an assurance of U.S. understanding for the inherent weakness of the Soviet position in peacetime Middle East, and thus the assurance of U.S. cooperation in backstopping Soviet influence in the area when its conflict-related basis had been eroded.

All in all, Soviet fear of Middle Eastern peace was caught up in a mutually frustrating imbroglio with the U.S. fear of Soviet participation in peacemaking. The amount of U.S. acquiescence in formal-procedural inclusion of the Soviets that was actually forthcoming in circumstances surrounding warfare or intervening between spells of military activities was equal to their de facto exclusion insofar as the acquiescence was chiefly aimed at demonstrating Soviet intractability on either the regional or "linked" extraneous issues. And exclusion fostered Soviet extremism, dedicated to keeping an irreducible foothold within the area, conjointly with the search for extraneous positions of strength outside the area for purposes of leverage on (and possible future "linkage" with) issues and events in the most conflict-torn regional theater in the Third World.

Such major and minor vicious circles became inextricably intertwined when acting on the postulate of disruptive Soviet intentions confirms the Soviets in policies that seemingly corroborate the postulate; when each upgrading of the anti-Soviet priority sets off a new chain of events that raise the stakes and enhance the risks beyond what made the priority initially seem plausible. A single-minded strategy of anti-Soviet containment then makes for America's self-containment. It generates a paralysis of strategic flexibility and imagination on the subject of the local sources of unrest. Moreover, self-containment will be easily attended by internal contradiction. A stance of painting the Soviets as the main threat is punctuated by bids for their (unrewarded?) cooperation in appeasing the less hypothetical, locally originated threats to regional peace and stability—such as the Syrian-Israeli contentions in and over south Lebanon. The fundamental contradiction cannot but defeat the fleeting discovery of the usefulness of cooperation.

The U.S. alternative to an anti-Soviet reflex is not dogmatic repudiation of any political group or ideological faction in the Third World. Managing decompression vis-à-vis the Soviets neither need nor could exclude cooperative alignments with other parties in a highly complex part of the world. Even if it shares a basic cultural disposition toward the West, it is a universe that is as pluralistic as the threat it poses is multifarious.

The change in the strategy toward the Soviet Union implies merely a special kind of flexibility when dealing with both intra- and interstate conflicts in the Third World. The United States need be only as principled in the face of a shifting U.S.-Soviet balance (and a perhaps fracturing world balance) as the early third-world policymakers were toward the United States—and the Soviet Union—in the period of a taut bipolar East-West balance favoring the United States: that is, not at all. A western policy tolerant of structural changes, such as that in regard to Pakistan, must be equally opportunistic in strategy when alternating between support for, and backing of local resistance to, indigenous actors intent on shaping national or regional balances of power to their advantage. There is ample reason for this. Ambiguously offensive and defensive local interplays will moderate ideological and cultural attitudes toward the West over time by creating compulsions to deal with indigenous interest issues and power drives. They will also preempt by local power struggles and configurations the geopolitical space, or the power vacuums, that would otherwise invite Soviet expansion or intensify U.S.-Soviet competition over reapportionment of influence. This will reduce the stakes of great-power conflict, not the least by making any (and especially Soviet) gains precarious.

As regards the regionally ambitious small or middle powers in particular, a relaxed superpower competition will encourage making support for them contingent on their self-limitation. Their function is to trigger the regional crystallization process, not to kill it off prematurely. Moreover, a United States that has moved beyond both containment strategy and an imperial role and posture would lessen its need for regional surrogates in checking the Soviets. Instead of devolving that task, a yet longer-term strategy would aim at dissolving cultural East-West polarity into a competitive, global *Realpolitik*. With better reason, "no more Irans"—of the Pahlavi as much as of the Khomeini brand—would join "no more Vietnams" in a negative view of the past. Past mistakes and misjudgments are still hard to assess justly and reliably; but they can be redeemed only by a positive hold on a future that safely may, and surely will, include "more Angolas."

U.S.-Russian appeasement and East-West accommodation from strength or weakness. Threat from Soviet Russia has come to be emphasized again over that from the Third World, in official western Europe only slightly less than in the United States. This distribution of emphasis has had its rewards. It allowed the United States to press dependent west Europeans for support in anti-Soviet measures and sanctions, and it allowed the west Europeans to maintain an apparently cost-free or immediately profitable pretense of independence in foreign policy on third-world issues. Jointly, the result has been that Atlantic solidarity appears greater than it actually is—an appearance sustained by two half-illusions: one, for the entire West, of a communitylike alliance among equals; another, for the west Europeans only, of continued statehood in the classic fullness of the term, implying the possession and exercise of a foreign policy that is commensurate with national resources (vis-à-vis the Third World for the European "middle powers," within the Atlantic Alliance only for the truly small states). Near-fictions work so long as harsh contrary facts are in abeyance. When they intrude, it might become clearer that Euro-American solidarity is more solidly based with respect to the Third World than it is vis-à-vis Russia; that it is more likely to be actively expressed toward the former under economic pressure than, under politico-military pressure, with respect to Europe's last major power and one closely contiguous with European middle and small powers.

It can be usefully a major premise behind a grand strategy that the central U.S.-Soviet contest over entitlement to role and status parity-in-situational disparity is easier to manage and less threatening than are the issues raised in and by third-world demands or disorders. In its critical segments, the Third World is high on the scale of immediate threats to the West (and eventual threats to both superpowers). It is low on the scale of direct manageability by routine measures of low-level strategy or tactics. This premise and the underlying perception place a premium on a circuitous approach to the Third World, via a U.S.-Soviet accommodation, rather than the other way around. They also warrant selective intimidation of currently unmanageable third-world elements, instead of viewing isolation from the Third World *en bloc* as the supreme evil and its avoidance as the highest priority.

The utility or necessity of the indirect approach—at first largely preventive—has been ratified by a failure. It has also been resisted on the basis of a fallacy. The failure has been one of policy: all of the U.S. approaches to the Third World so far attempted, from delegation of responsibilities onto the European colonial powers to the devolution of responsibility onto regional actors (the so-called Nixon Doctrine), by way of alliance proliferation (Dullesian "pactomania") and battlefield association (in Korea and Vietnam), have failed to produce the anticipated benefits, be they satisfactory results or reduced costs. The fallacy has been one of perception: it was just as misguided to reduce third-world actors to a common denominator, as states (or political parties) in the conventional meaning of the term, as it has been to either deemphasize or overemphasize the splits and divisions of interests and capabilities among them.

As things actually stand, America's west European allies have striven to recover in the Third World the lost external attributes of statehood by way of foreign policies directed at it; most third-world parties have not yet achieved such statehood based on the strength of effective domestic politics or policies. Consequently, in order to reverse the priorities between Soviet Russia and the Third World with regard to perceived threat and effectuated response, it is first necessary to fully take in the indeterminate, inchoately state- and nationlike character of most third-world entities; the next step is to draw consequences from this awareness. Until this has been done, continuing fallacies will make it attractive, and past western failures make it challenging, to treat all third-world actors as responsive objects of diplomatic and other initiatives. For the same reasons, it will be unappealing to treat any of them as a major threat.

Only if the evaluation of the threat is changed will accommodation with Russia become attractive: for its own sake in the short run; as a basis for accommodation with the third-world forces in the longer one—and then all the more lasting accommodation for its taking place from political strength. This is a brighter prospect than is one of having to purchase such accommodation in a precipitate fashion as the sole remaining means of continuing a rigid containment of the Soviets, at the cost of a final constriction of western influence.

The western sway expanded whenever expansion was the least costly response and remedy to systemic crisis or core-systemic stalemate, or was the most profitable response to weaknesses outside the West. As time went on, expansion could be also the least costly safeguard against the external weaknesses infiltrating the West. The nature of the crisis could and did vary and evolve. So long as the nonproductive economy of early feudalism put a premium on war as a source of wealth in the form of booty or ransom, the result was a military crisis; it was best drained off into the predatory thrust of the crusades. When changes in the techniques of land cultivation had proved insufficient to augment the food supply and the industrial revolution was in the future, the agricultural crisis of later feudalism was eased by the first drive overseas. The drive outward continued to be stimulated by the late nineteenth-century crises of industrial capitalism at mid-life, before relief came from intrasystemic remedies in the form of neocapitalist welfare statism.

Either misuse or maldistribution of the comparatively static agricultural surplus or the more elastic capital-industrial surplus were among the causes of the economic crises. Alternative propellants to expansion gained in importance whenever intranation or intra-West remedies were adequate to deal with the consequences of those crises. Then, expansion was due to the urge to escape from stalemate among the nation states in Europe, increasingly well-defined as they evolved out of smaller or relatively shapeless larger units via entitites of changing optimum size or scope, from imperial city-states to multistate empires. Or expansion could be triggered by instability or generalized insolvency of societies outside Europe.

The long-term record points to three main propellants: actual or anticipated economic crisis, politico-military stalemate, and peripheral instability. It is arguable how exactly they were distributed in the impetus behind the post–World War II restoration of the West-centered system around the United States. And it is questionable whether yet another spell of reexpansion might follow the latest of the likewise periodically recurring constrictions of the western sway.

Either actual shrinkage or, at least, slackening of the expansionist dynamic were due to two extreme conflict situations: an unusually intense and absorbing intrawestern conflict and an unusual moderation of central-systemic contentions. The first category is best illustrated by the discords among the crusader kingdoms, which helped Islam roll back the early western presence in the Near East. Later, the religious conflicts climaxing in the mid-seventeenth century delayed the full resumption of overseas competition and colonial expansion. And the latest example is the peak of multifaceted conflicts in the two world wars of the first half of the twentieth century. They promoted formal decolonization as a prelude to cold war–induced neocolonization. In the obverse, relatively conflict-free category can be likewise tentatively placed the half century or more following 1815, prefacing late-nineteenth-century resurgence of formal imperialism; the slightly more than a decade long post-1918 lull followed by the late-colonialist resurgence of the 1930s; and, most recently, the post–cold war détente and the related U.S. attempt at partial disengagement from the Third World in the mid-1970s.

Currently at issue is the sequel to the attempted disengagement associated with the retreat from Indochina, the "Nixon Doctrine," and the high-water mark of U.S.-Soviet détente. Will another reexpansion attend parallel or joint U.S.-Soviet responses world-wide to postindustrial American and industrial-agricultural Russian economic crisis; will this take place on the strength of a U.S.-Soviet politico-military stalemate that is more or less competitive, depending on the achieved degree and scope of parity between the superpowers; or, finally, will it occur in response to intensifying instabilities and upheavals or provocations in the third-world arena? Or else will the latest spell of semivoluntary western disengagement merge into further constriction of the western sway in favor of eastern predominance? Would such a constriction be imposed on the narrow West from the outside, or would too intense a conflict within the total Occident finally result in undermining the capacity of both of its superpower poles to exert significant influence outside it? And which trend is more propitious for the restoration of the international system as genuinely global (because mostly locally determined in its dynamics), if heterogeneous in terms of member values?

The unlikely event of an easy subduance of the Soviet Union would be likely to reduce the stimulus behind western self-assertion abroad. Barring that event, anything like western sway is apt to reexpand—or the international system is likely to be more enduringly recentered on the West—only if Russia has become part of the latter. While the cost might include some revaluation of prevailing norms and the redistribution of influence in the West, the method might include partial recolonization outside the enlarged West. The revaluation and redistribution would express the fact that peaceable accommodation of rising or resentful forces, such as Soviet Russia in relation to the traditional or narrow West, requires expansion of the political system, and that expansion entails change. The recolonization, in turn, while it is only one of the ways for generating the added margin of resources or space that facilitates accommodation, and while it is apt to be less direct and less onerous for its objects in each successive spell, would draw practical consequences from the fact that the expectations accompanying formal decolonization and prior disengagement efforts have failed to be fully realized in regard to the politico-economic development and foreign-policy behavior of many of the "new states."

Whether or not attended by recolonization, the reexpansion of an enlarged West could easily involve a shift eastward in the focus of international activity and competition. But neither would entail, and both would be likely to prevent, an eastward shift in the center of gravity of world politics and power. Not the least of reasons for this is that the bulk of what would be Russia's economic dowry to the West continues to be located west of the Ural Mountains. Somewhat the same effect would flow from the regional Russo-Chinese demographic and related balances in the east being stabilized at a lowered level of tension, while the Atlantic allies remained the key focus for Soviet diplomatic and strategic concerns despite (and in part because of) the shift in the balance from competition to cooperation within the greater West.

Accommodation between West and East would take a different course if it were consequent on some form of expansion of the eastern segment of the international system and a concurrent constriction of the western part. The expansion of the eastern system might result from reactions, chiefly military, to aggravated economic maladjustments within the Soviet Union (perhaps including a final failure to develop and populate Siberia), to a conflict-prone politico-military stalemate between the Soviet Union and a China aided and backed by the West, and to moral, political, and economic weaknesses and insolvencies in the West. It is true that the western political system was confined or constricted from the east before, by more or less nomadic invasions from Asia and by Islamic inroads or counter-crusades. New forms of inroads remain possible. But, for the first time in vivid memory, the West might also be constricted by virtue of a politico-militarily enacted dynamic among fully consolidated powers in the east. For the West to be so constricted would mark the end of an entire era of western growth, begun in the tenth century and accelerated from the fifteenth century on. The late drift to disengagement in the relatively minor or short-term cycles of western expansion and retrenchment would merge into an antiwestern turn in the major or long-term East-West cycle of rise and decline, advance and retreat.

Several scenarios are possible. The West might be constricted by a military Russo-Chinese interaction when a Russia still weak, and weakening further, is compelled to shift the main thrust of her military power against rising China. The West would then be reduced in size if Russia unleashed a massive Schlieffen Plan–type assault in order to neutralize her western European rear and free her hands against China in the east; or if the European part of the West chose self-neutralizing passivity in order to lessen the Soviet incentive to preemptive conquest while war clouds were gathering over the East. The center of gravity in world power would shift eastward as the residual West in the form of the United States shifted strategic attention to Japan (a substitute off Eurasia for the British islands in Europe) in an effort to maintain a stake in the Pacific balance of power after losing out in the Atlantic, and as it firmed up the alliance with China, in order to "stop" Soviet Russia in the Far East after failing (in the Middle East and elsewhere) to secure western Europe against either Soviet pressures or the Europeans' own propensities.

Under such a scenario, America would be all that was left of the West and would have to act precipitately from great weakness to accommodate the East, meaning China and whatever third-world country might still be up for auction. Under a different scenario, the West would also be curtailed, if only relative to its potential size and strength, and be likewise pushed toward accommodation with the East, if an augmented one. In such a hypothesis, an irresistible drive from overpopulated northern China into underpopulated eastern Soviet Union would reduce effective Soviet Russia to her inner, Eurasian heartland. A thus truncated Soviet Union would be likely to withdraw into sullen isolation, attended by intensified coercion especially within the non-Russian parts of the remaining core empire. As a volatile third force between China and the West, the Russians would be fixed only in a revived sense of western betrayal. Thus disposed, they would bide their time until they could exploit any sign of U.S.-Chinese conflict filling the vacuum of conflict across the quasi-vacuum of power created by Soviet regression. Such a situation would compel the West to propitiate at all costs a newly strengthened China or any other major third-world actor, in order to perpetuate the east-west encirclement of an ultra-revisionist Russia as long as possible. Just as under the previous scenario in which the feared prospect was Soviet victory over China, so now Russia's partial defeat would compel the United States to accommodate the East from a position of weakness. Although the weakness in the latter case would be more diplomatico-strategic than military-strategic, it would be weakness nonetheless.

Finally, Soviet Russia might effectively neutralize China, politico-ideologically or otherwise, in the face of a provocative but insufficient western support for China—or for anti-Soviet elements within China. Under this particular scenario, the West would become more than ever dependent on any third-world parties willing and able to align with it against a recombined

Russo-Chinese complex. It could hardly bargain effectively over the terms of either economic or political accommodation with potential third-world supports. Along with the chance for a U.S.-Russian appeasement from remaining western strength, the chance for reexpanding the influence of an enlarged West world-wide would also have been lost. It might be lost for good as Soviet Russia, triumphant in Asia, moved away from any inclination to Europeanize her outlook and herself; she would no longer need this partial protection against an Asia resurgent outside Soviet boundaries and, potentially, within them. It would be Japan's turn to run the risk of being neutralized, while the development would hardly galvanize western Europe into a closer and more active commitment to the western alliance. West Europeans would be likelier to fall gradually within the magnetic field of Soviet power: first diplomatically, then politico-militarily, and finally economically.

Henceforth, if gradually, as Soviet Russia rose in the east, changes in the focus of competition in world politics would prefigure the displacement of the center of gravity in world power as well. It would be part of a special form of convergence if the eastward power displacement were to accelerate the westward migration of the economic center of gravity inside the United States; a further speed-up in that migration already under way might be necessary for a strong U.S. stand in the Pacific arena. A parallel shift in the ethnic composition of Americans, away from the European stock, already matches the relative increase of non-Russians in the Soviet Union. A new, post-Atlantic era could thus open for the United States on the cultural plane as well as on the geostrategic and economic front. Russia more than America would then remain able to import whatever might still be serviceable in Europe's cultural treasury, either directly or indirectly across the transfer zone of her western-Slavic dependents. As for western Europe, commentators describing her condition would be free to choose between (politico-economic) "Netherlandization," (politico-military) "Finlandization," (socio-ideological) "Polonization," and—last but not least—(cultural post-Renaissance) "Italianization." But the West hailing from Rome, as we know it, would be no more. To survive in any form whatsoever, it would have to be, not for the first time, revived from the "Greek" east.

It is possible to prefer, over such a grim scenario, the quadrilateral pattern of balance wherein the two superpowers are flanked by China as ballast on one side and by western Europe as East-West broker and the bridge for Russia's Europeanization or westernization on the other side. Much provisional stability could accrue from such a pattern. It would generate the margin of time and safety necessary for determining, in relative tranquillity, which way the provisional equilibrium is to evolve for all. A world order centered on major powers (including what presently are only middle powers) might grow out of an initially only western, but all-occidental, concert including Russia. Europe's unity and the West's enlargement would become synonymous while western Europe and the United States moved closer together on the platform of a grand strategy keyed to fostering decompression inside Soviet Russia, and both moved closer to Russia thanks to the strategy's success in fostering intra-occidental appeasement. Only if the United States alone repulsed the efforts of the west Europeans to act as honest brokers in the relations with (and within) the Soviet bloc would European unity be taking shape at the expense of Atlantic community. The extreme and ultimate result of such an evolution might be the American and Chinese wing powers setting out to contain, from off-shore insular and rear-continental extremities, a genuinely amphibious Russia-centered Europe as the intermediate power.

Such a configuration is much less likely to result from western European secession from America in a quadrilateral context than from Soviet coercion of western Europe (or her gradual diplomatic subversion) in a triangular context. So long as peace reigns and prosperity is not at stake, tensions within the Atlantic area are not likely to translate into complete rupture, or strains into secession. Nor will tensions within the Soviet bloc generally, and upheavals in any one eastern European country specifically, be resolved into either integral domestic liberalism or completed westward defection. If there is instead to be some degree of overall convergence, the converging movement will have to engage all parties, even if each case differs as to motivation and particular manifestations. Equally inclusive would be a divergent movement toward more conflict and a war so major as to preclude progress toward interdependent valued ends. One consists of restoring the endangered international system in its new global and incipient community dimensions; another of recovering lost individual liberties in traditionally sustainable dimensions.

Long-range aspects of East-West accommodation: international-system restoration and interregional regeneration

A policy for easing the U.S.-Soviet competition will tend to divert Soviet Russia from taking the critical step in the by-now classic sequence, beyond the first phase of limited expansionism on land and sea to the second phase of an all-out drive for continental hegemony. A moderate Soviet global outreach serves in the more benign contingency as a medium for Russia's full integration into the international system, while her own political system is being internally decompressed and her regime is being encouraged to reduce acts of oppression within the dominated region. The third-world issue involves a different problem over a still longer period of time: how to relate resolution of the conflict between the West and Russia to dealing with cleavages between an enlarged West—including Russia—and the excolonial "East."

Only as the connection between the two sequences is realized will an East-West détente fit in properly with the so-called South-North dialogue and the international system move from revolution to restoration. The issues are not new. If détente is the more recent label for a state of great-power relations more graphically denoted as appeasement in the 1930s, interdependence, which presumably underlies the South-North dialogue, has been less a descriptive and more a prescriptive condition of revising the economic status quo in favor of the latest brand of "have nots." Both détente and interdependence have been subject to misconception and misrepresentation. This will continue so long as they depend for being more than clichés in a slogan upon conditions that are either absent or also treated as unnecessary or undesirable, be it by critics of détente or by advocates of interdependence.

East-West diversions and intercultural conversion. Preparing the ground for system restoration entails trying to save the contemporary western and eastern great powers from eventual collision. A clash can take place at the end of the rivals' movement away from a stalemate in different, including opposite, directions. An early example is supplied by the Habsburgs and the Ottomans. More generally, the maritime European powers moved repeatedly overseas in reaction to stalemates in the heart of Europe. The elliptical movement led them by way of west Africa and America eastward toward Asia. Russia's diversion from deadlock in central Europe was mostly overland toward Asia. It has been lately inflected increasingly southward as well as westward in the overseas realm. With the United States replacing the west Europeans, the elliptical movements have come to intersect in the Middle East cum Africa region and, secondarily, central America. So far, the intersection has been only moderately conflictual when measured against a potentially more explosive development. Such would be a massive diversion of Russian power eastward on land only, or its contrived deflection thereto.

A spontaneous Russian military assault on China would differ from peaceful Soviet promotion of a self-sufficient regional balance with China, aided by economic development in Russia's east Asian provinces. It would match Germany's assault on Russia in World War I, while incorporating the lesson from the failure of the Germans' West-first strategy. And a deliberate western attempt to deflect a Soviet thrust eastward would do more than complement the many past moves to block Russia in the west. It would replicate the hope of some western strategists before World War II that Nazi German expansionism might be directed away from western Europe toward and against Russia, en route to the two totalitarian powers' mutual destruction. The attempt might, however, also reenact the scheme's failure and aggravate the consequences of the Russians' ingrained suspicion that, while actors and plots may change, dealing with Russia through eastward deflection is a settled western policy.

Whether spontaneous or contrived, an overland Russian drive eastward would initiate a major crisis in the east, without the West being assuredly capable of significantly influencing a Russo-Chinese deadlock. The least likely western achievement is to make certain that the two powers do not avoid mutual destruction by coordinating their expansion in Asia. Similarly, a weakened France and an indifferent England were previously either unwilling or unable to prevent greater-power deadlocks in eastern Europe being resolved at the expense of the lesser states or peoples in the area. The basic scenario was the same when the deadlock was between Austria, Prussia, and Russia in the late eighteenth century and when it later resurfaced between Germany and Russia. Nor could the West parry on land a full-scale Russian move eastward even if it braced itself into resuming expansion there with full might and military muscle.

Times have changed since an earlier diversion from intrawestern strains eastward, but its consequences are still working themselves out. The drive began when rule and religion—or force and faith—as well as profit and power came together in the crusades in the "near" (European and Levantine) East. It was resumed largely for profit even before receiving added impetus from the new kind of stimuli secreted by the near-simultaneous French and Industrial revolutions. Napoleon's drive into Egypt was followed by Britain's accelerated advance beyond Egypt in creating the modern conditions for spreading beyond the near East the western compound of conquest, colonization, and conversion. However, much as the intensity of the West's drive defined the global scope of conquest and colonization, the incompleteness of the East's conversion has since defined the extent of the global crisis. So did the insufficiently foreseen consequences of accomplished, if often unintended, kinds and forms of westernization. The frequency with which conversion to techniques went hand in hand with the perversion of both western and indigenous values has done anything but mute the crisis. And the consequences of the crisis have been blunted only little by the outcome of the attempt by the communist East to convert ideologically first the West itself and then the modernizing East. The effort has proved no more—or no more lastingly—successful than had been the liberal-capitalist West's in the premodern East.

Anyone interested in ways of resolving the global crisis can usefully note yet another failure. Just before the French revolution, it seemed possible to appease the systemic turbulence attending the difficult transition from the primacy of land-based to the superiority of sea-based power and economy within and between states. Britain and France had finally settled their overseas accounts over North America. They might have been able at last to monitor jointly the protracted adaptations of societies and states at points east, at first in Europe, to the new order of things and their eventual inclusion in the new politico-economic synthesis. It was not to be, even after Napoleon's taming of the revolution made a new try possible (at the Peace of Amiens); the taming of France herself after Napoleon's fall made it irrelevant. The question has since been whether the restoration process, first interrupted and then set back after another (Anglo-German) attempt, could be consummated around a U.S.-Soviet core; or whether the process would be again caught up in, and frustrated by, a new wave of revolution having only superficial if any points of similarity with possible antecedents—be it the French bourgeois (let alone commune-type) social revolution, the so-called proletarian Bolshevik revolution, or the British industrial revolution in its causes and effects.

The West's hesitant undertaking to convert the third-world East to its values and practices was a pale replica of its one-time fiery zeal to convert eastern Europe to Christianity. Likewise less impressive than the earlier achievements in the same area by western Catholicism and eastern Orthodoxy have been the more recent competitive efforts of modern West and Soviet East to base a parallel delimitation of zones of influence globally on an irreversible triumph of either side's values. But if the twin modern failures have been the making of the ongoing global crisis in relations between the two superpowers, and between them and the Third World, the failures have also created the preconditions of excelling a mere conversion.

Superior to conversion from one source—and more lastingly beneficial than even mild recolonization by two superpowers acting jointly or in parallel—is regeneration shared by all parties to the East-West cleavages. Whenever indigenous and received values blend within culturally and otherwise defined areas or regions, they do as part of an interactive process between them. Thus, influences from the east had regenerated the West in Italy and in key ways helped the rebirth of the West in the Franco-Germanic realm before the western impact on the European East propelled its latent energy into a more purposeful enterprise. Although it was most pronounced between European parties, interregional regeneration through East-West conflict was not confined to them. Stopping short of utopia, the interplay between culture areas was beneficial in ways sufficiently real to contrast with the ultimate nemesis of competitive power-seeking as part of the schism between land- and sea-oriented powers. Theirs was a mutual, even when not simultaneous, destruction as states of the first rank and declension as nations from higher aspirations.

The historical omens confer long-term promise on every uncertain sign suggesting that the U.S.-Soviet activity in the Third World might become ever less defined and motivated by the land-sea power issue (aggravated by the "narrow" East-West issue) and be increasingly fitted into a transformed and globally expanded East-West issue. The promise would be greatest if resolving the first-mentioned conflict regenerated an enlarged West to the point where it might stand its ground in relations with the third-world East while respecting its strivings. Only by standing its ground will the West help firmly implant in the postcolonial world whatever hybrid compound of old and new, indigenous and alien (i.e., western, depending on one's viewpoint civilized or barbarian) values and forces the global "East" (or "South") may be able to evolve as part of *its* regeneration. As the interregional and intercultural East-West dynamic reaches outside Europe and gathers momentum, it will evoke recollections—and may revive some of the manifestations—of earlier, precolonial interplays. But it need not repeat them exactly.

System restoration or disruption. The international system can be restored out of revolution as late-entering key powers are socialized into its rules and key regions or cultures recover from regression. Or the system can drift into one more episode in the cyclically recurrent mutual destruction of successive rival parties to the land-sea power schism, which merely shifts a third party into the foreground. The difference is momentous at a time when it is easier to abstract from past instances the pattern of claims and denials attaching to the schismatic two-power relationship and to its triangular setting than it is to project the pattern past the U.S.-Soviet-Chinese triangle. That triangle can be described as terminal, given the limitation of the available geostrategic space and the scarcity of possible future role holders or incumbents that can be reliably identified. Inherent in this seemingly terminal manifestation of a recurrent pattern of conflict perfected over four centuries are possibilities of disruption quite independent of the aggravating effect of the ultimate weapon. Yet what that weapon might add to a climax in the next century does not make for more sanguine prognosis about what mismanaging the contemporary triangle would do to the expanding and diversifying East-West environment.

Mismanagement would dispose of the task of restoring a stable international system by a use of traditional methods that only improves on traditional outcomes. It would do so by shifting the task to the reconstitution of something resembling a system of states out of intervening chaos. If the major powers continued to undermine one another in competition, the familiar pattern could resume only in a quasi-system more depleted of organized power than is the present one. *Ex hypothesi,* such a "system" would lack Russia (or America) and, perhaps, any equivalent of Russia (or America) as, historically, the source of support for resistance to one-power hegemony. It might also lack China as an offset to a Russia (or America) entrenched in hegemony, or lack the equivalent of China as the continental counterpoise to a China that had succeeded Spain, France, Germany, and Russia as the aspirant to hegemony. Also lacking in the aggregate would thus be a configuration of major powers capable of imposing rational constraints on any revolutionary or rebellious forces for system dissolution. Rationality in interstate relations hinges in the best of cases on a prudent adjustment of means to feasible goals that are almost automatically induced by well-defined power structures. Its hold would be more than precarious on the forces of chaos that would dominate the scene before the attendant ordeals inflected the longest-term cycle of system dissolution and reconstitution again toward order.

It is a tactical, or low-strategic, difficulty that the road to a common superpower front against chaos will be paved with Soviet military initiatives aimed at consolidating regional dominion and reaching beyond it. Such initiatives will have positive side effects if the Soviet outreach extends "modernization" from the military to the economic sphere and promotes "liberalization" in the political sphere. It is paying the tribute due to circularity omnipresent in matters of this kind to argue that the beneficial chain reaction will be likelier within the regional Soviet orbit the less leadership roles in the economic and the military arenas are frozen into segregated compartments—with the United States dominant economically and the Soviet Union assertive militarily—in the world at large.

Anything that highlights the role of military factors in world order is welcome if it corrects the western tendency to lapse into shaping policies in keeping with economic factors (i.e., into economism) whenever political tensions have subsided ever so little. Even more desirable is anything that adds an economic dimension and distills in the process an antidote to Russia's history of militarism. Because the functional, economic and military, constituents of political *power* cannot be lastingly separated within either a national or the global order, it is just as well that the military-political and economic capabilities be joined in both of the superpowers. Their union is preferable to the two types of *powers* (primarily land-based military and sea-oriented mercantile) subverting one another as each superpower tries to monopolistically exploit one kind of power or acquire and assert the other kind. It may be a remote goal to foster a dual—politico-military and economic—equilibrium for world order around two coordinate points of gravity. But, even if such a goal contravenes past precedent, it is more realistic for a long-term strategy than has been much of recent practice. An economically stronger power, such as the United States, may try but will not succeed to purchase the geopolitical abstinence of a militarily strong and enterprising power, such as Soviet Russia, with benefits from economic transactions and technology transfers.

The more stable situation is one wherein the two superpowers share more equally in the influence arising out of politico-military and economic capabilities. The resulting equilibrium should weaken both of two unsettling tendencies: one is inherent in the urge of the first (politico-military) type of power to overextension; the other in the second (economic) power type being liable to self-liquidation.

The tendency for economic advantage to be expended as it is diffused grows with the use of the economic weapon in a politico-military contest; it will be intensified to America's disadvantage. Equally, Soviet Russia will display the tendency to overextension all the more if U.S. policy opposes Russia's use of her military-political assets in ways her leaders can view as provocative. When this happens, the Soviets will inevitably seek additional gains in order to secure older ones. More foreign successes will be expected to compensate, in internally enhanced regime legitimacy, for the outside world's denial of legitimacy to the regime's external gains. They will also serve to offset the rigors of internal austerity or stagnation, which the outside world, embodied in the chief rival, has refused to relieve as part of its policy of sanctions.

A U.S.-Soviet appeasement based on the principle of overall parity would reduce Soviet incentives to unending expansion. So would a controlled relaxation of internal Soviet authority, likely to attend such appeasement, to the extent that contraction of internally oppressive controls would replace diplomatic or other conquests abroad as a source of regime legitimacy. And the controlled manner in which gradual internal relaxation occurred would minimize any turmoil or dynamic within the society that might stimulate external expansion indirectly by way of defensive regime reactions. Nor would reducing the military-political contention with the Soviets augment the risks of the western economic and technological superiority being self-liquidating with regard to the Soviet Union. The latter is unavoidably the beneficiary of economic-technological diffusion, as a rival only somewhat less and later than as "ally." Furthermore, the risks would be reduced with respect to the Third World because cooperation—rather than rivalry—with the Soviets would make it easier to regulate world-wide diffusion and keep it optional in kinds and degrees.

Helpful in the adjustment of the material factors of economic and military power, appeasement would eventually also help erode the cleavage in socioeconomic values and ideologies. It would defeat even repeated efforts to retard or roll back the erosion. An aggravation of the conflict will instead intensify the impact of either the racially or the geopolitically conditioned belief system. Both are more vital and psychologically meaningful ideologies than is or can be any elaborately formulated socioeconomic one. On the East-West axis, China's ascent or a U.S.-Chinese alliance would reignite the racial-ethnic Russian complexes about Asia into a passional creed; and a prolonged contest over identical geopolitical stakes on the land-sea power axis would be once more rationalized by exaggerating the situation-related value differences into diametrical opposites. A new type of heroic anti-Asian idealism rooted in hallowed soil might then arise in Russia to oppose the image of the maritime-capitalist West as grossly materialist and opportunist. In the West, liberal and pacific values (quite possibly distinct from practices) would be reemphasized in opposition to Russia's aggressive militarism and anachronistic expansionism. These mutual perceptions—and in part misperceptions—would inflect the two leading nations toward a conflict all the more impassioned for their respective millennialisms being rich in parallels deeply rooted in ancestral religions.

East-West conflicts and conflict resolution. Perceptions and rationalizations can elevate what is a difference in degree into a difference in kind. What is true of adversaries is also true of conflicts. Thus, it is possible to attribute East-West conflicts in general to differences of creeds and beliefs that were traditionally only gradually concretized by material interests and pragmatic concerns as the local conflicts were caught up in the dynamic of the environing state system. Conversely, conflicts between land and sea powers originating in material or situational discrepancies can be seen as only progressively ideologized. Even if the difference is not stated in dichotomous terms and is reduced to differing nuances, the ideologies peculiar to each conflict type can readily feed into one another so long as the "narrow" East-West relationship overlaps with the land-sea power cleavage. The two-sided ideologization will then set back any progress toward "rational" or "realistic" politics that may have been achieved at the expense of the socioeconomic ideologies, both Marxist-socialist and liberal-capitalist.

As matters stand, value differences have already sparked conflicts on the expanded East-West plane, as between the North (including Soviet Russia as industrially developed as well as culturally, on balance, "western") and the third-world South. It would be more difficult for local power drives and locally compelling interests to make third-world politics more pragmatic if increases in superpower competition were to introduce into the local dynamics a growing multiplicity of ideological signals.

The interlock between the narrower and the extended East-West relationships is too real not to influence the chances for restoring the global system out of revolution and regenerating the several regions from the throes of their respective regressions. Because a strictly internal western issue is closely linked to the two East-West issues, all three can be viewed as part of a single conflict series, as well as each unfolding in specific ways and time spans peculiar to it. The common denominator is the role that the major polarities play and are likely to continue playing in conflict resolution.

First in line for accommodation was the class conflict within the narrow West. A new framework was created for its resolution when the issue of social justice, in the past wholly surrendered to the spiritual agency of Christian charity, could also become a secular concern. This change imparted a newly positive dimension to the sacral-secular polarity that had previously tended to tear apart the West in the narrowly political domain. The secular agency could be effectively engaged only when the interplays between the two types of land- and sea-based powers had amplified available resources, and when especially maritime power engendered the surplus to be doled out within a society. Changes toward representative government, associated with the maritime powers' contention with land-based powers, engendered in due course the political mechanism for redistribution. The role of the continental-maritime schism was moved one step further when the attendant series of global wars evolved and gradually mobilized the social force that energized the redistributive mechanism into an actually ongoing redistributive process. While it was being consummated, the change was consecrated by ideological rationalizations that transposed the land-sea power schism into a benign sequence in social dynamics, from an agrarian-feudal order to an urban-industrial and then to either a welfare capitalist or socialist one.

As yet another polarity, the East-West cleavage also played a part in resolving the intrawestern social conflict. The split made the West particularly receptive to socially enlightened individualism as one more means of marking its difference from a stagnant or backsliding, pseudo-feudal and autocratic, East. In the process, the East's organismic cum communal reaction found its way into the evolving western solution whenever the West absorbed, on a ricochet, selected elements of what the East had made out of seminal western ideas or marginal exploratory practices. One such element was the state-fostered social welfare policy amplified but not originated in Bismarckian Germany; another, the collectivist socialism institutionalized but not invented in Soviet Russia.

Successive resolutions of the second-in-line conflict (Russia versus the West) and the third-in-line conflict (a West including Russia versus an excolonial "East" that includes China) will unfold, if at all, through a series of comparable interplays. They, too, will be dialectical in mode and can be positive in outcome as they engage elements and attitudes clustering around the same polarities, however revised or redefined. The West and Soviet Russia will have to start adjusting to each other's divergent secular and spiritual values and aspirations, which are woven into the narrower East-West polarity. They will also have to narrow the divergences and disparities in military and economic endowments (and their ideological rationalizations) associated with the land-sea power polarity. As this preliminary process unfolds and the two sides begin to accept one another while their doing so underpins parity on a widening basis, it ought to be easier to come to terms with the constituents of the larger or global East-West cleavage. A resolution of the related, overt or latent, conflict will unfold as third-world cultures recover their particular spirituality by replacing the uncongenial elements of imported western secularism with disinterred autochthonous creeds, and as conflict issues meaningful to third-world states are territorialized in local or regional balances of wholly landlocked or also oceanic resources.

As conflicts expressing locally meaningful value differences become substantially secular and pragmatic in the Third World, they will make up for the loss of incentives previously generated by decolonization. Such conflicts might then help accelerate the psychological decolonization from seaborne western colonialism that is yet to follow upon the formal one. To be useful, the more difficult kind of decolonization must be mutual. And, to be mutual, it must do more than attenuate the sense of grievance or inferiority on one (third-world) side. It must also do away with both flaunted guilt and disguised condescension on the other (western) side. On the basis of either side's respectful awareness of the other side's values, a corresponding adjustment of policies and institutions might propel restoration of an orderly international system toward incipient world community. The stage might thus be set for consensual redistribution of material assets and vulnerabilities to material deficiencies, so long as this is done in ways compatible with continuing generation of wealth and welfare—and conducive to shielding interdependence from its built-in propensity to one-sided disruption or exploitation.

A last chance for conservatism against the wrong kinds of traditionalism. Even transactions that might benefit all are necessarily competitive in part. Aspiration toward utopian goals such as integral world community and harmonious interdependence must not lose contact with reality through the pursuit of modernity. To that end, it must incorporate traditional values and be guided by traditionally tested methods for combining gradual change with fundamental stability. Only then can the world be safe from the wrong kinds of traditionalism.

Forestalling one kind of relapse will require peaceable integration of the Soviet Union into an adequate role in the international system. Should this come to pass without a violent test of strength, it would be a major "first" for a third-generation power—a navally aspiring and equipped continental state, succeeding in salience to the maritime powers as they themselves had superseded the sacral monarchies. However, such a break with tradition is incompatible with invoking allegedly modern world-community or world-order standards in ways liable to impel the Soviets into a traditionalist bid for hegemony. It would not help matters if such a drive coincided with the revival of another kind of disruptive traditionalism: a reactive-to-reactionary way of behavior in the Third World that is suggestive less of social revolution and more of slave rebellion.

One or another kind of traditionalism would be easily denatured as it is renaturalized in its respective habitat: as one poses as social or moral reform within states, whereas the other triggers a systemic revolution among them. Ill-timed western innovations in defining either the legitimate goals of national policy or formulating the concepts of progressive international politics could well boomerang; traditionalist relapses in either the central system or in its peripheries could not but intensify the military and economic threats to the West from the outside. Trying to cope with the split between the theoretical modernity and reactionary actuality could not but depress western morale, whereas neglecting the third-world variety of the external threat too long is the surest way of eventually exacerbating defensive western reactions and thus dividing West from East on a global scale all the more radically.

Foremost among the casualities of the wrong kind of traditionalism would be the conservative idea; gone would be its "last chance" to be applied to a genuine postrevolutionary restoration of the international system. At least for the next phase, the philosophically conservative doctrine points to a need for rebalancing approaches toward Russia and toward much or most that transpires in the Third World. Necessary caution and irreducible amounts of skepticism are an essential part of *Realpolitik* in regard to both and all, including oneself; but authentic political realism would be wholly severed from humanism if it did not redeem the absence of illusions by a touch of romanticism. In the heyday of world-wide western supremacy, much of partially false romanticism was expended on the "mysterious East." The consequences were not wholly damaging for an East that became newly aware of itself through western ethnography and newly alive through western-style nationalism. Now may be the time to inject a romantic motif into a grand strategy toward the "nearest" of the Easts. Writing a conciliatory chapter in European and western history might then also mean turning a page in the longer book of world politics.

EPILOGUE.

Views of Reality and the Realist Philosophy

If the history-conscious realist is to tackle the task of international-system restoration with some chance of success, he will have to be equipped with a doctrine weaving many strands into a relatively simpler grand strategy; he will have to draw strength for an alternately subtle and firm execution of that strategy from an altogether simple—even a doctrinaire—sense of a kind of justice that transcends diplomacy.

When deserving to be called "grand," strategy: (1) takes into account the greatest possible range of phenomena (e.g., civilizations, cultures, or religions, and related norms and mores affecting dispositions); (2) is aimed at coordinating a wide range of instruments; and (3) does both in relation to several time ranges. Some of the considered phenomena will condition action and ought to influence strategy even though they themselves are not units of action on a par with states or social groups. As regards doctrine, a policy posture is doctrinal when it is guided by a set of premises and propositions concerning "reality" in its multiple aspects. It is doctrinaire to dogmatic when it is inspired by a single factor, or by a normative belief or an empirical hypothesis that is questionably reflective of reality while issuing imperative commands.

Although "doctrine" is slanted toward premises and presuppositions and "grand strategy" toward precept and prescription, there is no clear or absolute line of division between the two. One encompasses the other, most graphically in the notion of strategic doctrine.

Thus, the strategic precept for managed decompression and diversion, on the basis of shared capacity for geopolitically extended mutual deterrence, postulates as its doctrinal components: (1) a positive relationship between effectively expansive foreign policy and internal regime legitimation and authority relaxation in a rising power; and (2) the legitimacy of the drive of all, differently situated, major states toward self-assertion in all of the arenas critical for physical survival or status maintenance and role enhancement, independently of a revocable toleration by the rival great power or powers. The legitimacy of the drive implies that the tendency toward parity (of role and status) in diversity (of situation and resource endowment) is natural within a system that includes major powers differently located on the ascent-decline or system-integration continua, differently related to the continental and maritime arenas, and belonging to overlapping culture areas.

A grand strategy will also comprise lower-level strategy and tactics. If designed to accommodate the just-mentioned drive and tendency, the tactics may be those implicit in two powers encircling one another within several sectors of a wide area for the sake of delimiting individual zones of influence therein. If the aim of grand strategy is to restore order in an international system that gradually or organically evolves toward a balance of power between the major states and toward diffused power within them, the subordinate objective will be to avoid the acutely conflictual upheaval that would result from the preeminent power's sole response to a rival's drive for parity being a rigid denial of the natural tendency. By contrast, a strategy for indefinite containment will be predicated on assumptions adding up to an essentially mechanistic doctrine as to the interplay between intra- and interstate power dynamics. To wit, expansionism will be held to equal and to promote authoritarianism; a hard-line response, softening within. And the correspondingly slanted strategy—in favor of an outflanking alliance—will be rationalized by a moralistic doctrine as to entitlements, in that any serious challenge to preestablished advantages will be equated with adventurism in the rival and treated as the chief source of instability or anarchy in the world at large.

The one area where commitment to sound doctrine does not rule out being doctrinaire (and being doctrinaire may be the necessary condition of transcending mere diplomacy, while avoiding the only pragmatic policy's moralistic bias), is the area of historic justice. It is not a subject that is familiar to or a notion favored by a maritime West that is more preoccupied with social justice. One reason may be that "historic" justice among nations or states may lend itself even less easily to gradual and painless reparations or redistributions than does the "social" variety among individuals or groups; another, less invidious, reason may be that while the two kinds ideally complement one another, they may be mutually exclusive, if not contradictory to one another, in practice and in the short run. Only when both are on the way to being realized might their different requirements begin to move in parallel before merging in some kind of all-embracing equity. Meanwhile, questions abound of a both general and particular nature.

Ambiguously as Russia is tied up with an evolving Soviet system, is her access to power and influence reaching beyond her territorial limits consistent with historic justice? To answer that question, other questions have to be asked. Is there an immutable right of great nations to express themselves through the fullest draft on their potential power? Are great nations so entitled, notably if their self-expression is in keeping with the laws of power migration from one place to another? Are such rights and such laws sufficiently clear and compelling to warrant subordinating, at least for a time, procedural principles to substantive values and, among the latter, the demands of social to those of historic justice and the imperatives of individual rights to a corporate claim?

Or else, as the traditional American view would have it (with more instinctive conviction than does the revolutionary-Marxist dogma), are only those entitled to leave their imprint on history who can rightfully regard themselves as called to improve on past history—and thus in effect terminate actual, by necessary implication flawed, history? There is a related question. Is the American sense of providential entitlement if only to restrain and not to rule others—a self-perception firmed up by placing social over historic justice and individual over corporate claims—a sufficient warrant for wasting a decades-long investment? The investment, also the West's, is in the gradual softening of first a revolutionary and then a reactionary despotism. To be sure, the softening has not perceptibly been toward western-style democracy. It points only toward a politically as well as economically developing polity that, with time and patience, can reenter the mainstream of western political traditions. Is this enough? The question is not academic; along with the waste of investment in positive change would be lost one element of the existing world order, however "minimal." Blocking Russia as a world power would knock from under such order a support for its longer-term evolution, which is in part existing and in part potential; it would mean doing this, moreover, in favor of actual forces and would-be powers even less congenial to the West and less amenable to even partial containment by the West—a West, moreover, that in such a case could be reinforced with only the scattered fragments of a dislocated Russian-Soviet imperium.

If, as an alternative to the pursuit of appeasement, western instincts about the proximate, European East are allowed to dictate policy unreformed, the scales of historical justice will remain unredressed. When justice is not realized in history by actions that are deliberately keyed to satisfy its demands, it will be meted out only as it takes deferred revenge on those who denied its claims; when justice *is* realized between peoples or cultures, it is rarely if ever self-generating in ways wholly free of the intrusion of power. The winners may eventually lose their cultural or racial identity to the losers, but they had first to be victorious; the losers must have been defeated before they can absorb the victors. By the same token, a polity or culture must assert itself in the sphere of power before its values can lastingly influence others.

However, the West's eastern cousins need not bring it down to its knees before they can offer it, in the ways of both spirit and power, what they have long been giving it in philosophy. But neither should the West expect to go on indefinitely drawing fresh life from infusions of mind and heart without paying the price of legitimating eastern might. The free gift was preferred and long enjoyed by the modern Latin and Anglo-Saxon West when facing postmedieval Germandom and premodern Slavdom. When the "good Germans" became weary of being the fount of poetry and metaphysics, they turned with redoubled energy to materialism and militarism until an "evil Germany" was broken up with help from Slavic mass, and her reformed fragment driven into the welcoming bosom of a weakened West. The Slavic East was called more than once into provisional partnership to help redress the balance of the West, but has continued being held off more or longer than it chose to keep aloof whenever the balance of the West was reset and its turmoil quieted, apparently for good.

The arrangement has been too convenient for only one of the parties to last. It has been breaking down, all the more seriously because slowly; all the more lastingly because at first only latently. One side's convenience will sooner or later have to give way to a two-party compromise; partial compromises will endure only if they are stepping stones to the Great Compromise. In any future *Ausgleich* more widely beneficial than was weakened Austria's with Hungary, power (the foreign word suggests) will have to be shared more evenly not only inside Europe but also in the world at large; the balance of power will have to shift peaceably eastward inside the Occident if barely reviving civility is not to regress again into exhibitions of mere potency.

Only when eastern Europe has been fully integrated into Europe under the impulse emanating from Russia as a legitimated world power, and the incorporation has reshaped the power-political givens of the East-West problem in its European dimension, and set the stage for reshaping its psychological ones, will the conditions be present for disengaging *central* Europe again from its present limbo as a distinct culture area with its unsolved political problem of Germany's relations with her Slavic neighbors. Stressing meanwhile a separate central European identity in an effort to mark a cultural if no other distance from Russia is an affectation without positive effect on events. It does nothing for resolving, when it does not aggravate, the intra-European East-West polarity. That polarity being in part attenuated, along with Russia's regional security concerns, and in part displaced, along with changes in Russia's global role-resource-risk equations, is the precondition to central Europe reemerging into meaningful existence just as it is to Europe as a whole becoming again a center of world politics. She can be such a center when, as part of an all-occidental concert or as *its* precondition, Russia's diplomatic and cultural Europeanization makes America's functional and strategic European-ness more rather than less solidly rooted and lastingly viable—links her European vocation to a function that is still countervailing within the concert-implementing mix of reciprocal constraints, concessions, and compensations, but no longer strenuously or solely contentious; participant, but not one-sidedly protective; steadily influential without being half-heartedly hegemonic.

In such a relaxation of the East-West cum land-sea power polarity pointing toward a terminus in the cycles of East-West conflict first inside Europe, an important auxiliary role between the contemporary protagonists belongs to the preceding phase's principals, Germany—now mainly qua West Germany—and Great Britain. The first is physically as well as politically in the position of the key arc in the west European bridge for Russia's passage westward, as well as historically Russia's forerunner and pathfinder on the road to inner appeasement through the peripeties of confrontation and conciliation with the West; the second is America's culturally closest and politically least suspect interpreter of the all-European interest and Russia's global-strategic interests. Whereas West Germany has a role to play in making it gradually possible for Russia to pay heed to changes in the global balance of threats to her and opportunities for her, Britain has the matching role of making it easier, and if need be necessary, for the United States to adapt its policies to the ways the global shifts ramify into Europe. As for France, she could never make good outside Europe losses in role and status to superior German or Anglo-Saxon power: through third-worldism since leaving Algeria no more than through colonial imperialism after losing Alsace.

The range of strategic options shrinks as the perspective broadens; to recognize this is the beginning of wisdom in reviewing grand strategy. It is likewise necessary to recognize that thought on strategy can be no more fully separated from sentiment than prescription can be from premise.

There are some westerners, and a few Americans,* whose reservations about the Soviet system are of a piece with sentimental attachment to Russia. On the plane of deliberate judgment, this attachment and the sympathetic understanding of things Russian that it breeds easily lead to greater than average severity vis-à-vis the Soviet regime and rigor in defining policy toward the Soviet Union. The resulting mind-set prompts ruling out any real, in-depth conciliation or convergence between West and Soviet East—either at any time or in the "foreseeable future." Yet, however qualified, Russophilia will also prompt disapproval of policies that would deepen the cleavage between Soviet Russia and the West behind the ideological screen of anti-Communism, with aid from technocratic shibboleths of military strategics.

*A prominent example is George F. Kennan, as revealed in his two-volume *Memoirs* (Boston: Little, Brown, 1967–1972).

Ambivalent at its base, the resulting position is nuanced on the surface. It can be rationalized by applying general principles of statecraft to it. However, there is another reason for the ambiguity. If attachment to the real, non-Soviet, Russia makes lasting alienation intolerable, no more tolerable is the thought of convergence so long as to accept all that convergence entails is to inflict a lesion on the American ideal. It is an ideal that will be cherished and held to most loyally by those whom empathy for things traditionally and inherently Russian cannot but estrange somewhat from the American actuality, as one less than wholly congenial.

Unlike the American, or other western, outsider whose spiritual home is the real-ideal Russia, the expatriate from eastern Europe as she actually is or was will draw on inherited ethnic or other personal background when evolving his particular blend of positive-negative attitudes toward Russia and toward the Soviet regime. This will be the case not least when he tries to influence the positions of the emotionally less involved—or also factually uninformed—"average" westerner. The non-Russian east European will differ from both the ethnically Russian émigré from the Soviet Union and the American or west European Russophile, but he will be like both when what he sees, or foresees, varies with the particular angle of his vision—with how "globalist" is his detachment or "futurist" his speculative objectivity.

Even so, when the east European expatriate departs from the orthodox anti-Soviet line, he gives rise to questions about his more intimate motivations. Is his motive the loser's perverse need to exalt the winner's power just enough to dwarf the size of his own people's defeat and lighten the burden of its dejection? Or is his urge one of the perverse loser, intent on diluting the defeat by bringing others within the bounds of bondage? Or again, does the exile's emotional need to construe an imaginary country wherein to strike his only remaining, intellectual roots merely give life to the academic's cerebral outreach for ways of mastering the repetitive dynamics and the devious migrations of great power in behalf of an end that will mute both without doing violence to either?

An argument that is suspect of multiple bias will be suspect of being reducible to an interested apology for one party to a quarrel, inviting the other party to underwrite all the costs of the conflict's appeasement. However, in any defense of appeasement that looks past the remark echoing from the 1930s about peace being worth the price paid for it by a small country unfamiliar to the West, the question, Is not freedom indivisible?, may be turned aside with another query, Is not equilibrium made up of differing shades and dovetailing constituents of freedom and unfreedom? Moreover, a recipe for appeasing, if not the authoritarian East, then the conflict with it, is not simply an act of apostasy from the ideals and some of the realities of the liberal West. It can be more than anything else a plea stemming from anguish about the uncompleted West.

In the very year of the Anglo-Russian convention (1907) that appeased the rivalry between the two powers, Sir Eyre Crowe of the British Foreign Office wrote a famous memorandum arguing for the containment of Imperial Germany. The memorandum neatly blended some good structural analysis with a fair, if discreet, dose of patriotic-moralistic cant. Crowe ended on an optimistic note: the prospect was good for inducing German self-restraint—as, before, the French (and, presumably, the Russian) had been induced—by well-administered checks and rebuffs. The need was for "a prompt and firm refusal to enter into any one-sided bargains or arrangements, and the most unbending determination to uphold British rights and interests in every part of the globe." Four decades later, Sir Eyre's counterpart in the American foreign service, George Kennan, fathered a yet more celebrated containment doctrine.

World War I proved Crowe's optimism to have been manifestly wrong. The structure of power and interests took only seven years to prevail over sense and sensibility; "unbending determination" was not the "sure[st] or quick[est] way to win the respect of the German Government and of the German nation." The pliancy of the feeble French Republic after Fashoda (1898) could not serve as a meaningful analogy for a Germany more correctly comparable to a France of two hundred years earlier. By contrast, the course of the cold war proved Kennan to have been largely right, not least as to Soviet "mellowing." He remained right when, quite early on, he warned against the kind of rigidity and excess in applying the containment doctrine too often found in eager converts.*

There are similarities as well as differences between the two Anglo-Saxon containment theorists. Crowe had personal ties to German culture that were as intimate as those of Kennan to the Russian. This very closeness may have worked to sharpened their antagonisms for the official stance and policies of the authoritarian regimes of their day. So did an idealized view of their own societies or, at least, the professed values of these societies—as distinct (certainly in Kennan's case) from their policymaking processes. Both were of a more academic cast of mind than were leading intramural pragmatists: in the British Foreign Office, Sir Thomas Sanderson on behalf of a more relaxed attitude toward Germany's world policy; in the U.S. State Department, Dean Acheson on behalf of an invariably tougher posture vis-à-vis the Soviets. The great initial impact that the two men's doctrinal statements had at the very center and summit of government was (again notably in Kennan's case) not translatable into the author's continuing impact on policy. The discrepancy

*The Crowe memorandum is conveniently reprinted as selection no. 35 in Hans J. Morgenthau and Kenneth W. Thompson, eds., *Principles and Problems of International Politics* (New York: Alfred A. Knopf, 1950). The quoted passages are on p. 261. The text of George F. Kennan's "X" article in *Foreign Affairs* (July 1947) can be found, alongside subsequent reflections by the author and others, in Charles Gati, ed., *Caging the Bear: Containment and the Cold War.* Kennan's earlier dispatches from the Moscow Embassy are appended to the first volume of his *Memoirs.*

between inspiration and influence confirmed the difficulty of harmonizing, in the administration of democratic foreign policy, the universe of strategic thought with tactics mindful (among other things) of domestic politics and public moods. But whereas the deep and constant preoccupation of Sir Edward Grey, the foreign secretary, with feelings in Parliament acted as a brake on overt anti-German commitment, Acheson's condescension to Congressional moods and John Foster Dulles's ostensible deference to them made the anti-Soviet engagement on balance more intense or rigid.

The Crowe tradition of anti-Germanism in the British Foreign Office, seconded by Sir Arthur Nicolson, was carried on in the Hitler era by another permanent undersecretary, Sir Robert Vansittart. The appeasement from weakness that Vansittart opposed was (as officially rationalized) a kind of degenerate successor to the accommodation that greater strength might have made possible around the turn of the century. In a matching reversal, the Sanderson school of thought triumphed posthumously over the Crowe school when Neville Chamberlain ignored the would-be *spiritus rector* in the Foreign Office and supplanted him with a more like-minded personal factotum. In America, it was for Dean Acheson and John Foster Dulles to bring a simplified, institutionally digestible version of the Kennan doctrine to bear on Kennan's more complex thought. But the American pattern was moved an inch toward merging further with the English evolution when some of Kennan's fuller thought on U.S.-Soviet relations, especially in regard to eastern Europe, found its way, however fleetingly, into a semi-official doctrine widely criticized as a formula for appeasement (and disowned in those terms by its alleged formulator, the then State Department counselor, Helmut Sonnenfeldt). The notion of making it easier for the Soviets not to depend for regional control wholly on coercion by helping diversify the bases of that control could be faulted less for going too far too fast than as advancing only part of the way, on too narrow geographic (regional) and functional (economic) fronts, toward a doctrine of East-West accommodation in the original meaning of appeasement, to be implemented in time and from sufficient remaining strength.

It was *de bonne guerre* in off-and-on debates over U.S. policy toward the Soviet Union to tax Kennan with inconsistency in advice on policy rooted in incomprehension of the realities of power and its management. But it is also true that more than one view is possible as to what "power" and a "realistic" approach to it mean and, especially, comprise. While narrow in short-term application for immediate effect, their compass must perforce broaden as longer time spans and grander strategies are brought under purview. As ancient quarrels of schools continue amidst some new ones, more important than to settle them is to use the range of ideas they encompass for devising and refining a genuinely realistic doctrine and strategy for the present that keep in step with evolving elements responsible for both acceleration and attenuation in the Soviet "outreach for world power."*

A commonplace objection to "realism" as an approach to international relations has been that it deals with states and relations among them as an instance of intershocking billiard balls, ignoring the internal constitution of the actors, time, and changes related to both. The result, it is argued, is to represent interstate relations as an endless and unchanging game of skill and chance. The point is well taken *if* it is not forgotten or ignored that such an interplay *does* constitute the dynamics of interstate politics at any one time; that it *is* the essential hard core of such politics whenever it operates at a level of more than moderate crisis or tension. Only if this reservation is made, fully accepted, and intellectually assimilated is it theoretically legitimate to go beyond the inner-core mechanics of interstate relations; only then is it also useful for practical policymaking purposes to modify the rationally controlled and constantly motivated play of force and counterforce, pressure and counterpressure for individual advantage by concern for and with the organic factors of evolutionary change within and among actors.

In the short run, such "organic factors" are barely perceptible and are wholly distinct from only marginally or provisionally influential variations in internal impulses and in adventitious external inducements or constraints. In the long run, however, such factors as the changing power distribution among rising and declining social groups or classes (rather than anything like a fleeting "public opinion") internally, and among ascending and decaying political communities internationally, are ultimately determining for actors and systems alike. Yet just as only the most rudimentary realism can ignore the organic-evolutionary dimension with its operational and normative implications, so concentrating on this dimension alone would risk losing contact with political realities in favor of ideal states or imaginary utopias; vulgar pragmatism or actualism is then replaced with quixotic potentialism.

The line is thin between a correct simplification of the interstate dynamic being vital (because it is keyed to immediate survival in crisis situations, and conforming with its imperatives assures survival in principle), and its formulation and application in policy being vulgarized (because wholly pragmatic or opportunist and totally ahistorical). But, thin as is such a line, the intellectual space within which can occur the various attempts at reconciling or fusing the mechanical with the organic aspects of total political reality will be unavoidably wide. Attempting to do this is to be analytically stretched between the short run and the variably long run, between the essential simplicity of an elegant dynamics model and the elusive com-

***Griff nach der Weltmacht,* the title of Fritz Fischer's controversial revisionist treatment of German foreign policy and war aims before and during World War I. Published in English as *Germany's War Aims in the First World War.*

plexities of the change- and time-conscious mode. It just might be barely possible to span the two universes theoretically, although impossible to convey any resulting synthesis simultaneously by words that cannot but follow one another. The only recourse is then to successively identify the aspects and elements constitutive of the dynamic and evolutionary complex. Even then it will be difficult for the policymaker to integrate the insights and directives emanating from the long-term perspective into his short-term action program in a way that is either self-conscious or rigorous; difficult, that is, to qualify the compelling simplicities of the billiard-balls model (or, put differently, of interstate mechanics as an aspect of political physics) by the nearly unlimited, largely hypothetical contingencies that can be subsumed under the organic dimension. Yet without the antecedent intellectual, or "academic," effort, the policymaker's task is wholly impossible except where an inborn right instinct, a second sight, shows the way.

The academic student who does not recognize that practical statecraft will always be about four-fifths a matter of instant reactions to immediate pressures and opportunities is irrelevant to the practice of statecraft, and thus useless to society. By the same token, however, a policymaker will be practically ineffective and be an actual danger to society if he is temperamentally or intellectually incapable of bringing to bear upon his routine stewardship a sensitivity to the remaining one-fifth of reality, or concern about reality, that transcends the workmanlike mechanics of daily business one way or another. Be he scholar or statesman, the philosophical realist need not be for all that a full-fledged practitioner of the philosophy of history when he sets out to explore the historico-evolutionary aspect of a problem; nor, on the same principle, need he be a cultural anthropologist or country or regional specialist when exploring and attempting to evaluate the cultural modifiers of the constant features in either dynamics or evolution. But such explorations will be appropriate for the philosophical realist because, the more his doctrine directs him to abstract a simple model from the continuities underlying historical change, the more will he depend for verisimilitude on enriching that model by sensitivity to specific contingencies and variations. But again, just as the essential realist theory limits itself to supplying no more than a penetrating central insight into the dynamics, so the realist sensitive to history and cultural differences need not strive for a rigorous or coherent theoretical framework into which to fit the evolutionary and idiosyncratic variations. The only requirement of the academic effort is that it be phrased in terms that can be argued about with reference to identifiable assumptions and definable historical perspectives; it is not that the effort issue in an "elegant" theory or be sustained by elaborate methodology any more than by a sophisticated metaphysics.

BIBLIOGRAPHY

Adams, Brooks. *The New Empire.* New York: Macmillan, 1902.

Anderson, M. S. *The Ascendancy of Europe: Aspects of European History 1815–1914.* Totowa, N.J.: Rowan/Littlefield, 1972.

———. *Britain's Discovery of Russia 1553–1815.* London: Macmillan, 1958.

Cherniavsky, Michael. *Tsar and People.* New Haven: Yale University Press, 1961.

———, ed. *The Structure of Russian History: Interpretive Essays.* New York: Random House, 1970.

Coles, Paul. *The Ottoman Impact on Europe.* London: Thames/Hudson, 1968.

Curtiss, John S., ed. *Essays in Russian and Soviet History.* New York: Columbia University Press, 1962.

Daniel, Norman. *The Arabs and Mediaeval Europe.* London: Longmans, 1979.

———. *Islam, Europe and Empire.* Edinburgh: Edinburgh University Press, 1966.

Fadner, Frank L. *Seventy Years of Pan-Slavism in Russia: Karazin to Danilevski 1800–1870.* Washington, D.C.: Georgetown University Press, 1962.

Fischer, Fritz. *Germany's Aims in the First World War.* New York: Norton, 1967.

———. *War of Illusions: German Policy from 1911 to 1914.* New York: Norton, 1975.

Fischer-Galati, S. A. *Ottoman Imperialism and the German Protestants.* Cambridge, Mass.: Harvard University Press, 1959.

Gati, Charles, ed. *Caging the Bear: Containment and the Cold War.* Indianapolis: Bobbs-Merrill, 1974.

Gleason, John H. *The Genesis of Russophobia in Great Britain: A Study of the Interaction of Policy and Opinion.* Cambridge, Mass.: Harvard University Press, 1950.

Gollwitzer, Heinz. *Europe in the Age of Imperialism 1880–1914.* New York: Harcourt, Brace/World, 1969.

Graham, Gerald S. *The Politics of Naval Supremacy.* Cambridge: Cambridge University Press, 1965.

Grenville, Johns A. S. *Lord Salisbury and Foreign Policy.* London: Athlone Press, 1964.

Hellie, Richard. *Enserfment and Military Change in Muscovy.* Chicago: University of Chicago Press, 1971.

Hoetzsch, Otto. *Russland und Asien: Geschichte einer Expansion.* Stuttgart: Deutsche Verlags-Anstalt, 1966.

Kasperson, Roger E., and Julian V. Minghi, ed. *The Structure of Political Geography.* Chicago: Aldine, 1969.

Kehr, Eckart. *Battleship Building and Party Politics in Germany 1894–1901.* Chicago: University of Chicago Press, 1973.

Kerner, Robert J. *The Urge to the Sea: The Course of Russian History.* Berkeley and Los Angeles: University of California Press, 1946.

Korpeter, C. Max. *Ottoman Imperialism during the Reformation: Europe and Caucasus.* New York: New York University Press, 1972.

Lobanov-Rostovsky, Andrei. *Russia and Asia 1825–1878.* Ann Arbor: George Wahr, 1965.

Mackinder, Halford J. *Democratic Ideals and Reality: A study in the Politics of Reconstruction.* New York: H. Holt, 1950.

MacMaster, Robert E. *Danilevsky: A Russian Totalitarian Philosopher.* Cambridge, Mass.: Harvard University Press, 1967.

Mommsen, Wolfang J. *Max Weber und die deutsche Politik 1890–1920.* Tübingen: Mohr, 1959.

Monger, George W. *The End of Isolation: British Foreign Policy 1900–1907.* London: T. Nelson, 1963.

Pois, Robert A. *Friedrich Meinecke and German Politics in the Twentieth Century.* Berkeley and Los Angeles: University of California Press, 1972.

Pokrovskii, M. N. *Russia in World History.* Ann Arbor: University of Michigan Press, 1970.

Riasanovsky, Nicholas V. *Nicholas V. Nicholas I and Official Nationality in Russia 1825–1855.* Berkeley and Los Angeles: University of California Press, 1959.

———. *Russia and the West in the Teaching of the Slavophiles.* Cambridge, Mass.: Harvard University Press, 1952.

Rich, Norman. *Friedrich von Holstein: Politics and Diplomacy in the Era of Bismarck and Wilhelm II.* Cambridge: Cambridge University Press, 1965.

Ritter, Gerhard, *The Sword and the Scepter: The Problem of Militarism in Germany,* vol. 2. Coral Gables: University of Miami Press, 1970.

Rothwell, V. H. *British War Aims and Peace Diplomacy 1914–1918.* Oxford: Clarendon Press, 1971.

Spykman, Nicholas. *The Geography of Peace.* New York, Harcourt, Brace/World, 1944.

Stern, Fritz. *The Politics of Cultural Despair: A Study in the Rise of the Germanic Ideology.* Berkely and Los Angeles: University of California Press, 1961.

Stökl, Günther. *Osteuropa und Deutschland: Geschichte und Gegenwart einer spannungsvollen Nachbarschaft.* Oldenburg and Hamburg: Gerhard Stalling Verlag, 1967.

Strausz-Hupé, Robert. *Geopolitics: The Struggle for Space and Power.* New York: G. P. Putman's Sons, 1942.

Sumner, B. H. *Tsardom and Imperialism in the Far East and Middle East.* London: Humphrey Milford, 1942.

Von Laue, Theodore. *Sergei Witte and the Industrialization of Russia.* New York: Columbia University Press, 1963.

INDEX